The Man Who Saved Vancouver

THE MAN WHO SAVED VANCOUVER

MAJOR JAMES SKITT MATTHEWS

Daphne Sleigh

VICTORIA • VANCOUVER • CALGARY

Heritage House Publishing Company Ltd.
#108 – 17665 66A Avenue
Surrey, BC V3S 2A7
www.heritagehouse.ca

Heritage House Publishing Company Ltd.
PO Box 468
Custer, WA
98240-0468

Library and Archives Canada Cataloguing in Publication
Sleigh, Daphne
The man who saved Vancouver: Major James Skitt Matthews / Daphne Sleigh.

Includes bibliographical references and index.
ISBN 978-1-894974-39-4

1. Matthews, James Skitt, 1878-1970. 2. Archives—British Columbia—Vancouver—History. 3. Vancouver City Archives—History. 4. Vancouver City Archives—Officials and employees—Biography. 5. Archivists—British Columbia—Vancouver—Biography. 6. Vancouver (B.C.)—Biography. I. Title.

FC3847.26.M38S54 2008   971.1'3303092   C2008-900290-3

Library of Congress Control Number: 2008921327

Edited by Karla Decker
Proofread by Sarah Weber
Book design by Frances Hunter
Cover design by Ruth Linka
Cover photos courtesy of City of Vancouver Archives.
Front-cover photo by B.W. Leeson, CVA, Port P567.
Back-cover photos, starting at top: J. Laing photo, CVA, Port P1137; CVA, P138; CVA, Port N941.2; CVA, Port P352.3.

Printed in Canada

Heritage House acknowledges the financial support for its publishing program from the Government of Canada through the Book Publishing Industry Development Program (BPIDP), Canada Council for the Arts, and the province of British Columbia through the British Columbia Arts Council and the Book Publishing Tax Credit.

This book has been produced on 100% post-consumer recycled paper, processed chlorine free and printed with vegetable-based dyes.

To Francis

Contents

Acknowledgements

Thanks are due to a wide variety of people in the course of researching and writing a book, but in this case there is no doubt in my mind that the most fervent thanks of all should be extended to none other than the spirit of Major Matthews himself. Had it not been for Matthews' memoirs and his frank disclosure of the most pivotal episodes in his life, any attempt to interpret his career would have been that much more difficult. His wealth of correspondence, too, is a gift to any biographer, for he reveals himself freely on every page, and his natural spontaneity of expression gives his letters a character all their own.

The staff in the City of Vancouver Archives have clearly inherited the Major's dedication to heritage, and I think they must feel his presence as they work amid his cherished collection. Their enthusiasm for this biographical project has been encouraging throughout, and their professional expertise has been outstanding on all my visits to the Archives. Heather Gordon, Carol Haber, Megan Schlase, Jeannie Hounslow, Chak Yung, Nancy Mulligan, Pat Hanna—each one of these archivists has provided help for which I am enormously grateful.

I should also like to acknowledge the assistance of the BC Archives, whose staff have had the task of dealing with the unusual conditions imposed by the terms of Major Matthews' will. Special thanks are due too to the staff at the Vancouver Public Library, another of my haunts while researching this book. Other institutions that provided important material are the National Archives of Canada; the Cloverdale Public Library, Genealogical Section; the Family History Centre, LDS Church, Abbotsford; the Fraser Valley Library, Mission branch; the Newtown Local History Group, Powys, Wales; and the Newtown Public Library.

Several individuals have been crucial to the development of this biography. Evelyn Walser's kindness in lending me photographs and showing me family records and memorabilia was hugely appreciated, as was the help of her husband, Don. Another great impetus came from Millie Nelles, whose letters from Major Matthews and memories of him were very much an inspiration for this book. The continued supportiveness of my husband, Francis, almost goes without saying by now. I am also grateful to the late Anne Yandle, Leonard McCann, Margaret Brunette, Elizabeth Walker, David Pugh, and John and Helen Wi Neera, all of whom offered generous help in their different ways.

And to Karla Decker, my editor, I likewise extend my sincere appreciation for her painstaking work and constructive suggestions, which have undoubtedly been beneficial to this book and averted many a slip.

Foreword

James Skitt Matthews is arguably the single most important individual in the history of Vancouver. While others generated events, he ensured that a record of their activities would survive. Major Matthews, as he liked to be called in recognition of his military service, was both the city's first archivist and its long-time principal cheerleader and booster.

Daphne Sleigh's highly readable biography reveals Major Matthews as a complex product of his times. He fell into his archival niche, but once there used all the resources at his disposal, including a difficult personality, on behalf of the city he came to love.

Like the overwhelming majority of Vancouverites of the turn of the 20th century, Matthews was an immigrant, and, as had many others, having lit on the city he laid claim to it with all of the zeal of a convert. Not a man of half measures, he grew determined to give Vancouver a past to match its widely anticipated exuberant future.

Matthews arrived in Vancouver at the age of 20, just a dozen years after the city came into being as the west-coast terminus of the transcontinental Canadian Pacific Railway (CPR). Having secured a job to support his young family, Matthews began writing for local newspapers, increasingly about Vancouver. In part to get the information to do so, Sleigh tells us, he started "searching out old discarded maps and records, talking to old-timers and setting aside anything of historical interest for his personal collection of trivia." The home he built on Kitsilano Point in 1911 encouraged his avocation, "as he became the recipient of old unwanted documents and photographs, took in outdated military uniforms and weapons, and filled to overflowing the basement of his little house with the so-called 'junk' that would one day take on a far greater significance." Had he not done so, it is very likely that most of this material would not have survived.

By 1930 this "very knowledgeable self-taught historian" possessed, in his own estimate, a ton of material. Deciding it was time to put it in order, Matthews went looking for a home for his collection, ideally one that would also include him as city archivist. His persistence during the Great Depression was remarkable. Even more so was Vancouver City Council's agreeing to give Matthews a tiny purchasing budget and a niche in the former city hall.

Daphne Sleigh deftly chronicles Matthews' single-minded determination to expand this small beginning into a full-fledged city archives, with himself at the helm. By 1933 he had obtained the title of City Archivist, with a small monthly honorarium and a location in the city hall on Hastings Street, making Vancouver the first city in Canada by over two decades to have its own archives. His acquisition of the entire ninth floor in the new city hall completed in 1936 fed his ambition. The more he got, the harder he pushed not just to collect, but to make the past better known. Matthews was so convinced of his mission, Sleigh observes, that "he could not help making life difficult for himself by taking offence at the slightest hint of criticism or dissent, when no insult was actually intended."

Those of us who write about the history of Vancouver walk in Major Matthews' shadow. The critique levelled at him shortly after his death—that instead of "collecting the administrative records of City Hall" he chose to save, in Sleigh's words, "whatever he recognized as bringing history to life: personal memoirs, contemporary pictures and photographs, objects connected with great events or outstanding personalities"—is true. That shortcoming is precisely what makes the City of Vancouver Archives such a unique resource, making available virtually the entirety of the city's past. As well as paper, he collected objects relating to the city's history, whatever their size, and in doing so also laid the foundation for the Vancouver Museum.

Matthews understood the importance of documentation. The materials he acquired, including an abundance of photographs and other images, he annotated individually as to their provenance and subject matter in his very recognizable—and fortunately very legible—hand.

Matthews sought out long-time residents for their stories going back to the city's beginnings and earlier. He did not restrict himself to important figures or to members of the dominant society, as would have been usual at the time, but also talked at length with ordinary men and women of virtually every background, including many Aboriginal people. Matthews not only listened to what he was told, but also ensured that what he heard survived in permanent form. In an age before the tape recorder, he took detailed notes, had them typed and then checked back with their teller to ensure accuracy. He met with numerous people multiple times over the course of months or years, and the hundreds of transcripts that resulted await visitors to the City of Vancouver Archives.

Twice, descendants have encouraged me to tell their families' stories, but it was only because Matthews had got there first that I was able to do so. My book *The Remarkable Adventures of Portuguese Joe Silvey* is based on Matthews' conversations with Silvey's two oldest daughters and their contemporaries, with whom he met on more than two dozen occasions between 1938 and 1943; *Stanley Park's Secret: The Forgotten Families of Whoi Whoi, Kanaka Ranch, and Brockton Point* draws even more extensively on Major Matthews' conversations, as well as on the photographs, maps and eviction records he collected. He spoke at length with many persons who lived on the peninsula that became Stanley Park or in its vicinity at Kanaka Ranch, or who knew the park's history. Matthews' two decades of conversations with August Jack Khahtsahlano, a Squamish man who grew up on the peninsula and at the Kitsilano Reserve close to where Matthews lived, resulted in his invaluable book *Conversations with Khahtsahlano 1932–1954*.

Matthews' commitment to the history of Stanley Park went beyond the sources he collected or created. When the park's last resident, Tim Cummings, died in 1958, it was the 80-year-old Major Matthews who led the charge (ultimately unsuccessful) to persuade the Vancouver Parks Board to rescind its decision, made the day after Tim Cummings' death, to tear down his house. "I believe the board is called the board of parks and public recreation; it should be called the board of parks and public desecration," he proclaimed in his usual blunt manner.

Until now we have known far too little about the man who gave Vancouver its history. Without Major Matthews' persistence and determination, the city's past would have survived far less fully than it does. Sleigh perceptively observes that "always in his imagination, he remembered Vancouver as it was in those wonderful impressionable days, when he first saw and marvelled at his new surroundings." It is to Matthews' credit that he did not restrict himself to those heady first years, but understood that each new happening becomes, a day later, part of a past equally necessary to remember. Daphne Sleigh's engaging portrait reveals a remarkable man utterly committed to the city he loved. We are indebted to her as well as to Major Matthews.

Jean Barman
Vancouver, 2007

Introduction

How the city reporters of the 1950s must have loved Major Matthews. Eminently quotable, forthright and provocative in speech, he was a gift to any newspaperman attempting to liven up an otherwise boring account of the deliberations of the Vancouver City Council. His mere presence at any discussion of a contentious nature would be enough to ensure a wealth of good copy, and a strong, catchy headline as well. "Move me? Just Try it, Says Major"; "The Major downs the Sabre as he Wins the Archive Skirmish"; "Once more unto the Breach goes the Bristling Major"—such were some of the headlines of the 1950s, irresistibly inspired by the militant style of this formidable figure.[1]

Then in his late 70s, but still the City Archivist, he was a legend in his lifetime, tolerantly described as a "character"—perhaps a bit of a comical character by then, but most definitely not a person to be trifled with. It would not be an exaggeration to suppose that he would have been regarded with the utmost respect and possibly trepidation by all those at City Hall from the mayor on down, whatever their feelings of irritation at the Major's intractable ways. Many were the hints that it was now time for him to think of retiring, to appoint a successor—but all such suggestions were lost on him, as if they had never been uttered. If James Matthews had his mind set in a certain direction, it took more than a mere hint or suggestion, or even an order, to dissuade him: it had to have the finality of a legal decision.

In fact, he never did retire. Long after various mayors had come and gone, James Matthews was still there, presiding over the Archives and dominating the scene. He died at the age of 92, completely deaf, his memory a little faded, but still officially at the helm of his beloved Archives.

Every British Columbian owes James Skitt Matthews an incalculable debt. Had it not been for his extraordinary interest and persistence in searching out any item relating to the earliest history of Vancouver (and, peripherally, other parts of the province as well), we would have a much less graphic picture of the unique period when the city was born. No other contemporary of his was attempting anything like this in the City of Vancouver. Had the Major not made a point of noting down his conversations with every early pioneer he could meet, and then publishing the results in a series of volumes, we would have little but official documents to take us back in time. And we might not even have many of these either, had he not rescued them from musty basements and even wastepaper baskets.

His reputation for crustiness and aggressive behaviour was certainly justified, but it had grown up and become habitual partly because of the long struggle he had endured in order to convince officialdom even of the need for an archives department at all. It was only through sheer force of personality that he had succeeded in gatecrashing the sacred portals of City Hall and getting himself awarded the title of City Archivist, and it was only through persistent attacks in the ensuing years that he managed to extract the merest pittance of a salary or funding for the archives. All this had brought out the most combative side of his personality. But the truth was well expressed by his friend and champion General Victor Odlum, who made an eloquent address to City Council in a plea for their understanding of "this prickly officer with the heart of gold underneath."[2] James Matthews' patent sincerity and tireless passion for what was so obviously dear to his heart would eventually win over most people to support his cause. He was affectionate by nature, warm and expressive in his letters to his friends, good to his family, and soft-hearted toward all those brave enough to see through the gruff exterior.

James Matthews was one of Vancouver's great "characters." His life had its sorrows and its difficulties, which have to be understood in order to see his life in context, and he himself did not hesitate to face these issues. Setting down an account of his early life, he once wrote: "In recording this data it is the duty of the chronicler to state the facts, and from there, after consideration, we attempt to improve the present and future by observing and avoiding the errors of the past. Some may say that it is ill-fitting that the skeletons in the family chest be brought forth and exposed to the vulgar gaze, but the author disagrees, and would point out that … the germs of disease are most easily killed and so dispersed by letting in the full flood of sunlight."[3]

CHAPTER 1

A Welsh Valley

In the chronicle of human endeavour there is no story more inspiring than that of the resourceful courageous people whose initiative and energy, peacefully, and in the briefest period of time, created out of the silent emptiness of the primeval forest a monumental city of beauty and of culture. (From James Matthews' foreword to his history of the city, *Early Vancouver.*)

Vancouver has never had a more loyal citizen than Major James Skitt Matthews. Passionately absorbed in the city's history, obsessed by the need to save its records from extinction and defiantly fighting for its historical life, he might well have been mistaken for a native son of the Vancouver he loved. In fact, he was not. He was not even Canadian by birth. Matthews was a Welshman by origin, his family deeply rooted for many generations in the hill country of Montgomeryshire in mid-Wales. And when his family left Wales and emigrated, they headed not to Canada, but to New Zealand. James grew up as a New Zealander, educated in New Zealand schools and absorbing the New Zealand culture.

But when James suddenly left there for the United States at 19 and arrived in Vancouver a few months later, he appears to have instantly shed any hold that New Zealand may have exercised upon his allegiance. With his first glimpse of Vancouver, it was love at first sight. Intensely conservative in spite of (or perhaps because of) a restless family background, he attached himself passionately to this vigorous new city emerging from the shadows of the forest, and he gave it his lifelong devotion. He never returned to visit New Zealand, nor did New Zealand figure to any great extent in the family history that he compiled at the age of 49. His descriptions of his life there are minimal and often lack atmosphere or immediacy. By contrast, his childhood impressions of Wales (or Cymru) and his Welsh family are vivid and affectionate, and give a sense of belonging. Although he revisited Wales only a few times when he was stationed in Britain during the First World War, and again quite briefly when his father died, his memoirs give the feeling that his Welsh heritage had sunk more deeply into his psyche than his overlaid New Zealand experience.

James Matthews was nine when his family emigrated from Wales to New Zealand. From those impressionable first years of life, what sort of recollections might he have had of his earliest surroundings and the people who inhabited his world? His memory was of the visual kind—this much is obvious from the colourful imagery of his later writings. He must surely have retained an indistinct but very real mental snapshot of the distant green land of Cymru—images of swelling hills and gentle valleys, uplands blue with harebells in summer, hedgerows edged by meadowsweet, country lanes and little cottages, and a slate-roofed town in a hollow—the market town of Newtown, where he was born on September 7, 1878.

The part of Wales that had been the home of countless generations of Matthews ancestors was not the Wales known to tourists. Its landscape was not the scenic spectacle of Snowdonia. It was not the shimmering panorama of the northern mountain ranges with their wintry frosting of white and silver, nor was it as spacious as the broad vistas of the Brecon heights to the south. It was a cluster of rising hills and mounded contours and wooded river valleys, whose streams rushed eddying down to meet the River Severn at Newtown and Welshpool. Here and there the land was forested by little copses of native ash and oak and birch—any conifers were alien intruders—but mostly it was a landscape of sloping fields, sometimes tilting steeply at unexpected angles, sometimes undulating softly into folds of grassy meadows.

And everywhere, dotted white against the green hillside, moved the nebulous forms of wandering sheep, slowly drifting from pasture to pasture. Almost every field in this windswept country supported a scattering of hardy sheep grazing on the slopes, for these flocks were the mainstay of local farmers and represented prosperity in this part of Wales. The whole of Montgomeryshire was a sheep-farming district, and Newtown in particular was the centre of an important woollen industry.

The thick woolly fleeces of these sheep had once been the wealth of mid-Wales—and of James Matthews' immediate forebears. Spinning and weaving had always been the traditional fireside occupation for labourers and their families during the winter months, but in the early 19th century, what had begun as a cottage industry grew into something much larger and more organized. The invention of a carding engine for combing fleece and a jenny for spinning wool had transformed the process and encouraged certain forward-thinking individuals to build small mills. A proliferation of these brick-built factories began to fill the country towns of Montgomeryshire, and the most important centre of all was James Matthews' hometown of Newtown.

Newtown lies in a low dip of the hills. Slate-roofed in shades of grey and rose, it is a compact little town, its boundaries well defined by the loop of the Severn. Three bridges used to span the river, connecting

Sheep grazing near Newtown, a traditional sheep-farming area. (D. Sleigh)

the town to the surrounding countryside, but 20th-century flooding has forced changes to these systems. However, the wide main street (Broad Street) still makes an emphatic statement in the heart of the town and takes on the role of a city square, with a colourful street market that still does a lively trade twice a week. Brick buildings of superior size and generous ornamentation indicate times of some prosperity—but they are relics of a bygone era. Newtown's industrial age is over; the imposing Flannel Exchange is now a cinema, and Newtown Hall, once the country seat of the gentry, has a more functional use today as the town's municipal hall. New housing spills over into the outskirts of town. But soon the buildings become sparse and the roads begin to climb up into the farming country, running between dense hedges and fields. The urban areas recede, and the way ahead lies through the heart of rural Wales. Low green hills rise up on all sides, riffling the horizon. Clouds lie mistily on the hilltops. The fat white sheep graze everywhere, as they have done for centuries on end.

James's immediate family background was one of comfort and prosperity. The wool and flannel trade had become hugely successful, especially after the invention of power-operated looms, and by the middle of the century Newtown had a reputation as "the busy Leeds of Wales." In the first 40 years of the century the population more than quadrupled. Large public buildings embellished the town—a pilastered Flannel Exchange with "magnificent gas-lit hall," imposing banks and churches, new houses and massive new factories.[1] "At that time Newtown was a very rich little town and the wool trade a regular gold mine," recalled James's great-aunt Margaret. "The merchants and the manufacturers were gentlemen. In the old days the London merchants used to come all the way from there to Newtown, bringing the money with them. They were not troubled with banks and checks [*sic*] in those days."[2]

Both James's grandfather and great-grandfather were among these woollen manufacturers, and very well-to-do. Of their 18th-century ancestors little is known, except that they owned land in the hill country outside Newtown. Probably they were sheep farmers, like the other landowners around them. However, the Matthews family had plenty of entrepreneurial spirit, and some time early in the 19th century

BROAD STREET, NEWTOWN, SEEN FROM THE LONG BRIDGE. (D. SLEIGH, 2005)

James's great-grandfather John took advantage of the new opportunities in the woollen industry and started up a mill. It was a water-powered mill, built on the banks of the Severn. Major Matthews describes it as having been on the south side of town, "on the far side of the Short Bridge," though there is no such bridge today. When he revisited Newtown in 1917, he found the mill still standing and its water wheel still intact, with the name "Matthews" still just discernible in fading paint on the brick façade. The mill had then been out of use for 20 years, he writes. Today this whole area has been redeveloped, and the course of the river rerouted after massive flooding in the 1960s.

This was not the only mill the family owned. Another Matthews mill stood in the heart of the industrial area immediately north of the Long Bridge, occupying the southeast corner of Union and

Crescent streets. James did not know whether it was his grandfather William or great-grandfather John who had built it. Like the other small factories, it was a plain four-storeyed, red-brick building, but it had curious dimensions, being long and shallow, with a frontage of 101 feet along Union Street but a depth of only 27½ feet. Hand looms filled the upper floors, while the ground level was occupied by a row of two shops and several back-to-back cottages for the workers. Thought unsafe, this particular mill was demolished in the 1970s, but several of the neighbouring structures still survive, gaunt and unlovely, their brickwork grimed and weathered with age, but redolent of the industrial past that is part of Newtown's heritage.

All through the first half of the century, the profits poured in abundantly from Newtown's mills. Great-grandfather John "made a pile of money," according to family accounts, and was in a position to live a life of affluence. He was heard to say to one of his daughters-in-law: "Margaret, I have made £300 [about $1,500] this morning. Don't you want a new dress or something?"[3] He supported numerous relatives and was indulgent to his family—overindulgent, in the opinion of Major Matthews, who considered that John's children all turned out badly except for William.

William (James's grandfather) seems to have been a natural scholar. His father was in a position to give his children a superior education, and in his teens William was sent to the Grove Grammar School in Wrexham, many miles away. Being a clever student, he stayed till the late age of 19, absorbing such refinements as French, Latin and Greek.

During the first part of his career William, too, lived a life of affluence. His home on Park Street had a plain exterior, but within was much comfort. James had childhood memories of a huge stone-flagged kitchen with pot-hooks and antique fire tools, kept brightly polished, though no longer in use. Occupying an entire side of this room stood a great glass-fronted dresser, with shelf upon shelf of gleaming displays of magnificent silverware. The upstairs parlour he dimly remembered as a place of some splendour, with handsome furniture and "quaint old urns, pictures and draperies." Interwoven with these memories was a vision of his grandmother Ann, "a lady of some slight degree of haughtiness," always remembered as sitting

James's grandfather's woollen mill, Union Street, Newtown. The looms were in the upper storeys. (Newtown Local History Group)

there with her embroidery or her knitting, but never involving herself in any sort of active housework. All the work of meal preparations was carried out by servants.[4]

James was under the impression that his grandfather had at one time been the largest manufacturer of woollens in the whole of Wales. This was probably an exaggerated view, for the Matthews mills are not mentioned in histories of the industry, while some of the large mills, such as the Cambrian Mill, are listed as employing many more workers and containing many more looms. Nevertheless, William Matthews was evidently a very successful businessman who had every reason to anticipate excellent prospects for his two surviving sons.

James's father, Herbert, was born to Ann and William during the good times, in 1851, and he and his brother Charles grew up in an atmosphere of plenty. Herbert enjoyed the luxury of a private tutor to supervise his education, though he also attended a Mr. Cook's school in Newtown. But the future was not as rosy as it looked, for the wool trade was having its fluctuations. Suddenly, in 1865, came a major calamity for William. Heavy failures in business brought financial disaster, as a result of which he lost several thousands of pounds—a huge sum in terms of today's values. He did not go out of business, but from then on he and Ann ceased to enjoy their former sense of security. Ann in particular was horribly troubled, and began saving odd sums of money from the housekeeping and setting them aside in case of future need. After her death William would discover 300 sovereigns hidden away in all sorts of unexpected places.

In spite of Newtown's prosperous appearance, the woollen industry was no longer the reliable source of wealth that it had been in the early part of the century. It faced competition from the English mills in the northwest, and particularly Rochdale, the centre of the flannel industry. Rochdale had converted to power looms and other technology well ahead of Newtown, and also had superior transportation routes, even though Newtown was connected to three railways by the 1860s and had a link to the Montgomeryshire Canal. There was another factor too: cotton flannel was now overtaking woollens in popularity, and Rochdale had been building cotton mills since the beginning of the century. Besides this, Wales faced outside competition from the sheep farms of Australia and New Zealand, whose imports were steadily streaming into the British market.

Soon after William's financial disaster, the time came to decide on Herbert's future career and training. He had little mechanical aptitude and this, added to the uncertainty of the family business, may have influenced William to apprentice his son to a draper at some cost rather than set him to learn the operation of the mills. But Herbert soon grew to hate his work at the draper's and bought his way out with his own savings. He was a serious young man, good at figures and mentally astute, so he next took a position as a confidential clerk at a brewery, and in this more congenial occupation he did well. By the time he was 30 he had invested his savings in a rundown coal business and transformed it into a paying concern. He became affluent enough to own a fleet of railway wagons, a lime kiln and a canal boat; and for pleasure he could afford his own horses for fox hunting, as well as a driver and gig.

Herbert's life was governed by the controlling personality of his wife. He had married at the age of 20, having admired his future wife since he was only 14. Mary Skitt was seven years older than Herbert, but had evidently known her own mind all along, for she later said that she had waited for him to grow to maturity. She retained a strong influence and perhaps ascendency over him throughout their marriage. An attractive young woman with long curls and a deceptively delicate Dresden china look, she was in fact a strong, tough and determined character who had been running a successful millinery shop near the Short Bridge for several years.

James Skitt Matthews was the middle child of this marriage. He had a brother, Martin, who was five years older and another brother, Frank Woolrich, four years younger. There had also been a sister, Agnes, but she had died of scarlet fever at the age of four and a half. She was "a little fairy girl with golden curls," as James visualized her, though he must have drawn upon his mother's memories for this image, for he was not quite two at the time of Agnes's death.

It was a happy home for James and his brothers, financially secure for their material needs and blessed with parents who lived—as he sensed it—in absolute harmony. "There may be arguments against early marriages, but not against this one, for it was the most superlatively happy marriage I ever knew of," wrote James in middle age. "Never during their long life did I hear Mother utter one cross word to father … Their life as man and woman was a beautiful and perfect example of what married life should be."(The offspring of such a marriage are frequently handicapped by their expectations of an effortless state of bliss, as James was to discover.)

Nevertheless there are many indications that James's mother was the dominating personality in this happy marriage. Herbert had fallen in love with Mary when he was only a teenager, had looked up to this older woman and grown accustomed to accepting her judgement. "Mother's wish was duty for father. She ruled him with that affectionate rule which love alone can understand." There was evidently a strong sexual attraction too, for Mary retained her beautiful looks even into her older years.

James idolized his mother all through his life. His memoirs constantly tell us how lovely he thought her, and he writes intense descriptions of her "extremely prepossessing appearance"—her beautiful features, her long curls and her silken gowns and crinolines. Even at the end of her life, he considered her "the prettiest old lady in Wales." Equally he admired her courage and strength of will, qualities he inherited in no small measure. James took after his mother, inheriting a similarity of looks and character that created an instinctive sympathy in the relationship. This would be true as well of his youngest son, Hugh, whom he adored. All three shared the same cast of features and the same qualities of temperament. In a moment of self-analysis, James decided that on the positive side, they were all "affectionate and generous and loyal," though perhaps impulsive, but he confessed there was a certain "hastiness" that went with this type of personality.[5] (The Major's detractors would certainly have agreed with this last admission, though likely phrasing it in much stronger terms.)

He felt a deep affection for his father also, and considerable respect for his qualities of mind—his good intelligence, his financial ability and, above all, his "unqualified honesty" and integrity. In spite of this strength of moral character, Herbert had one weakness: he was too much inclined to put the interests of others before his own. He was

James's mother, Mary Matthews, in New Zealand. "My mother was extremely prepossessing in appearance." (Wrigglesworth & Binns photo. E. Walser)

unselfish to a fault. His was a quieter and softer personality than his wife's, and he could show emotion more easily, perhaps even feel it more profoundly. James had several memories of his father breaking down uncontrollably in the face of some terrible anguish concerning one of his family. Mary proved more able to endure the difficulties of life without emotional damage.

JAMES AGED FOUR YEARS. (J. LAING PHOTO. CVA, PORT P1137)

Their complementary personalities blended well, and Herbert and Mary lived in harmony together. They visited with their numerous relatives in Newtown, and they also saw something of Mary's family in Shropshire. She was brought up in Old Heath Grove, a village near Shrewsbury, where her father, James Skitt, was a farrier and veterinary surgeon. James remembered following him around and noticing his kindness to animals and his gentle way with them. He must have been very fond of this grandfather, for he could recall that as a child he sometimes refrained from some misdeed because he wanted his Grandpa Skitt to think well of him: "Dear old gentleman, my affection for him has been a comfort throughout life." It was very likely this grandfather who sparked James's original interest in things military, for James Skitt was an enthusiastic member of the Shropshire Imperial

Top: The "White House," where James Matthews was born in the hill country of mid-Wales, overlooks Newtown in the valley below. (D. Sleigh, 2005)
Bottom: A closer view of the "White House," still standing in 2005. (D. Sleigh)

Yeomanry for 43 years, of which he served 19 years as a quartermaster "greatly respected by all classes."[6]

All James's early memories appear to have been happy ones. He had a governess for his early education, Miss Halford, a beloved figure who occupied a cherished place in his memory (so much so, that he sought her out when he was in Britain again in the First World War and nearly 40 years of age). Following his educational start with Miss Halford, he and Martin attended a school run by the same Mr. Cook who had tutored their father; James has nothing adverse to say about this school.

The only disquieting element in these years was the Matthews' constant change of residence. When Martin was born, the family lived near the Short Bridge, but by the time James arrived, it had moved to a house about a mile outside the town. Called the "White House," it still has that name and is still painted white. Pink roses grow by the wicket gate at the entrance. The house stands alone on the edge of a steep valley that plunges down to Newtown in the hollow, and beyond the valley you look out to a dramatic sweep of the surrounding hills. Perhaps it was too far from town, for when the last child, Frank, was born, they were living close to the centre of Newtown. A pattern of perpetual moving was to be the norm throughout Herbert's and Mary's lives.

In this environment of loving parents, affectionate relatives and a comfortable prosperous home, James might have been expected to reach adult years in an atmosphere of continued security. So many positive factors in his life should have assured a relatively easy and untroubled emotional development, and his family's sound financial standing should have paved the way to a career with excellent prospects. But when he was only nine years old, something happened to change all this: it was the great gamble of emigration.

It is hard to explain why Herbert made this unexpected decision. Or was it Mary's decision?—she made many choices for him. On the surface Herbert had little reason to move away from Newtown. This part of Wales had been the family's home for generations; he had strong ties to Newtown in terms of relations and friends; he had a thriving coal business. On the other hand, even though Herbert's own business was doing well, his father's mill was not in such a happy state, for his hand looms could not compete with the mechanized weaving of the larger mills. (After William's death in 1890, the Matthews mill declined still more and had to be sold a few years later.) The insecurity of the Welsh woollen industry in general by the 1880s must have been very troubling to Herbert, for the economy of the town was dependent on the mills.

Even at that early date, in 1887, Herbert and Mary felt that Wales was "overcrowded"—this was the explanation they gave James many years later. They wanted better opportunities for their sons, and so they looked at other options in newer, less populated countries. According to James, it was purely for the boys that Herbert resolved to take this drastic step, to leave his family (his elderly parents were still living), give up a profitable business and risk everything to take a chance on the unknown. James always regarded it as an act of extreme unselfishness, typical of his father's nature. It is very possible that it was Mary Matthews, rather than Herbert, who pushed for this radical move. In later years, when recording his parents' lives in dispassionate hindsight, James came to the conclusion that his mother might well have been the instigator of their incessant changes of home and their unsettled lifestyle.

At first they considered western Canada as a place to start their new life, but were deterred by thoughts of the frigid winters that were the popular concept of life in any part of Canada. Perhaps they were unaware of the small sheltered coastal belt in the southwest, where James was eventually to make his life. In the end it was New Zealand, with its temperate climate, that attracted them the most and became their ultimate choice. It was really a much more logical choice than Canada, for the woollen industry was already booming in New Zealand, and Herbert, with his family background, might hope to make use of his specialized knowledge and launch seamlessly into his new life. Rather strangely, however, he did not intend to continue in the family tradition and operate as a woollen manufacturer. Instead, he decided to embark on a different type of career and start up as a sheep farmer. Sheep farms abounded, for the lush green slopes of New Zealand were already proving ideally suited to this type of land use.

But it was one thing to have the financial expertise of a businessman and quite another to live the life of a pioneer farmer, and Herbert's plans were not to work out as expected. James was later to make the sorrowful comment, "The pioneers always pay."[7]

A formal portrait of the Matthews family just before they emigrated to New Zealand in 1887. Left to right: Herbert, Frank, James, Martin, Mary. (J. Owen photo. E. Walser)

CHAPTER 2

Youth in New Zealand

The migration to New Zealand, though an extreme measure, was not at all out of character for James's parents. It epitomized one of their instinctive modes of behaviour—to move away if conditions at home or at work failed to meet expectations, not to look for compromise or exercise patience, but to disconnect completely from the negatives that had been an irritant in their lives and hope to experience a happy metamorphosis in a new setting.

It was a pattern that had been apparent from the time of Mary Matthews' decision to move miles away from her hometown of Shrewsbury to set up her milliner's shop in Newtown. A curious restlessness had marked her life and Herbert's from the time they first married. In the course of their nearly 15 married years in Newtown, the couple had changed house no fewer than seven times. The move to New Zealand was merely an extension of this on a grand scale. Unfortunately, it would be no more of an answer to their problems than any other of their moves, nor would it be the end of their journeys, but only another beginning.

James gives no indication of his grandparents' reaction to this bombshell. It must have been shattering news for them when they learned that their reliable and serious-minded son was about to throw up a thriving business in Newtown and go out of their lives—probably forever—leaving only their other son, Charles (known for enjoying a good time) to take care of the mills and other business affairs. James did recall that old family friends and servants were shocked and concerned, prophesying storms at sea, shipwrecks and other dreadful disasters. These anxieties were not completely fanciful either, for although the family was to travel by steamship, it was a small vessel by today's standards and a slow one (capable of a speed of only 11 knots), and accidents at sea were not uncommon. In that era there would be no means of sending out an SOS, and in any case few other ships would be passing their way.

They were to leave from Plymouth, but on the way the family made a special visit to London. Herbert and Mary wanted to give the boys a good educational experience and leave them with edifying memories of the historic sights. Frank was only 5, but Martin was 14 and James was 9—old enough for some of these images to imprint themselves on the memory. No doubt the boys were exposed to the usual cultural sights of London—the Houses of Parliament, Westminster Abbey, the Tower of London, and so on—but what made the greatest impression on young James was none of these. The marvel that literally dazzled his imagination was a display of the newly invented electric light in the Lowther shopping arcade just off the Strand. Great crowds always stood across the street, viewing the wondrous sight of the names illuminated in golden light (actually rather a dull yellow from the carbon lamps.) With its array of toy shops, the arcade itself must have held great allure for a child, but what chiefly lingered in James's memory from this tour of London was the marvellous electric light.

The voyage to New Zealand was uneventful, contrary to all the depressing predictions. They put out from Plymouth harbour on October 6, 1887, on the Royal Mail passenger vessel *Tainui*. This was a steamship, but because steam machinery was not entirely dependable, it was equipped for sail and did sometimes make use of sail power in a favourable wind. After six weeks at sea they arrived without mishap at Port Chalmers, Dunedin, disembarking on November 20. From here they travelled up the coast on another ship to their ultimate destination, which was Christchurch on the South Island. Much of their baggage was to follow on the sailing ship *May Queen*, including some of Mary's special treasures that she had insisted on keeping. But the *May Queen* was less fortunate than the *Tainui*. After travelling safely across two vast oceans, she was just approaching Christchurch when the weather turned stormy, and as she struggled to enter harbour, she foundered and sank. The sodden cargo was eventually raised, but it is doubtful whether many of Mary's cherished possessions survived the immersion.

The family stayed a short time in Christchurch while deciding their future plans—long enough for James to spend January to July of 1888 at St. Alban's School, the first of several schools he would be shuffled around to in the new country. Herbert's first priority was to discover what land was available and which region would be best suited for sheep farming. He came to the conclusion that the North Island held the most promise, so with the couple's usual swiftness of decision the family quickly transferred itself to Wellington to consider the next step.

It did not take them long to explore the district before taking the plunge and investing in the acreage that was meant for their sons' future. About 50 miles north of Wellington, on the west coast of the island, lay the small rudimentary settlement of Te Horo. Known today as a holiday resort by the sea, the community now advertises itself with attractive colour photos of a beach and tourist lodges. But on the east side of the railway line, Te Horo has a different character, for you are now nearing the foothills of the Tararua Ranges, which run parallel to the coast. It is hiking and walking country, with forested trails leading to the Otaki Gorge and the Mangaone River. This was the spot where Herbert Matthews chose to carve out a farm in the heart of a jungle-like forest.

The whole of this area was then an untouched wilderness: acres and acres of forest extended for miles around. Even the little flag station of Te Horo itself was hemmed in by trees to within a few yards of the railway platform and up to the very edge of the tracks. To reach the Matthews' acreage, two miles east of the station, you had to ride horseback through a wilderness of fronded green jungle, following a muddy trail where horses sometimes sank up to their knees in winter. When the trail petered out, you were obliged to take to a rough creek bed, which sometimes had to function as a route for carts and pack animals.

Herbert and Mary had picked out a choice site for their home. It stood on a natural terrace, 40 feet above the surrounding land, and a little stream, known as Mangaone Creek, flowed around this terrace on three sides. Behind the house the land rose higher yet, to form a hill called Little Kapakapanui, and a broad sweep of more distant ranges filled the horizon. Herbert immediately had the whole acreage clear-cut, since it was intended for agricultural use, and in those days the forest was the enemy. He had paid £2 an acre for the 178 acres, and he then paid another £2 an acre for having it logged and cleared of brush. Finally the forest lay vanquished, the felled trees massed in chaotic piles over the whole site, 10 feet deep in places. It was burned off; seed was thrown onto the ashes of the fire, and soon it all greened over, and young steers were put out to graze the land. Sheds were erected, fences put up. Sapling fruit trees were planted. Lastly, they built the house, a simple, timber-framed cottage, which they named "Glenhafren" as a sentimental link with an old family estate in Wales. (It became a Matthews tradition to give their subsequent homes the same Welsh name.)

Unlike many of his fellow pioneers, Herbert had the advantage of having emigrated with sufficient capital to employ labour and jump-start his farming enterprise. Whereas the majority of immigrants were obliged to work for years to clear their land *and* put up buildings by their own labour, Herbert and Mary were in the happy position of creating a pleasant home setting and a working farm in just about a single year. But there the benefit ended, and the difficulties of the new life began to make themselves felt.

The first thing that happened was a grass fire. It was the end of their first season; a scorching summer had come and gone, and the fields had all dried out. Then someone carelessly tossed away a match, and in a minute flames were creeping through the brittle yellowed grass. The family fought desperately hard to save all they could of their year's work. James was proud to remember how he had rushed in to help—only 10 years old but "with the vigour of a man." They laboured to the point of exhaustion, but the fire moved too fast, and in the end they could only stand and watch as the flames rolled away into the distance and swallowed up their fields. In the space of just a few hours Herbert had lost the greater part of his new pasture. What was left could barely support his herd, and inevitably the cattle weakened and

Top: The Matthews' home in Te Horo, New Zealand, viewed in 1934. Like all the Matthews' homes, it was named "Glenhafren." (CVA, Add. MSS 54, 508-D-1, file 5, #13)

Bottom: The Te Horo home in 1934, a closer view. (CVA, Add. MSS 54, 508-D-1, file 5, #12)

some died. In the face of this disaster he maintained a quiet courage and told his son, "Jimmie, there are greater losses at sea."[1]

Herbert and Mary were a brave couple with plenty of resilience and staying power, and they were determined to make a success of their farming venture for the sake of their boys, but their upbringing had not equipped them for the life of the pioneer. Herbert had never even cleaned his own boots in the old country, and Mary's skills had lain more in the manipulation of pretty hat trimmings than in the outdoor routine of a farmer's wife. Both were well educated and had interests beyond the isolated homestead where they were virtually imprisoned, "walled in on all sides with the beautiful fern-floored forest."[2] Herbert in particular felt the lack of mental stimulus, and he struggled with the strangeness of life in the adopted country. Beautiful as it was with its fantastic tree forms and subtropical flora, its exotic birds and its jagged waves of mountains, New Zealand still represented more of a challenge than a solution.

Stoically the family set out to recover from the setback of the fire. The following year they managed to acquire the sheep that they had planned for; their orchard trees began to fill out and the grass grew back. The nearest store was seven miles away, but they were able to live off the land to some extent, shooting pigeons and wild pigs and taking honey from wild bees in the bush. Mary experimented with palatable herbs and edible greenery from the native vegetation. They caught and sold the wild horses that ran in droves over the sandhills near Te Horo.

The three boys adapted to the strange new lifestyle. The nearest school was 13 miles away at Paraparaumu, so each day James and Frank had to ride horseback through the forest to the station at Te Horo and take the train from there. With few other immigrant families in the area, James and Frank found themselves the only non-Maori children in the school. James picked up a bit of the Maori language, and was even taken for a Maori himself at times because when he got sunburned, his skin turned brown rather than red.[3] Their older brother Martin never attended school at all once they reached New Zealand. At 14 he was apprenticed to a carpenter in Christchurch, and after the family settled at Te Horo he spent his time working on the farm with his father.

For three years they lived in this way. Each year the farm became more productive and Herbert, in spite of the drawbacks of Te Horo, was rewarded by the knowledge that he was developing a potentially valuable asset for his son or sons. Martin would be 19 in July of 1892, and Herbert already thought of him as a future partner in the enterprise. But now Herbert's plans began to unravel in an unforeseen yet very natural turn of events. To his dismay, he found that Martin did not even want the farm. His oldest son was beginning to feel restless and cooped up in the limited confines of the Glenhafren farm and needed to get away on his own, to meet new people, to live in a wider society. Appalled and desperate at his son's desertion, Herbert vainly offered Martin an immediate partnership, or even to lease the farm to him on the most favourable terms, but Martin was adamant. "Like all young men [he] had plans of adventure and travel of his own, and did not take kindly to being the obedient foreman," James recalled.[4]

It was an impasse but not an open clash, for the Matthews' maintained strong family feelings that persisted throughout life in spite of many stresses—and indeed Martin was later to combine forces with his parents in other ventures. Herbert and Mary appear to have placed great reliance upon Martin, whom they may have regarded as more stable in character than the enthusiastic and emotional James. Fourteen-year-old James passionately urged his parents to let him take Martin's place and make it possible to keep the farm in the family, but although they responded kindly to his offer, the suggestion was never taken seriously. It is curious that they should not have considered it as a solution, for Martin had been not much older when they first began to farm the Glenhafren property. In any case it would have meant a wait of only a few years before James was of age to take over much of the work, and Herbert himself was far from aging—he was only 41 when Martin left. It can only be inferred that Herbert and Mary had doubts concerning James's volatile nature and the likelihood that he would never be able to tolerate the uneventful life of an isolated sheep farmer. Possibly too they had already recognized in James a superior intelligence and decided that his quick brain and talent for expression were qualities that lent themselves more to a career in business than to the rural life.

Without stopping to ponder their decision, Herbert and Mary abruptly sold the farm in which they had invested so much labour. It was a good investment for the neighbour who bought it, for it was just about to come into full production and was sold again a few years later at an extremely good profit.[5] (The same ironic sequence of events was simultaneously unfolding on the other side of the world in Canada, as the first generation of pioneers aged and the second generation rejected the farming life. James was later to draw the parallel: "It is the old story of the injustice of fate to pioneers. It has been the same in millions of instances in Canada. The pioneers always pay."[6])

Herbert never completely recovered from the sudden collapse of his hopes. Why had he made the sacrifice of emigrating at all? he asked himself. He was a deeply sensitive individual, and the shock of this tremendous disappointment affected him in all his future actions. Nor did the family ever regain its original sense of unity and stability. The repercussions of the Te Horo debacle were to have a permanent effect on James in particular, as his parents lost their motivation for the future and moved restlessly around from one city to another. After a succession of homes and a succession of schools, as soon as James became of age to make his own decisions, his basic requirement was for permanence and security in his own home life.

After leaving Te Horo in 1892, Herbert and Mary moved to Wellington to consider their options, and James and Frank transferred to the Thorndon School there. But this was to be only a nine-month interlude. In 1893 the family were off again, this time to Auckland. (Martin, after a brief period on a sheep station, had rejoined the family in Wellington and then remained there to work as an electrician.)

In Auckland James had to get used to two more new schools, first Point Chevalier, and after this a prestigious grammar school known as Auckland College. Assessing his own educational standing at school, he acknowledged that while he was "eminently successful in mathematics and chemistry," he was "deficient in languages"—a surprising conclusion from one who displayed such a natural gift for the written and spoken word. He cannot have attended either of these schools for more than a term or two, for he tells us that he left school for good in December of 1893 at the age of 15. His parents, coming from a business background, had never contemplated an academic education for any of their children, and the lack of such credentials was always to cause James a certain unease in his dealings with those who could put degrees after their name.

Because James was in poor health when he left school, it was thought that an outdoor job would do him good, so he spent most of 1894 employed as a farmhand at Warkworth. He learned to drive oxen and how to plow and shear. He worked first for a farmer named Morrison at Red Bluff Orchards, then at a Mr. Macklow's, where he was apparently very unhappy. Finally he found an occupation that suited him much better than farm work—he was hired as a clerk for a large timber concern, the Kauri Timber Company, whose office was in Auckland. James was now able to live with his parents again at their home in the neighbourhood of Mount Eden Road.

Now came a second terrible event in the lives of the Matthews family. It was July 1895, and exam time was looming for James's younger brother, Frank. Because of missing several weeks of school while on a visit to Sydney, Australia, with his parents, Frank had fallen behind in his studies and had decided not to go to school on a day when he was supposed to take one of his exams. He wandered around the property looking for something to do and thought it might be exciting to blast a small log with gunpowder. He bored the hole, filled it, lit the fuse and ran behind a tree to watch it go off, but as he ran he disturbed the log, which rolled over at an angle. A small stone blew out from the tamping and struck the side of his cheek. After a week the wound had still not healed and a doctor was called in; the diagnosis was tetanus, then untreatable. Frank died on July 10, just nine days short of his 13th birthday. "His last calmly spoken words to me," wrote James, "were 'I think I'm going to die.' "[7]

Frank and James had always been good companions, for Frank was a quiet and nice-natured boy—a perfect complement to James's vigorous personality—and in spite of their age difference, they had been very compatible. Frank's death was saddening for the whole family, but the person who appeared the most ravaged by grief was Herbert, whose extreme display of sorrow made a lasting impression on James. Mary, as always, appeared stoical and calm in the face of

FRANK, JAMES'S YOUNGER BROTHER, DIED OF TETANUS AT THE AGE OF 13 AFTER AN ACCIDENT WITH GUNPOWDER. (E. WALSER)

trouble, and seemed better able to resign herself to this new blow. It was all the sadder in that it was their second loss of a child. Little Agnes lay far away in St. David's churchyard in Newtown; Frank was laid to rest in the Purewa Cemetery near St. Heliers.

The death of Frank marked another turning point in their lives. In the three years that had gone by since they left Te Horo, Herbert had never found the confidence to commit himself to any further enterprise. He had investigated certain prospects, but his cautious nature had held him back from risking his capital a second time. Now all his remaining drive seemed to desert him. He had no heart for planning the future, and even began to have doubts about his choice of New Zealand.

Restlessly, he and Mary left for Wales to spend several months visiting family and friends, but on their return at the end of 1896 they did not go back to Auckland. Instead, they headed straight for Wellington to be near Martin. James, in Auckland, was left out of the equation completely, and was so from that time forward. In spite of Martin's earlier defection, he still seemed to be the son whom his parents depended on. Possibly James was seen as difficult, headstrong, impetuous and better left to his own devices. Although he was the younger son—only 17 when Herbert and Mary had abruptly embarked for Wales—they more or less abandoned him. From then on he hardly saw his parents, though there were occasional visits throughout their lives, and always regular letters. It was hurtful to James, unquestionably. He wrote in his memoirs that he "protested and protested—there seemed no way to remedy it."[8] As for Martin, apart from a few days spent with James in early 1897, the brothers were never to meet again. It had never been a close relationship, but rather one that was tinged with competitiveness and even latent antagonism. In all James's references to his elder brother in his genealogical notes, he never once includes any positive word of affection, but only an aura of veiled criticism.

This was essentially the break-up of the Matthews family, for in the spring of 1897 Herbert, Mary and Martin all left the country—this time with no plans to return. Their destination was South America, where Martin wanted to take up ranching. Deserted by his whole family, James remained on his own in New Zealand with no relation to turn to in case of need. It is a matter of speculation as to the cause of Herbert and Mary's apparent indifference to the welfare of their younger son, whom one might suppose to have been more in need of parental support and encouragement than Martin, who was five years older. The fact that they had removed themselves from James's life from the time he was 17 and were now leaving him behind altogether would seem to indicate a tough-love relationship, even though a very affectionate one (as their letters clearly show), and possibly a sense of frustration in their inability to deal with his temperament and his strong will.

Once in South America, with its alien landscape and, especially, the major hurdle of learning a new language, Herbert and Mary quickly decided that this was not the place for them after all. (Martin did remain for many years, and became the manager of a huge cattle ranch at Punta Arenas.) The older couple journeyed on to Britain, and settled in a spot not far from Wales, at Rock Ferry near the estuary of the River Mersey—though they would eventually tire of this home too. At Rock Ferry Herbert bought some cottages and was content to live on rental income, converting his assets into an annuity. He never worked again, and he and Mary continued to spend their lives moving from one place to another, forever in search of the perfect home.

In view of James's passionate attachment to his mother, he must have suffered greatly from her absence now. Alone in Auckland, he felt the lack of family and friends more acutely than those around him might have realized. (Later, in his Vancouver years, when he became notorious for his hasty temper and intimidating front, few people suspected his deep inner need for a close relationship, nor his profound gratitude to those who offered him warmth and support.) Yearning for affection and old enough for romance, he was in a susceptible frame of mind when Maud Boscawen walked into his life.

He had had a chance meeting with Maud once before. It occurred at the time when his family was living halfway up Mount Eden, the high volcanic plateau in the centre of Auckland, from whose summit you look down on a city surrounded by sea. It was early evening; James heard the sound of rifle fire from up above and decided to climb to the top and see where the soldiers were practising. At the summit, however, he could find only one person, and this was Maud's sister Gladys. "The wind was blowing her beautiful tresses in a stream behind her, and she made a pretty silhouette against the sky." He spoke to her, and they ended up walking down Mount Eden together until they reached the end of the path, where it joined Mount Eden Road. This was where they came upon Maud, who had gone out to look for her younger sister. Even after the passage of many years, James never forgot the charm of that first encounter. "I still have fond recollections of that meeting. It was a beautiful summer's evening, and she was pretty and petite."[9]

Maud's family lived so close by, on Mount Eden Road, that it is not surprising that she and James would eventually have met again. It happened in November of 1897, and this time there was instant infatuation on James's part. The two of them began to meet secretly, and in no time at all were engaged to be married. They spent a blissful Christmas together—where, he does not say, but it certainly could not have been at the Boscawen residence, for none of this was taking place with the knowledge or sanction of Maud's father.

The obstacle—and the reason for such secrecy—was that the Matthews family and the Boscawens moved in very different social circles. The Boscawen family was of such standing that it could justly be termed aristocratic. Maud's father, Colonel John Boscawen, was the nephew of the 6th Viscount Falmouth. The family seat in Cornwall was (and is) an impressive country house at Tregothnan on the River Fal, where Maud's relations at a later date were to entertain royalty in the persons of King Edward VII and Queen Alexandra.

(The Tregothnan gardens, overlooking Falmouth Bay, are famous for their rare camellias and rhododendrons, and are on the tour list of garden enthusiasts today.) Maud's grandfather had been chaplain to Queen Victoria, and Maud herself was named after Victoria's daughter, Princess Maud, whom her father would have met during his childhood. Maud's second name, the unusual and beautiful name Valentia, also had noble connections, for her great-grandmother, Catherine Annesley, was the daughter of the 10th Viscount Valentia. (This was an Anglo-Irish peerage: the Island of Valentia lies off the southwest coast of Ireland.) Clearly, the son of a coal merchant was in no position to compete with such antecedents.

At the time of James's meeting with Maud, Colonel Boscawen was serving as an honorary aide-de-camp, or secretary, to the governor of New Zealand. His previous career had been in the navy, but now his excellent connections had secured him this position, which he would occupy in three successive governorships from 1888 to 1910. He had been living in New Zealand since the 1870s, and Maud, his first child, was born there in 1877 in Thorndon, Wellington.

In her own way, Maud had experienced just as unsettled a childhood as James, and she was equally in need of security and affection. Her mother, Katherine, a "brilliant, talented and vivacious" young woman, had died in childbirth in 1884 when Maud was only six or seven.[10] At first Maud was boarded out, but eventually she and her siblings were offered a home by her mother's sister, Gertrude Hamilton, at Dannevirke, where Captain Hamilton ran a sheep station—"a beautiful place," according to James. Two years later her father remarried and soon had a new family to raise. It does not appear that Maud rejoined him then. Possibly she stayed on with her aunt for some time, but eventually seems to have been boarded out once more with various friends or acquaintances. James records: "The story of Miss Boscawen's life up to 1895 is a repetition of one boarding-house after another, at some of which she was ill-treated."[11]

Maud was living at Napier when the news came that her stepmother had died in January 1895, and she was asked to come back to her father's home in Auckland to manage the household for him. Though still only 17, as the oldest daughter she was obliged to take on this responsibility. Irksome as it may have been to a young girl of this age, at least it offered her a secure home and the opportunity of being introduced to a wider social circle. However, her father had not intended this circle to include such outsiders as James Matthews.

Any thought of inviting James to the Boscawen home had been effectively extinguished at an accidental encounter with her father. James and Maud were meeting secretly by this time, but one evening, when he was escorting her home, they unfortunately saw Colonel Boscawen coming in their direction. It was too late to avoid the encounter, so James was introduced. The colonel's manner must have been icy indeed, for it made a profound impression on James. He was left with a lasting memory of a man with an "aristocratic appearance and haughty demeanour" and a personality that was "obstinate, self-loving and proud."[12] It was to be their one and only meeting.

It was a severe rebuff, but James was not so easily deterred. He followed up this meeting with a letter to Maud's father, in which he evidently explained his feelings for Maud and his hopes for the future. His thoughts must have poured out with great eloquence, if one is to judge by his style of letter-writing in later life, but they nevertheless met with the coldest of responses. All the colonel sent back to him was a postcard, which included the words: "I never discuss the affairs of my family with a total stranger."[13]

Although Colonel Boscawen behaved kindly to his own family, as James was to admit, Maud cannot have found her life in the Boscawen household particularly comfortable after the widowed colonel married for the third time in 1896. Maud continued to live with them, but by 1897 when she became engaged to James, she may have felt displaced in her own home and may have been only too eager to make a new life for herself through marriage. James, impulsive and passionate, was desperately anxious to do the same and recreate the home and affectionate atmosphere which he had been robbed of by his own family's absence. During the next few months the couple made firm plans for the future.

Life in New Zealand seemed to hold few prospects for them, and so they decided on the most extreme solution: they would emigrate and start life in a new country together. For James this was not such a difficult step, having moved around from place to place all his life and seen his parents travelling from continent to continent, but Maud had never known anywhere but the North Island of New Zealand, and for her it was a much bigger decision. James's enthusiasm must have swept aside any hesitations, for Maud found herself willing to risk it.

The plan was that James would go ahead and find work and then send for her as soon as he could raise the money for her passage. (We do not know if this was to be an actual elopement, or whether it was merely to be kept secret until the last moment, but certainly they realized that Maud's father would never agree to finance such a scheme.) James was still working as a clerk for a timber firm, though by now it was a different company, the Waitemata Sawmill Company, and with this experience he thought he might find similar work in the United States.

He embarked on the *Alameda* on March 19, 1898, and arrived in San Francisco on April 6. Writing 30 years later, he states with rueful amusement that he went "to make a fortune in America" (the quotation marks are his, for he was wryly echoing the proverbial hope of so many young emigrants). This was not to happen; no fortune was made, and his first few months in North America were far from successful financially. His dream of sending passage money for Maud was going to be harder to realize than he had imagined.

After a couple of weeks he left San Francisco and sailed up the coast to Tacoma, having heard of opportunities in the timber industry. In May he briefly held jobs in Tacoma, probably clerical jobs in the offices of timber companies. His description of the next month or so is confused. He mentions both Seattle and Whatcom (present-day Bellingham) as places that figured in his travels. By mid-June he was working for the Whatcom Falls Mill Company, but by August he was back in Tacoma and employed by the Tacoma Sawmill Company in what he calls the "Old Town."

He worked there for a few months, but it was becoming increasingly obvious that saving $100 to send to Maud was going to take far too many months of waiting, and patience was a quality that was notably lacking in James's makeup. He was obsessed by his need to see her, and his ever-volatile spirits sank into a miserable state of depression.

In desperation, he was reduced to asking his father for a loan, though without telling him what it was for, and in fact deliberately giving him a wrong impression. Herbert felt obliged to help out with the money, even though it meant drawing on capital—a cardinal sin to his prudent mind—but when he later realized that some of it had been spent on Maud's passage, he was extremely upset to discover that he had been misled. Although he and Mary assured James that they would look upon Maud as a daughter, they told him repeatedly that he should have waited and clearly felt hurt by his deception. A subsequent plea for further money met with lengthy lectures on his extravagant ways—"money thrown away"—and the need for economy and patience in a new country. (James says that he later returned the money "and $200 in addition as interest," which sounds excessive for a family loan.[14])

By now something had gone wrong for him at his place of work. "Misfortune had troubled me in the interval," he writes vaguely, "and … I left Tacoma, no employment." (Presumably he had been laid off or dismissed, but his father was under the impression that James had given up the job solely to meet Maud's ship in Victoria. Herbert pointed out that Maud would have been perfectly capable of travelling that further distance to Tacoma on her own.)

Whatever the circumstances, James now left the United States for good and entered British Columbia.

Had it been his plan all along to make his way to Canada, to live in what was then a British dominion like New Zealand, under the British flag?—for he was intensely loyal all his life to the concept of the British Empire. He merely writes that, after living in the United States for nine months, he "didn't like it" and "had an urge to get beneath the folds of the good old Union Jack once again." Strangely, he has no further explanation of this seemingly arbitrary decision that was to determine the whole course of his life. We are left only with the terse statement that from Tacoma, he made his way to Victoria on Vancouver Island to wait for Maud's arrival.[15]

CHAPTER 3

The Magic City

As a cold, steady rain poured down and the darkness of the November evening closed in, the two new immigrants stepped ashore at the Vancouver wharf. Night hung over the city; long tiers of mountains loomed obscurely on the north side of Burrard Inlet, and a ragged outline of trees pressed in on the southern edges of the town itself. The plank sidewalks were slippery from the incessant rain, and the roadway itself was nothing but a sticky morass. On that day, November 3, 1898, a *Daily Columbian* reporter complained that he didn't know which was worse, "the awful rain or the mud."

But James and Maud were happy just to be together after months of anticipation. James's patience had been strained to the utmost waiting for Maud in Victoria, for her ship had been delayed many hours due to a misunderstanding on the part of the harbour officials. A health officer and a pilot officer were supposed to meet the ship, but no one came, and it turned out that the *Aorangi* had not been expected for another two days. It took further time before they were given clearance to emerge from the quarantine station and the passengers finally allowed to disembark. At last James and Maud were reunited.

Late as she had been in docking in Victoria, the *Aorangi* was still due to sail on to Vancouver that afternoon, so James immediately joined Maud on board for the final leg of her journey. "Miss Boscawen" is listed in the *Province* of November 4, 1898, as one of the saloon passengers proceeding on to Vancouver, but there is no mention of James. He may very well have been one of the lowly unnamed individuals who were travelling steerage, and therefore did not rate a newspaper entry. It was a lengthy passage through the maze of Gulf Islands and around the tip of Stanley Park to the Vancouver wharf, and it was seven o'clock on this dismal, dark, wet night when James and Maud peered out at the lights of their chosen city and disembarked into the rain and mud of the ill-made streets. Nothing of course could deter this honeymoon couple, as they virtually were, and with hope in their hearts they made their way to one of the nearest hotels, the old Leland Hotel on West Hastings, and spent their first night in Vancouver under its roof.[1]

When they explored the city next morning, they may have been favourably surprised by what they saw. It had been only 12 years since the Great Fire of Vancouver, when a freakish windstorm had swept through a pile of debris where someone was burning brush and sent flames racing through the town. The wind had whirled into life with such deadly speed that within the space of 20 minutes every building in town was reduced to a smouldering heap. But the city had rebounded instantly with a defiant vigour. Only five weeks later a photographer recorded dozens of commercial buildings already lining each side of the main shopping street—Cordova—and by the following year, a photo showing a bird's-eye view from Hastings and Dunlevy reveals a spread of houses and wooden shanties as far as the eye can see.

Brick and stone structures went up in rapid succession, and by the time James and Maud first walked the streets of Vancouver, they would have seen an astounding array of very impressive buildings, obviously designed to be worthy of a city with an important future. The baronial turrets of the Canadian Pacific Railway station, the Old-World stonework of Christ Church, the dome of the Courthouse, the many gables of the first Hotel Vancouver, not to mention the Palladian-style pillars and pediments of many banks and offices and hotels—all these were already ornamenting the city by the end of 1898. And many of them were to be rebuilt on an even grander scale during the golden age of Vancouver's pre-First World War architecture.

In only a dozen years Vancouver had metamorphosed from the shantytown of the Great Fire to a vastly ambitious, almost pretentious, west-coast centre of commerce—by 1898 some people were suggesting hopefully that within a decade the city would become "the Liverpool of the West." And the city's ambitions were not merely confined to commerce. Arts and entertainment, basic needs of any civilization, had always found some kind of expression even in the early days, but with the new Vancouver Opera House and the nucleus of a museum and art gallery, Vancouver was clearly aspiring to a position as a centre of culture as well as commerce. Its population by 1898 had jumped to 25,000.[2]

Imposing as the heart of the city might be, its sophistication was confined to a relatively small district. The city was limited to a very concentrated area of development. Today's West End, with its soaring condos, was still a forested wilderness; no building had penetrated west of Burrard. On the south shore of False Creek beyond the area of Vine Street it was also a tangle of brush and woodland, where the occasional bear or cougar was still to be seen, and deer were hunted. It was the same on the outskirts south of town—the dirt roads petered out and faded away and merged into shadowy forest. Little creeks flowed plentifully into English Bay from Kitsilano Point, and small lakes and sloughs and muskeg formed a watery network near the shore.

This was the Vancouver that James Matthews discovered as he first explored the city, and it was the Vancouver that he lost his heart to. He never forgot the early sense of revelation that coloured his whole vision of the city in the years to come. Always in his imagination, he remembered Vancouver as it was in those wonderful impressionable days, when he first saw and marvelled at his new surroundings and attempted to reconcile the strange contrast that he was witness to—the contrast of a young city struggling to arise within a pristine setting of untamed nature. An unrepentant romantic, James never ceased to be stirred by this image of the city he loved. Throughout his life he retained the perception of having lived at a special moment in history—"the concluding chapter of an epoch … and with that comes the supreme achievement of the magic city which grew out of a forest whose trees were taller than our monumental buildings. It's a chapter in the history of the world that may not come again."[3] For James, Vancouver was always to be the "magic city."

From the moment he arrived, James never once appears to have entertained the idea of any further move. It was as if all his past experience had faded into insignificance as soon as he set foot in Vancouver, and life had taken on a freshness and colour that overwhelmed his past existence. There were to be no experimental relocations to any other province, or even to any other part of British Columbia. Both he and Maud had experienced too many different homes in the course of their formative years to wish for any perpetuation of this sort of life—James spoke pityingly of his parents' "continuous world tour in search of Utopia" and their wishful belief in "the pot of gold at the foot of the rainbow"—and he had no desire to emulate what he regarded as a pathetic and unsatisfying mode of existence.[4]

Once reunited in Vancouver, the couple might have been expected to marry immediately, but, surprisingly, it was almost three months before the wedding took place. The problem was almost certainly James's age. Maud was 21 and of legal age to marry without her parents' consent, but James had only turned 20 in September. He knew it would be useless to write to Herbert for his permission, since both his parents had been sending him a series of disapproving letters begging him to wait before thinking of marriage. They were too young, James had no job and couldn't support a wife, they told him; and he received another lecture on his "madcap hastiness."[5] There were also hints that his parents were concerned about the obvious difference in social status between the two families, and worried that Maud thought she was too good for him. It was all very negative and discouraging.

By January the situation was becoming even more pressing, for Maud was now pregnant. Finally, James found a way out of the difficulty by applying to the Supreme Court in New Westminster for special dispensation to marry. On January 30, 1899, the *Daily Columbian* reported the following item in its "Local and Personal News":

"In the Supreme Court, on Saturday morning, before Mr. Justice Irving, permission was given James Skitt Matthews to enter the matrimonial state. The young man being under age, his parents 'beyond the sea,' as the statute puts it, and having the necessary inclination, the order was made."

The Saturday of the hearing was the 28th, and on the very next day, January 29, the couple were united in marriage at last. The ceremony took place in the historic setting of Christ Church, but it must have been a very plain and inadequate affair, a painful contrast to the pretty wedding Maud might have enjoyed in an approved marriage in New Zealand. Still, their immediate problems were now over. Their relationship was legalized, James had a job and they had found a one-room apartment to live in.

Five months later, the twins were born.

It had taken James a little while to find a permanent position. He does not describe what sort of rough work he might have had to take in the meantime, or if he found any work at all. However, on January 2, 1899, he was lucky enough to be hired for an office job that was reasonably congenial. Repetitive manual labour had no appeal for him and would have resulted in great boredom, but his new position as a clerk with Imperial Oil provided sufficient mental interest to suit him. It must have involved bookkeeping, for he grandly described himself on his marriage document as an "accountant," but he was actually hired on the strength of his ability to type and take shorthand, both of which skills he had taught himself. His knowledge of typing had been somewhat illicitly acquired when he worked in the timber company office in New Zealand. "When our [stenographer] went to lunch he locked his machine, but sometimes he forgot, and when he did we two office boys took advantage. One stood guard at the door to warn if 'he' was coming, while the other typed—or tried to. This was how I learned," he told his friend General Odlum many years later, adding, "This is my sixtieth year as a two-finger typist."[6]

The company's office in 1902 was in the DeBeck building on Hastings Street, but the warehouse was at the south foot of Cambie Street. Its wagons and barrels of coal oil were stored there; it was the only warehouse in the city that supplied oil for the purpose of lighting. (The edges of Vancouver were still semi-rural, and just beside the warehouse, close to the dome of today's BC Place, was a large tract of bush where workhorses were put to pasture on Sundays, part of the vast holdings of the Canadian Pacific Railway and leased to Standard Oil. The undeveloped land stretched from Cambie to Homer and

James, aged 20, just before he left New Zealand "to make a fortune" in North America. (E. Walser)

down to the edge of False Creek. Any large trees had long ago fallen to the logger's axe, and it had since greened over with natural grasses, willow brush and alder.)

Before long the business developed a new and revolutionary sideline. James told the story in later years: "There had arrived in Vancouver a queer-looking vehicle called an automobile. We had read about them in magazines. One day the telephone rang. The call came from the Hastings Sawmill and the speaker asked me if we had any gasoline which could be used in automobiles." This was a novel consideration. After weighing up the merits of the three different types of gasoline available, they decided to send the office boy down to the warehouse to order a can of "74-brand" Baume gasoline, which was normally used for cleaning ladies' gloves. It was the first can of gasoline ever sold in BC for the use of a car.[7]

Back in these early days of automobile history, the filling procedure was a matter of trial and error; some American gas stations used watering cans; others merely dipped a can into a large barrel of gasoline. At James's place of business they were more inventive, for they set up a length of garden hose and attached it to a kitchen hot-water tank. When the first gasoline-powered car arrived in Vancouver in 1904, the arrival of about three cars at the pump might signify a busy morning at the gas station. Only when the volume of traffic involved seven or eight cars did they decide it might make life more pleasant for the attendant if he had some kind of shelter, and they put up a very basic corrugated iron shed, pronouncing it Vancouver's first gas station. This Imperial station at the southeast corner of Cambie and Smithe came into existence about 1907 and is believed to have been the first one in Canada.[8]

The senior bookkeeper and manager in James's office was Charles Merle Rolston, a man about five years older than James, who soon became a close friend of the Matthews family. A kindly individual, he lent the couple the considerable sum of $50 for them to buy a much-needed table and other items to supplement their makeshift bits and pieces of furnishings. The one-room apartment on Howe where they started out had soon been left behind for living quarters on the west side of Burrard near Pacific Street, where they shared an old house with one other couple. James and Maud had the whole upper floor, but they were still more or less camping out, with boxes for furniture and a minimum of cheap cutlery and kitchenware. It was hardly a fashionable part of town, down in a clearing at the foot of Burrard, where everything to the west of them was still a wasteland of stumps and Pacific Street could not be termed even a pathway.

They were still making do with these rooms when the twins were born on June 22, 1899, though the actual birth (and christening) took place in St. Luke's Home on Cordova, a hospital run by nursing sisters under the mandate of the adjoining St. James' Church. Because of potential complications—the twins being premature—there was a physician in attendance, and the delivery was also presided over by the formidable director of the hospital, Sister Frances (a high-profile figure for her many good works in the community).

The babies received the highly distinctive names of James Evelyn Huia and Herbert Llewellyn Terua, each child requiring a great many to fulfill his father's sense of family history. The first-born twin was named James after his father, Evelyn from the Boscawen side, and Huia because it was a Maori name denoting the sacred bird of the Natives. Herbert, the younger twin, also acquired a Maori name, Terua, meaning "second," as well as the Welsh name Llewellyn and his grandfather's name, Herbert. Each twin took the surname of Boscawen-Matthews.

The birth of not just one child but two, so soon after emigration and in such meagre circumstances, must have represented a major challenge to both Maud and James. She was only 21, "a lady of gentle birth and accustomed to live in affluence and vice-regal circles,"[9] as James was only too well aware, while he at the age of 20 was suddenly faced with the need to be the breadwinner for a family of four. His salary was $40 a month, and family needs now swallowed it all up. The romance of their secret engagement and their reunion in the beautiful setting of Vancouver—"an earthly paradise," to James—was now replaced by the reality of the heavy burden of childcare and hard work in very basic conditions. Worse still, after just a few months, Maud was pregnant again.

With the birth of the twins, it became urgent to find a place of their own, one with a yard for the children. The poor state of their finances severely limited their choice of available properties, so that in the end the best they could afford was something small and rundown, invariably described by James as the "shack." This was in the Fairview district, on 6th Avenue near Ash Street, right on the edge of False Creek and close to what are now the southern approaches to the Cambie Street Bridge. It was an old house that had once belonged to a mill owner, "a three-room affair, comfortable enough, but not very grand." In this "shack" their third child, Hugh, was born on July 31, 1900. Funds would not allow a nursing-home for this confinement, and so a doctor delivered the baby at home with the help of a midwife.

The infant's string of given names was again a lengthy one: Edward Hugh Pryce Boscawen-Matthews. Pryce was the Welsh element in the collection, while Edward and Hugh were both from his Boscawen forebears. (Evidently James could not bring himself to incorporate Maud's father's name of John.) After Hugh there were no more children, an unusual state of affairs in that era, when most women gave birth in a pattern of two-year intervals.

All three of the children acquired pet names within the family. James Evelyn went by his second name, abbreviated to "Lyn"—using his first name would have been too confusing. Herbert Llewellyn was rather strangely known as "Merle" after Charles Merle Rolston, who was not a relative, but merely a good friend. (It may be that Rolston was Herbert's godfather.) As for the little one, Edward Hugh, he was always "Hughie"—or even, playfully, "Chewie."

The twins being only 13 months old when Hugh was born, Maud's life must have been an exhausting test of endurance for the next few years. They were living in semi-rural conditions, for Fairview was only just on the cusp of development. Although all its giant trees had been logged in the very early days, it had gently reverted to nature and greened over again. "It was a most beautiful spot with grass in between the trees," remembered James. This access to a rough pasture meant that it was possible for the family to keep livestock, and now the workload grew to include tending a small flock of chickens and a Jersey cow, which provided good rich milk for the children. In addition, there were the constant trips to the beach to gather and cut firewood.

James never forgot how bravely Maud rallied to make the best of the hard life she had been plunged into so soon after the first idyllic days of marriage. Even after the years had brought embitterments, he was able to write: "The greatest of credit should be given to a lady of gentle birth, who [made] accommodation to the extremely straitened circumstances in which we found ourselves ... While here I was attacked with typhoid, and I shall never forget the unremitting attention she gave me." James was very ill indeed when he came down with typhoid, so ill that he spent June to September of 1902 in the old Vancouver City Hospital at Cambie and Pender streets. He was not an easy patient, but one nurse looked after him exceptionally well, a Miss Emily Edwardes, a recent addition to the hospital staff that spring. Emily, his favourite nurse, would unexpectedly re-enter his life in a different role one day.

Believing that his typhoid infection had been due to living in an unhealthy location (they were close to China Creek, which may have carried a certain amount of pollution, as did False Creek), James decided they should find somewhere else to live without delay. In short order they moved to Mount Pleasant until they could find something better, but it was only a very brief stay, because they soon heard of a place that appealed to them much more—a little cottage at 918 Pacific Street. It stood in a row of cottages near the north end of today's Burrard Bridge, where second-growth trees, stumps and blackberry thickets straggled thinly where once the forest had been. The couple liked the district, the rent was only eight dollars a month, and the family lived comfortably there for the next eight years. This was their first real home.

By now James was doing nicely in his job. Around 1905 or 1906, the company had given him a promotion that greatly expanded the scope of his work. Business was booming for Imperial Oil, and they were about to open a succession of new branches all around British Columbia. James's take-charge personality made him a natural choice to get things moving in the new areas, and he looked forward to his new position as a welcome opportunity to explore the province. One of his first assignments was to be responsible for oil storage tanks in parts of the Okanagan. Decades later, speaking to a Penticton audience at the age of 89, he recalled that in those early days there was not a single automobile in the Okanagan, and he had to reach Penticton by taking a boat down the lake. He described the drive to Hedley as a 12-hour trip, "occasionally meeting a six-team wagon on the narrow trail. We saw coyotes and once in a while a horse trod on a turtle. The entire distance was a wagon trail up and down the contours, little or no levelling, and a telegraph wire on short poles beside it."[10] It was all new experience, and he savoured it. He became the company's first agent in Victoria in 1907, and went on to travel widely around the province as far north as Prince Rupert, setting up branches and supervising the construction of warehouses. Between 1910 and 1915 he claims to have "occupied almost every position, except manager, in the gift of the company."[11]

James had proved himself to be a hard worker, but so far his story might have been that of any other enterprising immigrant. Beneath the superficiality of his working life, however, two great new interests had taken over the creative side of his personality, and a different persona was struggling for expression. In fact, almost from his earliest days in Vancouver he had begun to lead two other lives. In the city directories he was to be found listed as "J.S. Matthews, salesman Imperial Oil," but in his private life he could well have been described as "J.S. Matthews, writer" or "J.S. Matthews, militia officer."

Given his enquiring mind and his extraordinarily high level of energy, it was almost inevitable that he would have been unconsciously searching for some way of fulfilling the other sides of his nature. Although his work with Imperial Oil was beginning to offer more scope, his business career was not completely satisfying, nor did it represent a meaningful life. Much else was absorbing his interest and developing his largely untutored mind—it was as if the stimulus of living in a new country had suddenly jolted him into a heightened awareness of the world about him. Within a year or so of his arrival in Canada he began to channel a great deal of his energy into two unexpected enthusiasms: journalism was the first, followed shortly after by a passionate immersion in all things military. These two avocations, which developed into the equivalent of secondary careers, soon absorbed most of his spare time and attention. Devoted and loyal as he always was to his wife and children, he began to take his home for granted, accepting it as a natural, comfortable background for a more active life.

His natural flair for words began to find an outlet almost as soon as he settled in Vancouver, and he was barely 21 when he began to submit articles to the newspapers. Within a year or so of his arrival, his first piece was accepted. It was a history of the northern New Zealand timber industry, which can only have been based on his rather sketchy experience of it as a junior clerk—but he was not one to let this deficiency stand in his way.[12] Then, as he began to focus more on his new surroundings, he found himself powerfully gripped by the romance of west-coast history. Soon he was writing more pieces, but now they were inspired by his excitement in the discovery of pioneer adventures and exploration: the amazing drama of British Columbia's history had seized hold of his mind.

His first local contributions, published in the *Daily Province* in 1903 and 1904, concentrated on the historic paddlewheel steamer, the *Beaver*. They were merely short news items with no byline, but James later listed them as being his work, and they were a useful means of introducing himself to the paper's editors. He soon formed an amicable working relationship with the *Province*, which led to frequent and valuable publicity on its pages in the years to come. Dropping into the newspaper office with his material, he became friendly with the paper's circulation manager, Louis D. Taylor, who was then in the early stages of launching himself into city politics. James could hardly have guessed then how crucial the support of Taylor, as a longstanding mayor, would be to him nearly 30 years later.

Whether spoken or written, words came to James naturally and compulsively. They came bursting forth in an irrepressible flow, as his highly charged thoughts and emotions insistently demanded expression. Gifted with the ability to write vividly and convey atmosphere, he was a capable journalist and his stories still read well, even though his syntax does occasionally go astray and some of his more florid expressions inevitably have an old-fashioned ring. At its best his prose has a true poetic quality. He was also a great letter writer, often writing far into the night to unburden himself of his feelings, and his letters were as often a way of expressing affection and gratitude to his friends as they were a cathartic release for indignation or a therapeutic outlet in times of trouble. Correspondence with his parents in Wales was frequent, and throughout his life he received an affectionate weekly letter from his father.

Equally important in his life was his new-found passion for military affairs. It all began on March 17, 1903, forever memorable to him as the day he joined the Vancouver militia. The 6th Regiment of the Duke of Connaught's Own Rifles (DCOR) was just expanding to form two new companies in Vancouver, and James was there to enlist at the very first opportunity. It was always a source of pride for him to declare that he had been the first man to be sworn in to G Company on that March day within the turreted walls of the new drill hall on Beatty Street. G Company would never have a more enthusiastic recruit.

Sworn in as a private, James was soon displaying such energy and drive that he received rapid promotion. After just a few months he was a corporal, the next year he was a sergeant, and with yearly promotions he reached the rank of lieutenant by October 1907. His outstanding zeal was so obvious that it can have surprised no one when he received promotion to the rank of captain in August 1912.

From the moment he was sworn in, regimental affairs absorbed the whole of his time outside the office. He faithfully attended all drills and exercises, and he went off to army camp with as much enthusiasm as if he were going on holiday. He was later to record that in 27 years with the regiment he had never once missed the annual inspection parade. He was secretary of the Rifle Association from 1904 to 1907, and its president in 1911 and 1912. Keen to improve his marksmanship, he would hurry out in the evening to meet his friend Charles Merle Rolston so that they could practise target shooting together in some unpopulated spot. This was usually somewhere along the ill-defined trail designated as the line of 13th Avenue. They would carry along a four-foot square piece of canvas, which, roughly propped up, would form their target. It was possible to fire quite freely in a westerly direction, James recalled, since there was nothing west of Ontario Street except second-growth woodland.

Army exercises and rifle practice absorbed much of James's physical energy, but his interest in the military went far beyond this. His intellectual curiosity soon led him to study military history and traditions, and before long he was searching out old military records and memorabilia, frequently salvaging odds and ends that were in danger of being thrown away. This ever-expanding mass of material gradually evolved into a collection of wider scope and one which amounted to a private archives of his own—it would later become the nucleus of the Vancouver City Archives itself.

His absorption in military history was so obvious that only a year after he joined the regiment (and still only a sergeant), he took on the job of producing the military notices that were sent in to the *Province,* and for the next five years, between 1904 and 1909, he edited a regular column for the Saturday paper under the heading of *Military News.* Basically this consisted of news items about forthcoming military events, but was sometimes stretched to include longer reports.[13]

Very quickly he slipped into the role of regimental historian and archivist for the DCOR. By 1907 he had collected and studied so many documents that he undertook to write a history of the regiment. He does not describe what form this history took—and possibly it was never printed in separate format as a booklet. Very likely he was referring to his long article on the history of the BC Rifle Association, published in the *Victoria Colonist* on July 21, 1908, and later in the *Province* on July 21, 1910. From then on his reputation grew, and by the 1920s he was a recognized expert in the field of military history in western Canada.

The question arises: why did this fixation on military lore take such a powerful hold of James's life? The answer lies in the quality of his imagination, which imbued the whole of military life with an extraordinary glamour and significance. His fascination with the tactics and history of warfare did not derive from the day-to-day routines of the drill yard or even the expertise the recruits gradually acquired, but was a fascination experienced at a much deeper level. Part of it was the sense of camaraderie with his fellow soldiers, and part of it was the sense of carrying on a family tradition in the footsteps of his admired grandfather, James Skitt, who had served as a quartermaster for so many years. But beyond these elements was a more profound concept of service in the military. To fight under the flag of Empire was an ethic that appealed to his strongly developed sense of patriotism. It resonated with his love of history and the old tales of chivalry and valour and glorious battles fought for the honour of one's country. He also enjoyed tradition for its own sake: the uniforms and the medals, the bands and the parades, and all the ceremony of military custom and procedure. For Private James Matthews the whole of military life, down to the most tedious of army routines, was enveloped in a kind of mystique that ennobled it with heroic visions and high ideals. During the next two decades he would write many articles based on these values.

James would not have rated himself a true historian at this period of his life, and certainly not as a professional archivist. He probably did not even think of himself as a serious collector, even though he could not resist the lure of anything antiquarian and was beginning to amass a small hoard of relics and old papers. Gradually, his network of friends began to let him know when anything of interest turned up. He started to spend time deliberately searching out old discarded maps and records, talking to old-timers and setting aside anything of historical interest for his personal collection of trivia.

By the end of the decade, the family's lifestyle had improved greatly. James's salary had risen from $45 a month to $65 as he took on more managerial responsibilities, and he began to broaden his life with more varied outside interests. In January 1910 he was initiated into freemasonry as an apprentice of the Western Gate Lodge No. 48, and the brotherhood of the Masons became another important element in his life. For many years he was their representative on the Vancouver Masonic Cemetery Association, and when the time came, he and members of his family would be buried in the Masonic section of Mountain View Cemetery. Around 1910 he also joined the Vancouver branch of the Canadian Club.

James thrived on all these demands. However much he was to complain that it was all too much and the demands were too heavy, the truth was that he would have felt restless and unfulfilled without them. A compulsive worker and an innovative thinker, he could not have lived happily without giving expression to this side of his nature. But with ceaseless activity filling every free moment and many weeks spent away from home, he could have had little time left to share with his family.

And what of Maud? For her, the first 10 years in British Columbia may not have been such happy ones—on the contrary, they must have been difficult and lonely, full of hard work and privation. She responded gallantly, but with James continually absent it must have been a lonely life indeed, isolated on the outskirts of town and limited to the company of her three young children. True, if you walked along Pacific to Granville Street, there was a streetcar that took you into town, and sometimes there would be a family outing to some local destination like Greer's Beach. (This beach, off what is now Kitsilano Point, was one of Vancouver's favourite picnic places, and it had become far more accessible since 1905, when the BC Electric Railway put in a new streetcar route running as far as Vine Street. One of Kitsilano's visitors at this time was Emily Carr, who loved to paint this sequestered beach and its shady trees, or walk into the Native reserve beyond the beach.)

Sometimes the family ventured further afield. James describes a boat trip to Moodyville and a camping trip to Bowen Island, and there is a photo showing Maud and the children on a little boat on some creek or slough; but nothing more ambitious seems to have been arranged. Did Maud sometimes miss her more varied life in New Zealand and the well-educated, affluent society of her father's diplomatic circles? Unfortunately, her husband's memoirs offer no insights into Maud's personality or temperament, nor do they attempt to probe the conflicts of her inner life in these or later years. In spite of James's affectionate instincts and loyal qualities, it is doubtful that he ever had the ability to put himself inside another person's thoughts and see things from their perspective.

MAUD MATTHEWS (THE ORIGINAL PHOTO IS DAMAGED, HENCE THE POOR QUALITY OF THIS IMAGE). (CVA, PORT N94)

By contrast, his attitude toward his sons is more obvious and would offer considerable scope for a psychological study. In his family history, written in 1927, he outlines the life of each son to that date. In the case of the twins, he adopts a strangely cool and factual turn of phrase, but when it comes to his third son, Hugh, the account suddenly warms into life and passionate love. "He was a dear little boy—just a little cherub, active, earnest, and honest,

James and Maud's three little boys in a canoe on the south shore of False Creek, 1902. (CVA, Dist N15.1)

and truthful … We had been chums almost from his birth. We looked alike, we thought alike, our tastes were alike." The physical likeness alone would have formed a strong bond, for reflected in Hugh was what James saw in his own adored mother, and in her father too, Grandfather Skitt, whom he had been fond of as a child. Hugh's open straightforward nature mirrored his own, and made it easy for him to understand this son and see him as the perfect companion. Whereas James writes dispassionately of Lyn, "He was an indifferent scholar," and little else except the details of the schools he went to, he says of Hugh: "He made good progress at school, kept all kinds of animal pets, and was regarded as a young lad of some character. He was a leader in many sports … and a member of the [all-schools] champion rifle shooting team."[14] Even less is written of Merle than of Lyn, but James does reveal that these two boys were inseparable until the time of Lyn's marriage. James of course was very young at the time of their birth and ill prepared to be a father, especially of twins. It must have been a difficult period of adjustment to parenthood. By the time Hugh arrived, James had developed a more natural acceptance and was able to allow his affectionate nature to take over. This is not to say that he did not have a true affection for his two older boys; he encouraged them to be buglers at a very young age, and was proud of them when they joined up during the war. It was just that it was not the almost unbalanced closeness that he felt (and was increasingly to feel) toward Hugh.

It was while they were living on Pacific Street that James's parents suddenly decided to come for a visit. It had been 10 years since they had seen their son; they had never seen their grandchildren, and had barely ever met Maud either. Much had been going on with Herbert and Mary in the interval. When Martin decided to leave Patagonia and return to New Zealand in 1905, they had taken the fancy to go back with him, abruptly abandoning their life in Rock Ferry. Herbert and Martin had gone into partnership in a farming enterprise, which should have been Herbert's dream come true, since this was what he had originally intended at Te Horo. Unfortunately, it had not worked out and they had dissolved the partnership. Now, in March of 1908, the unpredictable couple were on their way back to Britain again, and stopping on the way to visit James.

The visit was not a success. Mary's sweetly controlling style must have met resistance from Maud, for James sadly noted that his parents were critical of his wife and disapproving of certain unspecified actions of hers. They were also disappointed that James was so preoccupied with business and had to be out of town for so long at a time, and these absences must have made Maud's position even more difficult to maintain. After a trying month, Herbert and Mary thought it best to move out and find other accommodation on Howe Street for the rest of their stay. Besides the upset of these tensions in James's home, neither of his parents felt comfortable with North American ways; they felt strange in Vancouver and uneasy with the pace of life in a large city—a more brash and strident city than those they had known in Britain or New Zealand. If they had originally planned a more

MAUD MATTHEWS (RIGHT) WITH AN UNIDENTIFIED FRIEND. (ONLY TWO PHOTOS OF MAUD COULD BE LOCATED, BOTH OF VERY POOR QUALITY.) (E. WALSER)

extended visit, they no longer had the wish for it, and with their usual hastiness they made an abrupt departure. By the end of May they were already crossing the Atlantic, bound for Britain and eventually a new home on the north coast of Wales. They would not see any of James's family again until the middle of the First World War.

Fortunately for James and Maud, their first decade in Vancouver coincided with a great upsurge in Canada's economic growth and prosperity. The city exploded into a grandeur of purpose that expressed itself in an orgy of new construction and proliferation of architectural decoration. Buildings of no great age were ruthlessly torn down to make way for more imposing edifices, and a growing network of roads pushed further and further into the bush as the residential areas began to fill. The automobile was gaining such popularity that 104 miles of Vancouver's streets were paved by 1908, though 12 miles of road were still woodblock paving.[15] Electric streetcars now trundled along many more thoroughfares than merely such basic routes as Granville, Hastings and Main, and the BC Electric Railway (BCER) tracks were extending along Broadway, through Fairview and southward to the fishing village of Steveston. And along with Vancouver's growing prosperity came a corresponding improvement for James and family in their material circumstances of life.

By 1911 their financial position was so much better that they were finally able to build their own home and move out of the rented cottage. The district that appealed to them so greatly—and where James would live for the rest of his life—was Kitsilano, with its open beach and its airy views out to the blueness of sea and mountains. A mind-boggling choice of site was available to the Matthews family, for Kitsilano Point had only recently been cleared for development, and the Matthews home at 1343 Maple Street was one of the first to go in. James must have been doing well at the time, for he bought not just the lot at 1343 Maple for himself to build on, but another lot for investment. The two lots together cost him $2,800, and such were the boom times of that era that he was able to sell the second lot afterwards for $2,300.

They started building in the spring, and by early winter their new home was ready to move into. It was designed in the Craftsman style so popular at the time (and now, nearly a century later, enjoying a vast popular revival). Wood-shingled, with an inviting full-width front porch, sturdy splayed-out columns and a quaint dormer window with a balcony, it was a home that looks just as attractive today, clustered in a lavish massing of greenery and bright flowers. It stands near the north end of the street and, at the time of construction, its back windows would have looked out on an uninterrupted view of English

Top: James and Maud's home at 1343 Maple Street, Vancouver, BC., c. 1913. The low-lying swampy area on Kitsilano Point had recently been filled with sand from False Creek, and the few houses on Maple Street raised to street level. (E. Walser)

Bottom: 1343 Maple Street, still standing today, is surrounded by many other attractive heritage homes. (R. Balfry)

Bay and the North Shore mountains beyond. The forested green headland of Stanley Park completed this lovely picture.

The couple's early years on Maple Street may have been some of the happiest ones in their marriage. Their living conditions were comfortable, their oceanside surroundings were as beautiful as one could find anywhere, and James appears to have been contented in his work and manifold interests. His competitive streak was satisfied by his sales job with Imperial Oil; his need for activity was met by his commitments in the militia; and his creative side found expression in his writings. And all this time, his artifact collection was growing as he became the recipient of old unwanted documents and photographs, took in outdated military uniforms and weapons, and filled to overflowing the basement of his little house with the so-called junk that would one day take on a far greater significance.

CHAPTER 4

The War Years Take Their Toll

When he moved into his new home in Kitsilano, James Matthews seemed to have reached a point in life where he might have been expected to settle into a comfortable routine and look to the future with reasonable certainty. Vancouver was in the grip of a huge surge of development, and the Matthews family was more prosperous now. His job was going well, he was full of keenness for all his outside interests, and his family life seemed to him normal and contented enough—although no one knows what stresses Maud was beginning to feel. He could not possibly have foreseen that within the next 10 years every aspect of his life would change unrecognizably and his whole world would be filled with strange and different elements. The political intrigues of Europe, which still seemed far off and irrelevant to Canada, would eventually have an impact on every aspect of his life.

But in the summer of 1912, the sun shone on James's life and prospects. His new home combined the advantages of city and country. He was only a few hundred yards from the sea and Greer's Beach, and he was also close to a wild, woodland area where deer and raccoons still wandered the forest trails. Yet, although there was still such a rural feel to the area, the Matthews family were certainly not cut off from the city, since they lived only a block or two north of a streetcar route. Essentially a city person, James would never have been happy without the stimulus of city life—he remembered all too well the stifling loneliness of Te Horo—but it was also a great joy to him to have the inspiration of the natural setting that gave Vancouver its beauty. The grand sweep of forest and mountains had captured his heart from the very first—"an almost interminable green carpet of boundless forest ... pierced at wide intervals by white streaks of snow-capped ranges, like foaming crests of billows breaking in green seas"—James saw the world about him in terms of the most poetic imagery.[1] Kitsilano Point would always be his chosen place, the place he would make his home for over 60 years, and where one day the name Matthews would become part of Kitsilano's history.

At the time when he and Maud moved there, Kitsilano enjoyed an almost holiday-like atmosphere, for it was one of Vancouver's favourite spots for picnicking and swimming. Its beaches had always been a favourite with West Enders, who used to row across from the other side of English Bay for day trips, or even put up tents and camp. The beaches were so popular that in 1905 the BCER put in what was known as an "attraction" line, as opposed to a "commuter" line, especially to service the crowds of holiday makers. It was called the Greer's Beach line (later the Kitsilano line), and it ran beside the trees as far as Vine Street, where it ended at a terminus indicated by a wooden platform and a shelter. Popular as these excursions were, few people actually wanted to build homes out here in the bush until 1909, when a new tramline went in along 4th Avenue. From then on, the area quickly filled up with housing.

During the Matthews' first year or two here, Kitsilano Point still had vestiges of its recent wilderness atmosphere. Maple Street was still in such rough condition in 1911 that it couldn't be negotiated by wheeled traffic, and when the family moved in, all their belongings had to be carried by hand from Cornwall Street onward. A deep slough slanted northwesterly across Laburnum Street to the beach and was the natural habitat of a colony of muskrats, which young Hugh Matthews used to hunt during the family's first year on Maple. Behind the beach lay a low swampy area, where the noisy croak of the bullfrogs rose in a nightly chorus. "Full of sluggish water," wrote James, "the muskeg was rank with coarse grass, small bushes and willow ... The banks were overhung with vegetation, the ground was black loam, the decayings of centuries, a veritable muskrats' paradise."[2] But this little wilderness corner was not to last for long. In 1913 it vanished before the onslaught of urbanization, and the dank, fecund hollows disappeared, filled in with the sand that was being dredged out of False Creek. The few homeowners on the point were given the option of having their houses raised by the City at no cost, though the dredging company charged $100 for putting in fill. Each of them, including James, accepted.

But even after the muskeg disappeared, there remained another almost untouched area—the Squamish Reserve on the east side of Chestnut Street. The reserve was still largely a wilderness of deep, old forest, deserted by now, for its few occupants had been obliged to disperse to other reserves when the government purchased the acreage in 1913. It became the natural playground for Hugh and the other young lads of the area, who used to spend happy hours roaming the trails, playing at being Indians or hunting raccoons in the trees.

The family still enjoyed their camping trips or boat excursions outside the city. One of these outings in 1913 turned into an adventure that could have had serious consequences. It happened on an expedition to Bowen Island—a rather poorly planned expedition, as it turned out. James had organized a group of eight people, all women, small children and babies, and had set off in a motorboat from Vancouver, but he had failed to pack any supplies of food and water or other necessities, nor had he considered that it might be prudent to have some oars on board. As they neared Bowen Island, the engine broke down. It looked as though they were about to drift into the Gulf of Georgia, and there were some tense moments before they somehow managed to make it to shore near Cowan Point, but now it was nightfall; the forest closed in all around them, and they had no idea where to go to get help. James and Hughie set out together; for five hours in the darkness they pushed their way through woods and gullies until at last James slumped to the ground in sheer exhaustion to wait it out till daybreak. But 13-year-old Hugh wouldn't let him give up. "Dad, think of those in the boat," he insisted. This courageous attitude on the part of his young son so impressed James that he got up immediately. Soon they came upon a fence and other signs of habitation, and the marooned party was rescued by boat at four in the morning. James' pride in Hugh was redoubled: "I saw the excellent mettle he was made of." He never forgot their dreadful slog through the bush that night all the way from Cowan Point to Snug Cove, nor the courage that Hughie had displayed. Forty years later James would create a park on the island in memory of his son's brave spirit.[3]

The boys were all encouraged to take part in sports at school, first at Henry Hudson School and later, in Lyn's case, at Langara College, and in his family notes, James dwells much more on this aspect of education than their academic studies. Hugh once again was a source of pride to his father, for he had an aptitude for sports. He played on the hockey team, took a leading part in other sports and was such a good shot that he had a place on a champion rifle team of eight boys representing all the schools in Vancouver. Where classroom studies were concerned, James seemed less interested, merely noting that Hugh made good progress, but his older brother Lyn was not particularly successful. Of the other twin, Merle, little is said, but around this time he became afflicted with a disability that was to permanently impede his life in various ways: he was diagnosed with epilepsy. Treatment for epilepsy was rudimentary then and remained so until after the Second World War, so with no effective drugs available, 14-year-old Merle must have had his activities significantly restricted.

James continued to pour a huge amount of energy into his devotion to the regiment and military affairs. The demands of his sales job had forced him to give up the editorship of *Military News* in 1909, but he still contributed the occasional feature article. He turned out regularly for weekly rifle practices, and eagerly looked forward to the international rifle contest in Washington State, one of the big events of the year. Selected for special courses, he qualified as a machine-gun instructor and in 1910 taught at the Maxim Gun School, the first machine-gun school ever held in British Columbia. He still never missed a parade, and was eager at any time to take off for army-camp training. Not surprisingly, he was also elected president of the regiment's recreation association in 1911 and 1912.

James could hardly wait to get Lyn and Merle enrolled in the regiment, and in 1912 he managed to get the twins taken on as buglers in the DCOR. They were still only 13 years old, and James admits "they were well known on account of their extreme youth," but it is to be hoped that they enjoyed it, for in 1913 he took them along to army camp on Vancouver Island, where they were obliged to endure an 80-mile march all the way from Cowichan Bay to Victoria. Apparently they did enjoy it and found it all very exciting, or so Lyn told his daughter in later years, and the boys went with James again to camp at Vernon in May of the following year—but this was the eerie summer of 1914, and by August soldiering was no longer an exciting game, but about to become a deadly reality.

It may seem strange that James did not join up in an active regiment right away after the outbreak of the First World War, but for once financial prudence had to overrule his patriotic impulses. He did not see how he could leave his wife and three young sons without a reasonable income (and by now he was in an excellent position with his firm and would have had to give up a good secure salary). In the early stages of the war, there were more than enough single men already lining up in the enrolment offices, and in any case, it was generally thought that the war would be over in a matter of a few months. However, as Christmas went by and the new year of 1915 unfolded, it became grimly apparent that victory would not be the quick triumph the public had anticipated. Disturbing stories from the battlefields began to filter into the newspapers, the casualties mounted and still no decisive outcome foretold an end to the bloodshed, even after the long series of onslaughts at Ypres and Loos. In spite of the heavy losses, neither side had gained appreciable ground in the actual lines of the trenches. James was torn by the stress of weighing his two conflicting obligations—how was he to decide between his country and his family? Throughout the year his thoughts were never far away from this problem, as he began to rethink his original decision.

In March of 1915 he went with the militia to Union Bay on the east coast of Vancouver Island, but it was only garrison duty, and more and more he was agonizing over the need to do his part at the front. By June he could stand the guilt feeling no longer, and he offered to join the 62nd Overseas Battalion. He doesn't say what came of this, but September brought a welcome development—Imperial Oil made a commitment to pay its employees a half salary while they were away on active service. At once he volunteered for active duty.

The only use they found for him at first was to assist in recruiting for the 158th Battalion, DCOR, and he felt as if he was only marking time during November and December, and still no nearer to getting to the front. In reality, however, the tempo of preparations for getting men to the battle areas was accelerating enormously during this period. On November 3, 1915, Lieutenant-Colonel John Worden had been given the job of creating a new battalion for overseas—the 102nd Battalion—and he was energetically recruiting all over northern British Columbia and the Interior. This was the start of the Canadian Expeditionary Force (CER), which officially came into being in December 1915.

James registered for service with the CEF on January 1, 1916. His military papers give an exact description of his physical appearance at the age of 37. He was of medium height at 5 feet 9 inches, but a little on the heavy side at 172 pounds; his hair was dark brown, his eyes were hazel and he was of medium complexion. A photograph of James in uniform shows a man of commanding, confident bearing, with strong and striking features.

Before going to training camp, men stayed at home or were billeted locally, and it was fortunate for James that he was able to stay in his Vancouver home for the next six weeks, because life at the isolated training camp was harsh indeed that bitterly cold winter. The windswept headland of Comox on the east coast of Vancouver Island did not enjoy the friendliest of climates, and this was where the 102nd Battalion were going through their training period before going overseas. A wretchedly cold bleak place it was, out on Goose Spit, where the men had to construct their own camp. Nothing was ready for them on arrival, and because it was an isolated spot, their camp seemed to be the last one to receive basic supplies. "Frankly, conditions were deplorable," wrote Sergeant Leonard Gould, author of *From B.C. to Basieux; Being the Narrative History of the 102nd Canadian Infantry Battalion*. "That [the winter] passed without any fatality from disease ... was a striking credit to the physical fitness and calibre of the men."[4]

"The winter of 1915-1916 was one of the coldest in the history of B.C.," wrote future impresario Ivan Ackery, who found himself there for training. "Many of us arrived at Comox in thin clothing, and there wasn't enough warm underwear to go round ... To add to the misery of the cold, wet winter, there was an outbreak of measles in camp." Ackery well recalled this Captain Matthews who "used to cup his hand around his ear and shout 'Ackery!' at me, when I'd done something I shouldn't. He later became the City of Vancouver's fighting archivist, where he carried on his war with City Hall, and I knew him well."[5]

James arrived at the camp with the Vancouver contingent in mid-February and at once transferred from the 158th Battalion to a permanent position in the 102nd. This involved giving up the rank of major, which he had enjoyed with the 158th, and accepting the lower rank of captain—"This is the best we can do for you," apologized Worden—but James had for some reason taken against the 158th so strongly that he preferred the demotion. The date of his enlistment in the 102nd Battalion was February 19, 1916. He was now second-in-command of No. 3 Company.

He quickly distinguished himself the day the recruits from Prince Rupert came into camp. As he happened to be the senior officer on duty, it fell to him to greet the troops. It was quite a stirring sight as they all marched in, and on the spur of the moment he gave a rousing cry of "The North British Columbians! Three cheers for the men from Prince Rupert!" The name stuck, and from then on the entire force at Comox was entitled "The 102nd Battalion, North British Columbians," replacing the original name of "Comox-Atlin."[6]

Life at Comox was something of an anticlimax, consisting chiefly of drill and more drill, and it was hard to create much variety in this, other than offer it in different forms—section, platoon, company and battalion drill. The only alternative was some tedious route marching. The month of May came and went, and by now the men were thoroughly bored and impatient to get overseas. Then, quite suddenly, they were on the move at last. Their departure had been hastened by the news that the water supply (a spring on the mainland) would not support them much longer, so in June, with no time for leave, they found themselves on their way to France. "We marched down from the Spit to Comox, singing 'Worden's Weary Warriors' to the tune of the 'Battle Hymn of the Republic,'" says Ackery. "Everyone was out on the streets waving goodbye to us." James was not there to record this proud moment, for he had been sent ahead to Ottawa to take another course in machine-gun warfare, and he only rejoined his unit on its way through to Halifax. They embarked for Europe on the SS *Empress of Britain* on June 18, 1916.

According to Sergeant Leonard Gould, it was a revolting journey—not because of submarine attacks, but because of the gross overcrowding on the ship. With about 4,000 men on board, it was not possible for everyone to find a place to bunk below, and since the 102nd Battalion was the last to board ship, many of its members had to sleep on deck regardless of weather (which was fortunately benign). "We had to eat in the bowels of the ship where the atmosphere was stifling, [and] every article of food was permeated with some disgusting preservative which caused all dishes to taste alike, all being equally objectionable ... Conditions were well-nigh intolerable, and this is written after two and a half years in France and Belgium," wrote Gould feelingly. They were thankful to arrive at the well-kept Bordon Camp in Hampshire on June 30.

Coinciding horrifically with their arrival in Britain, headlines broke the news of the dreadful carnage of the first offensive on the Somme—that tragic event from which only 69 of the 801 men from the 1st Newfoundland Regiment emerged alive and unwounded after the appalling massacre of July 1. The men of the 102nd Battalion were urgently needed to reinforce the position on the Somme, yet still had to be held back on the wrong side of the Channel for another six weeks while they took a crash course in musketry and bayonet fighting. During this period it turned out that five of their officers would have to be replaced, since new medical tests made it clear that these men could not meet the high physical standard that would be demanded of them on the front. It was probably as a replacement for one of these officers that on August 9 James received a thrilling promotion—he was made Acting Major, in full charge of No. 3 Company.

Departure for the front was imminent, but before they sailed the battalion was given a short weekend leave. James had just enough time to fit in a 28-hour visit to his parents in Prestatyn. Amazingly, he had never let them know that it was in his mind to volunteer for the battlefront or even that he had enlisted in the CEF, so obsessed had he been with the need to spare his mother any anxiety. Still less did they have any idea that he was now in England, so he had to find a way of breaking the news gently. He did this in a letter, but he put it off until a few days before his visit, and even when he arrived at the Rhyl train station, he still thought it necessary to send the wagon driver on ahead with his parcels to give them some warning. "I was afraid the excitement of meeting after eight years might startle Mother."[7]

It was a meeting filled with emotion from start to finish, and he remembered it with nostalgia. "I found a pretty little bright street of red, brilliant red, brick houses. There was the prettiest one. I approached the little silver gate set in the bright red brick wall, and above which towered the brilliant green of the hedge within. I read the name 'Glenhafren,' and looked up and over it, and peeped in … A profusion of pink rambler roses climbed over a white little cottage, stuccoed with quartz crystals which glistened in the bright sunlight; snow-white curtains hung within the rustic windows; a mass of blossoming flowers coloured a field of tall verdant greenery; and there, half hidden by the tall plants, their snow-covered heads just visible, stood Mother and Father, Father's beard now as snow-white as Mother's curls. It was a beautiful picture—a fitting subject for an artist's oils."[8] Like many of James's most vivid memories, it stayed in his mind in a painter's terms of colour and imagery.

The parting at Rhyl station was even more charged with emotion when Herbert gave way to his anguish completely and passionately as they said their final goodbyes. It was a harrowing moment—"that unforgettable scene," painfully embedded in James's memory. "Mother stoical and calm; father overwhelmed with the thought of what happened to most men who went [to the trenches], and these, these were the last moments."[9] James could only once recall seeing his father so appallingly overwrought: it was the day in 1895 when Frank had died of tetanus.

With the image of that bright pretty little rose-covered cottage still fresh in his mind, James was wrenched almost immediately into a grim and different world. His unit crossed the Channel to Le Havre on August 11, and soon he was in the battered landscape of ravaged Belgium, stationed in the remains of a village near the St. Eloi trenches, a few miles south of Ypres. Two great battles had already reduced Ypres to a scene of rubble, its historic buildings destroyed, and a further huge onslaught the following year would complete the devastation. When James and his unit arrived, military action was comparatively low, and the object of the their month-long stay here was chiefly to give them an introduction to war.

Their first venture into the trenches was an experience marked by total ignorance of battle conditions. "We had not been issued with steel helmets; it is to be doubted whether anyone at Brigade Headquarters had ever given a thought to steel helmets; such things [did not exist] in the early days of the war when our veteran leaders had seen their previous service," wrote Sergeant Gould.[10] But the new troops learned fast, and by August 19 they came under actual fire, with a heavy bombardment and the shock of the first injuries and loss of life. James proved fully equal to this—he writes that he was always cool under fire—and under his command No. 3 Co. remained so steady at their posts that they were ordered to remain an extra 24 hours.

James on the war front near Ypres, Belgium, 1916. (CVA, Port P1216)

From mid-August till late September the battalion lived in this curious world of low-scale warfare. From time to time they were assigned to move up to the trenches, but mostly it was a mundane routine of moving around to various camps to rebuild shelters and parapets or drain the trenches. In general, they spent their time moving around the ruined villages and farmhouses south of Ypres, getting on with the crucial work of improving the defences as fast as possible before winter. Although the battalion never had to withstand any dramatic sort of offensive during this spell of duty, they were still at constant risk from shells and shrapnel, and always on the alert for a sniper's bullet or a sudden burst of machine-gun fire. They experienced the first shock of losing some of their number in these incidents (including the well-loved commander of No. 1 Company). The one thing they did not experience was gas attacks. As part of their initial training here, the troops had had to run through a small cloud of poison gas (with and without respirators), but fortunately, the 102nd never had to endure the real thing.

One moving incident remained fixed in James's memory for its sheer incongruity and its strangely pictorial quality. The battalion, still in the region of Dickebusch in Flanders, was about to be moved into the war zone of the Somme, and the padre (or chaplain) asked James to assemble the men for a church service the Sunday before they left. When Sunday came, most of the company were catching up on some sleep after a tiring week, but about 20 men were rounded up, and obligingly shuffled off with the padre to the remains of a garden behind a broken building. The padre dragged an old barrel out of the debris and this became an altar. He covered it with a fresh white cloth, laid out the gleaming silver chalice, put on his white robe—and suddenly the dismal ruins were transformed into a place of sanctity. Shellfire broke out in the distance, the guns roared and boomed, but within the garden all was peace. "We felt safe," wrote Matthews. "No hurt could befall us there, we were not afraid. Oh, what a picture for a painter." As always, he remembered the scene pictorially: "The shattered buildings, the broken glass ... the snowy robe, the little knot of kneeling worshippers. unkempt but reverent, the roar of the guns, the crash of the shells, and God's minister. The occasion is ineffaceable from the memory of those whose privilege it was to be there."[11]

Miles away, the battle of the Somme had smouldered on throughout August and September. The campaign was originally planned as a diversionary tactic to draw some of the enemy force away from Verdun, where the French were desperate for relief. Field Marshal Douglas Haig had been convinced that a sweep of massive proportions would quickly wipe out the German line north of the Somme, but it had turned out very differently. It had not at all been the decisive victory he had hoped for, but had become a war of attrition. The German line of trenches that ran along 25 miles of the French countryside was strongly fortified with very deep dugouts, and these afforded their artillery an almost unassailable position from which to repel advancing troops. The slaughter on both sides was horrendous, and all for pitiful gains of only a mile or two of meaningless muddy ground.

The Canadian Corps was not part of the action until mid-August, when the fresh troops of the 1st, 2nd and 3rd divisions moved in as replacements in the northwest quarter of the line. By mid-September they had moved well forward and taken the village of Courcelette. Their main objective now was a position known as the Regina Trench, a long defence line that still resisted their advance. By early October, however, these troops needed a rest period, and at last it was time for the 4th Division to be called into action. James's company, which had been in reserve in a village in France, suddenly found itself on the train for the battlefront, and after a week's travel marched into the almost deserted town of Albert on October 10, 1916.

James's spell in the inferno of front-line fighting was to last precisely 11 days, but the effect on him—body and mind—was indelible.

Now that the 4th Division had arrived, everything was set for a major onslaught on Regina Trench. This was not a meaningful strategic position in itself, but it had become a marker of military success or failure and a test of military superiority. The senior corps had attacked it on October 1 and again on October 8, but still it had not fallen. Now it was up to the 4th Division to make another attempt. By now the physical conditions of battle were appallingly bad, for the weather had been steadily deteriorating throughout September, and constant rain had reduced acres of once productive farmland to an expanse of mud, so deep in places that a man could be sucked into it up to the hips and have to be dragged out by his friends. Shellfire had battered the villages into nothingness—sometimes all that remained to identify a hamlet and its human habitation was a scattering of red-brick dust, a few cellar steps or some scattered blocks of stone. Huge craters pockmarked the landscape, and the jumble of shell holes sometimes made the trenches indistinguishable from the rest of the torn-up earth. The line of enemy trenches had, in fact, become so

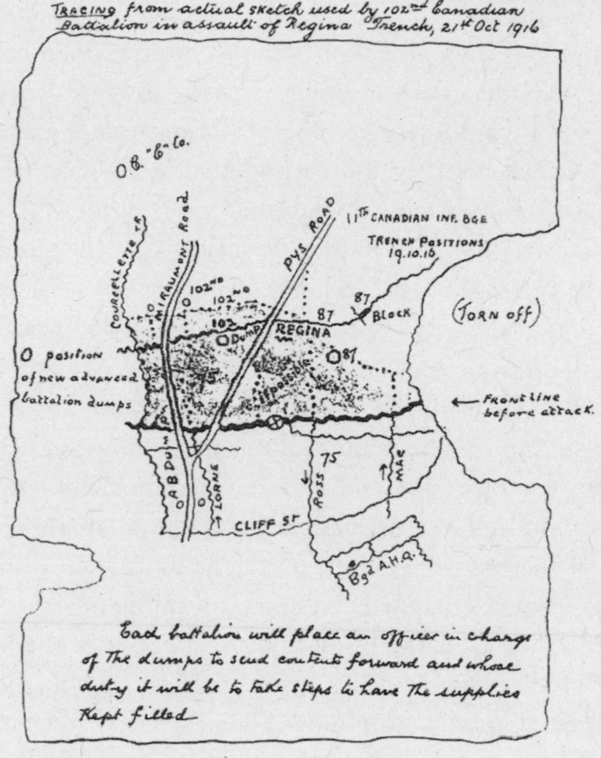

A SOLDIER'S SKETCH MAP OF THE REGINA TRENCH AREA. THIS TORN SCRAP OF PAPER, CRUMPLED AND SPATTERED WITH MUD, WAS PRESERVED BY JAMES AFTER THE BATTLE. (CVA, MIL P322.1)

hard to recognize that Canadian assault parties had been known to advance beyond their target.

The 102nd took over from the 87th Battalion on the evening of October 18. It was a dark night of heavy rain, the ground was a morass, but they were ordered to hurry forward at the double, as the Germans had suddenly launched a major shelling attack on the 87th's left flank. Once arrived, there was still no rest to be had, for the order came that they must spend the night in preparations for the dawn assault, while all the time the rain poured down and the shelling continued. When morning broke, the rain was still coming down in torrents and the ground was hardly passable, so the raid was called off and the tired men had to tramp all the way back to camp, leaving just one of the companies (not James's) to hold the line. They had barely been in the support camp long enough to get over this ordeal when the weather began to clear, and on the evening of the following day (October 20) the three companies repeated their laborious journey back to the front line. Once again, they had no opportunity for sleep. The order was given that trenches must be dug that night. James explains that these trenches were intended to provide shelter after they took Regina Trench, since the nights were extremely cold by now. The 200 men are said by James to have dug 350 yards of trench, four feet deep, by the time daylight came.

The morning of October 21 shone clear and bright, and the assault was on. At six minutes after noon the Canadian barrage broke out "with one tremendous crash and roar as if all the two or three thousand guns behind us had let loose at once," remembered James. As the echoes of the first volleys died away, the first wave of the assault party was over the parapet and pressing toward Regina Trench. Major James Matthews was at the head of his company on the left flank, with Major Homer-Dixon's company on the right. "Look, look, look!" James shouted excitedly, as Homer-Dixon's party advanced, completely steady and purposeful, and magnificently calm, even though the ranks would soon begin to thin. Four waves of Canadian troops bore down on the enemy lines at intervals between the rounds of shelling. "It was the grandest sight I ever saw," said Matthews reverently of that assault on Regina Trench.[12]

The losses were heavy. The men were out in the open, horribly exposed to enemy fire, unprotected by any kind of cover in the flat and treeless landscape. As the battle progressed, the casualties mounted and the four separate waves of attack started to blend, and to add to the confusion, it was soon impossible to identify the trench lines accurately, since they had been so shattered and churned up by shellfire. The Canadians continued their charge regardless, and with such bravery and determination that by the end of the day they had carried out their mission and a large portion of Regina Trench was in their hands. "The assault was carried out with such dash, vigour and impetuosity that the Germans were completely demoralized," wrote Sergeant Gould.[13]

As always, James remembered the scene in visual terms: "The picture of those grand men pushing back the frontier of France was a scene that would make a noble subject for a painter. About 500 men started in the attack at noon, but, according to the officer who made the count at sundown, only 140 men could be found in the trench. Of 17 officers who took part, not one escaped injury, and nine lay dead."[14] In his memory it would always stand out as a grand, heroic experience. The hardships, the squalor, the suffering and the waste of life—none of this is left out in his various accounts of the day, but it all seems transmuted into a brave and chivalric drama, a kind of ennobling vision of a scene in the panorama of Canadian military history. To add to the glory of it in James's mind, the battle of Regina Trench happened to coincide with a special date in history: the anniversary of the Battle of Trafalgar.

But the fight for Regina Trench was the end of James's own active war. Just as the battle was at its height and he was in the heart of the confusion, he found himself trapped with a machine gun at his back, and a bullet tore through the side of his head. He fell to the ground, helpless. "I was lying on my back in the bottom of muddy Regina Trench, soaked in my own blood. All officers were killed or died of wounds. I alone escaped," he recalled dramatically, if not accurately. It was very fortunate for James that his batman, Private Albert Taylor, happened to be by his side at this moment. Taylor, with incredible coolness, whipped out a supply of bandages, and—with bullets flying around on all sides—proceeded to administer first aid and do up the wound just as calmly "as though in a hospital ward."[15] Lieutenant Wilson gave James a sip of water; Captain Nicholls offered something stronger; and Private Taylor never left the Major's side. Without waiting for any medical unit to arrive, Taylor himself took on the responsibility of getting James to the dressing station, which was at Courcelette, about half a mile away. How he did it is hard to understand, for James was in terrible pain and shock and clearly quite incapable of making any move to help himself. Taylor was a large, powerful man, but it took him all afternoon until sundown to coax the injured man to traverse that dreadful half-mile through the mud, and many times the Major swore at his brave attendant and begged him to leave him alone to die in peace. "I had no desire to live; life was too painful."[16]

But Taylor, his "gallant comrade-in-arms," as James afterwards called him (with lifelong gratitude), persisted in his efforts, in spite of the fact that he himself had suffered a jagged shell wound on the back of his right hand. At last they reached the dressing station at Courcelette, where the army medical services took over. James was placed on what was known as a "mud sleigh" to begin his painful journey through the night, transferring later to a horse-drawn ambulance, and finally a motor ambulance. They arrived at the casualty clearing station at dawn, only to find it overwhelmed by thousands of casualties. It took two days to reach a hospital unit at Le Touquet and another three days to reach Britain, and all this time he was in the same bloodstained uniform and his wound had not been dressed.

He became a patient at the 4th London General Hospital, but sepsis had already set in, and the wound needed constant draining for some time. The bullet had pierced his right cheek, torn a path over the right mastoid process and made its exit behind the right ear, damaging the cheekbone. These injuries had caused incurable nerve damage and distortion of the ear canal. It took over two months before he was fit enough to be discharged, and the hearing in his right ear was permanently ruined. Fortunately, his wound caused minimal disfigurement, as the visible signs amounted only to a scar and a slightly misshapen right ear, with a hint of paralysis on the right side of the face. The paralysis did improve, but he was never to hear anything in the right ear unless the person speaking was just a few inches from his face.

It was while he was in the hospital reflecting on the ordeal he had gone through that he conceived the idea of a device that would give some small degree of comfort to the men in the trenches, and so he invented the "trench candle." It was just a small cube whose chief ingredient was paraffin wax, but it would boil a quart of water or heat food in the worst of conditions. It was light and portable, water-resistant and smokeless. It was also cheap. "Can you realise with what zest men would relish something hot or even a little warm after they have spent a night in a sewer-like trench, soaked to the skin, chilled to the bone, plastered in mud, exhausted from labour and lack of sleep, and the cheerless prospect of breakfasting on hard tack, bully beef and ice-cold water?" he asked.[17] Thousands of these cubes were distributed experimentally to certain regiments, and the ladies of the Imperial Order Daughters of the Empire in Vancouver started to work diligently at manufacturing them, but the war ended before the device came into general use.

When they discharged him from the London hospital on January 6, 1917, his one desire was to get back to his home and family to convalesce, so he immediately bought a passage on the SS *Grampian* at his own expense, and on January 9 he boarded the ship for Canada. Back in Vancouver, there was apparently nothing in his first reunion with Maud to indicate any sign of future trouble (James, however, was not a very perceptive man), and soon he was well on the way to a fair degree of recovery. In fact, he soon became so restless that within two or three weeks he was eagerly volunteering to give public lectures about his wartime experiences. He addressed the Canadian Club on February 11 in a talk that some of his hearers rated as one of the most interesting addresses the club had ever heard, and that brought him a hearty ovation. With his dramatic take on events, James was beyond doubt a riveting speaker. On February 13 he spoke to a crowd of 300 employees of the BC Electric Railway, and a few days later issued a circular letter to the effect that he was available as a speaker at any local military unit. His impaired hearing must have caused him some difficulty when it came to interacting with his audience, but nonetheless he was such an effective speaker that his disability never fazed him, either then or later.

He was far from fit at this stage, in spite of his wound having healed, and the army medical board twice extended his leave on account of his physical condition. But with almost total deafness in one ear, it was obvious that he would never be able to return to the front. Even when he was pronounced generally fit, he had to recognize that he would be restricted to lighter duties.

He was appointed company commander of the BC Regimental Depot for a time, and he also served as president of the district courts martial. However, during the summer, he found himself voyaging the Atlantic again, conducting new drafts of recruits over to France at Etaples. This seems to have gone on for several months, for he was getting monthly medical examinations at Seaford in Sussex, England, from July to October.

From time to time while he was in Britain, he was able to get up to Prestatyn to visit his parents at their pleasant little cottage, Glenhafren. Once he even managed to include a special visit to the dearly loved governess of his childhood, Miss Halford, and spent four or five hours with her at her home in Preston, Shropshire. It was a most affectionate and satisfying reunion, for he was afterwards to describe this as "one of the most happy days of his life."[18] (His detractors in later life could never have guessed at this tremendous capacity for affection and need for reciprocation.)

But the end of his wartime service was not far off. His active career with the CEF came to a close that year after a session of duties in the Canadian federal election. Most of December 1917 he spent travelling around the military zones as a deputy returning officer to assist with the armed forces vote. First of all he carried out duties in Belgium, though his headquarters were just the other side of the border, at Dunkirk. Bombing raids here kept the town on constant alert. After this he went on to northern France to Rouen and Caen. This spell of duty was the last time that James was exposed to enemy fire. At this point his usefulness to the army overseas came to an end, and the conclusive words appear on his record: "Ceases to be overseas on duty and is surplus to the establishment."

On January 11, 1918, the medical board at Seaford confirmed the obvious—that he was still deaf in one ear and still "somewhat nervous as result of strain of service," was still sleeping poorly, and was altogether permanently unfit for general service. The army would have to find a use for his services back in Canada. On January 31 he boarded the SS *Olympic*, happily on his way back to his home and his loving wife—as he still thought. But on the February day when he walked expectantly into his Kitsilano home on Maple Street, he got the shock of his life. Without any previous warning of her intention, Maud Matthews announced that she was leaving him. She moved out of the house four hours later.

CHAPTER 5

Maud and Emily

When Maud confronted James with the dreadful news that she was about to leave the marriage, it genuinely came as a revelation to him that there had been anything amiss in their marriage. In his memoirs James is terse and private in his allusions to this painful episode, but he prided himself on relating the facts honestly, and when he writes that "same day [of his return from the war] wife left his home, giving him great shock and surprise," it may be taken as an accurate record of his own reaction.[1] He *was* shocked and he *was* surprised. A more perceptive individual might have suspected already that there was something wrong, but James did not see personal relationships in terms of subtleties. Had he never sensed any constraint in his wife's attitude when he was home on sick leave? Had he never tuned in to any feeling of reserve in her letters? Perhaps he preferred to be in denial. At all events, he had not seen this coming.

The sad, indisputable fact was that while he was away, Maud had found someone else, someone she was far more comfortable with. James made heavy demands on all those who were close to him, depending as he did on their support and sympathy, yet at the same time expecting them to defer to his egocentric behaviour. Maud must have been accustomed to making allowances for his moods of despondency and his overbearing ways, but it cannot have been easy for her, and if she had now met someone with a happier, more restful temperament, the appeal of a new life must have been very great. How long she had known her new friend is a matter of speculation. Could the affair have started when James was away at Comox in 1916?

Had she deferred telling him when he was wounded and in hospital? Had she still felt unable to tell him when he came home for his convalescent leave in early 1917? By the time he was more or less fit again and on lighter duties overseas at the end of that year, Maud must have known that she could not go along with the charade any longer, and made up her mind to confront him with the truth once he returned to Canada.

James, completely stunned, could not shake her resolve. And so the awful day ended, and Maud was gone from the home, leaving behind her husband and her three sons, the youngest still only 17. In the light of James's parents' harmonious marriage and his own naturally faithful nature, the total unexpectedness of this revelation from Maud must have made it traumatic in the extreme, and the repercussions must have taken time to sink in. Yet in spite of this wounding defection, James found that he still loved his wife and wanted her back. He convinced himself that it was an aberration, perhaps induced by loneliness and the abnormality of wartime conditions, and that family life as he remembered it of old could somehow be restored. Romantic memories of his first meeting with her on the windswept slopes of Mount Eden still lingered in his mind and coloured his vision of their marriage. And after two years exposed to the hardships and horrors of war, he was desperately craving the kindness and affection of the loving family he had expected to rejoin. Throughout March he appealed to her to change her mind. James could be very eloquent and very impassioned when he was pleading a cause, and his forcefulness and patent sincerity had its effect. Somehow he persuaded her to return.

Maud came back to him in April, and agreed to go with him on his lecture tour of Oregon and Idaho. The Canadian government had decided to make use of James's abilities as a speaker by sending him south of the border to assist the Americans with their fundraising campaign for a Third Liberty Loan. As a wounded officer returned from the battlefront, he drew a sympathetic response and connected well with his audiences, and reporters stated that he was listened to "with deep attention."[2] James could always be relied on for a good, compelling address, and he probably carried out a very effective tour in those few weeks.

Besides satisfying his sense of patriotism, his tour of the northwest United States must have presented itself to James as a golden opportunity to have Maud with him and re-establish their relationship. Perhaps he hoped that absence from Vancouver might help Maud to forget her wartime infatuation, and if so—if the couple could effect a reconciliation—their trip might even be in some form the honeymoon they never had. Maud, on the other hand, might have had considerable reservations about the prospect of this tour, looking upon it more cautiously as a sort of trial period. If this was the case, it was a more realistic view than her husband's: their "holiday" together did nothing for the marriage and failed to bring them together. If anything, it may have been the decisive factor in making it clear to her that life with James was something she could no longer tolerate. Maud now knew for certain what she wanted to do, and once again she refused to stay with James.

James was now left alone with his youngest son Hugh, for his two older boys left home in May to join the army. Lyn and Merle had responded excitedly to the military fervour that had swept the country and could hardly wait until they were old enough to join up. They had turned out for the very first parades in August 1914 and had spent all their school holidays in uniform, training. They were so very eager to become soldiers that after their 17th birthdays in the summer of 1916, they had insisted on leaving school, much against their father's wishes. He himself had left school early, and perhaps he regretted this, for he wrote to his sons from France that August and voiced strong objections to their plans. It made no difference—he was too far away to influence them now—and from then on they paraded regularly with his old regiment, the DCOR. On his return in 1918, seeing how determined they were, James managed to get them into the 68th Battery of the Canadian Field Artillery, though only in time for the last few months of the war. As it turned out, they never saw action, and got no nearer to the front than their camp at Kimmel Park, near Rhyl (which happened to be near enough to their grandparents at Prestatyn for them to make several visits). An outbreak of measles put the camp in quarantine, and after that the war was over. They were demobilized in July of 1919.

James poses with his sons in 1918. The twins, Lyn and Merle, flank Hugh, the youngest. (George T. Wadds photo, CVA, Add. MSS 54, 508-D-1, file 5, #10)

May and June of 1918 were sad months for James and Hugh, still hoping that Maud might return. They were intensely close, almost abnormally close, companions, and James was passionately fond of this youngest son. "He wrote me weekly while at the war, oftener sometimes, and his childish letters were cherished as only a soldier in the field can cherish letters from a dear one," James says. But although Hugh's company helped him through this difficult time, James still longed for his wife. Hugh did his best to effect a reconciliation. "He did all he could to mend matters. He did all in his power to bring his mother to reason and get her to return home. His conduct was worthy of the highest approbation, for while he did all he could to help me, he never forgot her."[3]

By July James had worked himself up into such a state of desperation that he must have been almost out of his mind with grief and outrage, for he concocted a most extraordinary plan. In one last wild gamble to restore his marriage, he decided to kidnap Maud. He is extremely reticent about the details of this mad operation, only referring to it cryptically as "incident at Ladner." Surely he must have had some assistance in carrying out his plan, but however it came about, he succeeded in abducting Maud and bringing her back home. It was for the last time. Her stay ended after only three days. In Maud he had found his match for willpower, and she defeated him by the simple device of refusing to eat while she was there. With a sad heart he finally released his captive and recognized that his marriage was over.[4]

After his final medical examination in May of that year, James had been released from the army altogether. On May 16 the medical board had concluded that he was obviously unfit for military service, for as well having lost his hearing in one ear, he was suffering from other health problems—poor appetite, insomnia, dizziness and other symptoms resulting from his wound. They also noted that he was "very nervous and irritable ... and has a much worried appearance.[5] All this was at the time when he was under great stress over the uncertainty of his marriage. He was discharged on May 29, 1918. He had been an acting major throughout the war, and afterwards he was allowed to keep the rank of major.

While the crisis over Maud was still consuming all his thoughts and energies, he seems to have been too restless and strung out to go back to regular work, but by July, after the final scene in his marital drama, he had to recognize that he must accept what had happened and move on. Imperial Oil had promised him his old job back, and they kept their word—but only up to a point. The job they gave him after the war was not equal to his former position, which had been that of district manager. Instead he was now described as an executive clerk, and this demotion upset him greatly. Several years later, replying to a letter of James's in 1930, his former senior officer, John Worden, wrote: "What was the reason you never was [*sic*] given your position again which you held with the Imperial Oil Coy. of Canada on your return from the war? I was directly responsible for your asking and receiving leave to go out to France and do your bit for Canada and the Empire [and] I feel I am in some way responsible for your loss. I was promised by some responsible official ... that your place and position would be held open for you until you returned, when you would be put back in the same position, unless you were either killed or wounded badly, and in that case you would be taken care of."[6] John Worden himself was unable to find any permanent position at all until the end of the 1920s. Both men harboured intense feelings of resentment over the injustice of having fought for their country only to find themselves disregarded or deceived by empty promises once they tried to take back their place in civilian society. Following so soon after Maud's defection, the loss of James's seniority with Imperial Oil was yet another source of bitterness.

His great mainstay throughout the coming months was his 18-year-old son Hugh, and James unthinkingly put an immense burden of emotional responsibility on this conscientious and sympathetic young man. There had always been a strong bond between them, but James now depended on this to put his life back together. His need for closeness was heartrending at this time: "[Hugh] was my helpmate, my friend, my companion, and my advisor. Together we lived in comfort and loneliness, doing all our own housekeeping in that big house, sleeping in the same bed, cooking our meals together."[7] For a while their roles seemed to be reversed.

His son's encouragement was crucial to James's emotional recovery. Hugh would not hear of their leaving their old home, but helped his father to reconstruct his life into some semblance of normality. They set about the process of organizing a new household routine and sharing of chores. James welcomed physical activity, and together they kept up the house and garden, and prided themselves that the Matthews home presented the most immaculate appearance of any house on the street. His long army training in order and discipline, and the army's insistence on a smart turnout, may have helped him to focus his mind on these blessedly superficial routines, instead of wearing himself out with endless brooding.

As summer gave way to fall, the armies in Europe were slowly exhausting themselves and it was becoming apparent that the war was dragging to a close. Though the armistice was expected, the actual announcement of it on November 11, 1918, electrified Vancouver and brought forth an incredible mass rejoicing. The news came through in the middle of the night. James, asleep in bed, became vaguely conscious of unaccustomed noise outside and slowly realized that what he was hearing were the shrill blasts of steamer and factory whistles, sounding off at one o'clock in the morning. He and Hugh hurried to open the windows. Lights were on all over Kitsilano, and happy revellers were already heading for town. Firecrackers were exploding, pistol shots ringing out and there was shouting and beating of cans and other noisemakers.

In James's excitable mind, many emotions struggled for expression, but the most imperative was the sense that this was one of history's important moments and that—for some not fully understood reason—it was his personal duty to record it. Why did he allot himself this task? He had no official position as a war historian or an archivist, but his immediate impulse was to put the experience into words and describe how Vancouver responded. Before anything else, he thought it fitting to recite the Lord's Prayer. Then, "I got up, and recorded for the benefit of those who follow me, the first impressions of one mind at the receipt of the news that the greatest of all wars had ended."[8]

For an hour or two he wrote. Words poured out in a spontaneous flood of release, as he sat there writing paragraph after paragraph in a state of high of emotion, racing to keep up with the chaos of thoughts that demanded expression—thoughts of thankfulness and sadness, memories of heroism and of brutality, the whole disturbing microcosm of war. It was still dark when he heard a newspaper boy calling out. He went down to buy a paper, tipping the boy 10 cents for the good news. "Oh, how thoughtless of me. I should have given him $5," he wrote. Finally he lay down and slept, but only for four hours, for he wanted to be up and about and celebrating with everyone else on the streets of Vancouver.

November 11 was a day to be remembered. The city was in a state that bordered on pandemonium. All around Granville, Hastings and Main, thousands were milling around, singing and shouting and forming impromptu processions. Prohibition was conveniently forgotten, and bottles that had been carefully set aside for Christmas cheer were brought out to share with neighbours. Only one fellow worker had reported for work at James's office, so by mutual agreement the two of them promptly closed up, went out and bought flags to decorate the friend's car, and spent the morning driving around Vancouver to see what was going on in the streets.

James remembered the afternoon as the proudest in his life. It was the occasion of the veterans' march, and as the senior officer remaining in the 11th Brigade, he had the honour of marching at the head of his men. Huge crowds filled every inch of the sidewalks, blowing horns, whistling and waving flags. The bands and pipers played; the soldiers roared out the old war songs as they went, and James sang at the top of his voice with the rest of them. But after it was all over and the units had been dismissed, he lapsed into a more thoughtful mood. He knew the casualty lists (about 35,000 Canadians dead), and he had personal acquaintances who had lost brothers and husbands. Later that day he went out of his way to contact two of these friends and speak a few words of sympathy.

It was a day of mixed emotions, but the one uppermost in his mind was a glorious sense of pride in his country and a pride in the heroism of the men he had served with. He never doubted the service his country had done for the world, nor that he had served his country in an honourable cause. On a personal level, he felt an enormous thrill of satisfaction that he had been privileged to lead his company in the horrifying charge on Regina Trench and to have been at the head of such a gallant body of men. The result of his war service was to leave James with a heightened sense of patriotism. Although he was as much affected by the dreadfulness of war as any other thinking person might be, his most certain conviction—in spite of the price that had been paid, and the price he himself had had to pay—was that it had been a noble cause and justice had prevailed. "Yes; it was worth it, every bit of it was worth it," he wrote. "The epoch in British life in which it has been my fortune to live will go down to posterity and history as one glorified by the nobility of mind of those in that period ... Great deeds always call for great sacrifices."[9]

By the end of 1919 it was perfectly clear that Maud was not coming back, and in fact James records that she was becoming impatient for him to start divorce proceedings and set her legally free. He knew that he would have no difficulty in offering legal cause, since she had been living with another man as his wife for nearly two years. All this time, James had never brought himself to tell his parents the truth about Maud's absence, but had concocted the not very credible story that she was on a visit to New Zealand—a story that quickly began to wear thin and cause them more anxiety from being kept in the dark than if they had known the facts. Now the truth was out at last, and all James's family and friends (including father, mother and brother) were united in urging him to overcome his reluctance and take the final step. A strong sentimentalist and conservative by nature, James had to fight against all his instincts to sever the tie of marriage, but in January of 1920 he accepted the inevitable and instructed his solicitor to set the divorce process in motion.

James glosses over the circumstances surrounding Maud's personal life in this period and offers no information concerning his wife's lover. He appears to lay the responsibility for her defection more on this man than on Maud, for when he touches upon this episode in his memoir nine years later, he thinks of it in terms of "She was more sinned against than sinning" and "Judge not lest ye be judged." He never forgot her courage and resilience in the hard-up times of their early married life, especially in view of her aristocratic and affluent background, and he always remained grateful for the care she had given him when he was recovering from typhoid. Where her lover was concerned, he made no attempt to suppress his feelings. Even 40 years later James found himself flaring up with the old anger and bitterness. "Barry the bastard" he called him, and he scribbled on a card in 1964: "Mike Barry ruined his wife's home, his only child Rita's, and my wife's home."[10]

Maud had made a very unexpected choice in her new partner. An immigrant from Ireland, he had little money, his social background was very different from her own, he had no professional occupation and he was far older than herself—but he must have had the Irish charm. Michael Barry was almost 20 years older than Maud, and would have been 60 years of age at the time when she told James she had met someone else. It seems likely that he represented emotional security to Maud, in contrast to the turbulent atmosphere of life with the unpredictable Major. Interviewed at a St. Patrick's Day celebration in 1948, Mike Barry comes across as a light-hearted, jokey sort of character, with a sense of humour far more playful and good-natured than the Major's own, and this may have come as a considerable relief to Maud after the intensity of James's temperament.[11] She and Michael are said to have adored each other throughout their life together.

Michael was born in Limerick, Ireland, on September 25, 1858, to Patrick and Ellen Barry. He emigrated in his 20s, spent two or three years in some other part of Canada and arrived in British Columbia in the mid-1880s. He was working as a carpenter in New Westminster at the time of his marriage to Barbara Kilgour on January 11, 1892. Barbara was a woman about his own age, possibly a year or two older (there are discrepancies in the dates given), and had arrived in British Columbia from her native Ontario at about the same time as Michael. Directory listings show that Barbara Barry was living separately from Michael from at least 1921 onward.

Michael and Barbara were both Roman Catholics, hence neither could divorce. Although this could have presented a problem, the religious taboo evidently did not matter to Maud, who had always been a woman of independent ideas. She had married outside her own social circle and against her father's wishes; she had more or less eloped with James, a young man with few prospects; and she had resolutely led an unconventional, almost pioneer lifestyle with him in the early years—so she was willing to ignore the orthodox morality of the times and live with Michael without the marriage ceremony.

Several years went by, and on November 16, 1927, Barbara Barry died of peritonitis in St. Paul's Hospital after an unsuccessful operation. Her death did not affect Michael and Maud's situation and allow them to marry, since in the eyes of the Catholic Church, James was still Maud's husband, and James was very much alive. With James's longevity, no marriage would ever have been possible for Maud and Michael but for the fact that eventually Michael cut his affiliations to the Catholic Church. When they did marry on June 29, 1937, his religious denomination on the marriage certificate is described as "none." Maud did not seem overly concerned about religion either, for although she stated she was an Anglican, they were married in the home of a United Church minister.

Michael was not an ambitious man. For several years he had worked as a bridge carpenter and was hired by the city works department in 1899, first as caretaker for the Capilano waterworks, then a year or two later as caretaker for Mountain View Cemetery. The cemetery job satisfied him for the next 10 years or so, but his employment record becomes obscure after this. He may have been the Michael Barry who worked as a teamster around this time, but his line of work when he became involved with Maud is very much a matter of speculation.

Certainly, Maud did not improve her material lifestyle by moving in with Michael. Money was scarce and they lived in rented quarters, but by 1929 Maud and he decided that they could make a better living as apartment caretakers, an initiative that must have been Maud's idea, as she is listed as the apartment manager. Michael would have been about 70 by this time. They took on at least two appointments in this capacity—first at the Greythorpe House Apartments on Nicola, then at the Macdonald on Bidwell Street. After this they lived at the Driard Hotel on West Pender, followed by Hamlin Court on Jackson, though it isn't clear whether they were managers or merely tenants at these two. Her son Merle, who had not yet married, lived with them and became a long-time employee of Dominion Bridge. Finally, in

1938, the couple moved into a house of their own—James claimed that Maud asked him for financial help at some point in the 1930s, possibly at this juncture—and they settled into a home at 3428 East 23rd, where they lived for the rest of their lives.

James's divorce case came before the court on October 23, 1920, nine months after he had brought himself to accept the finality of Maud's departure. He was spared much of the publicity, as the case was privately held—apparently as a special courtesy on the part of Judge Morrison, who returned to the courthouse that Saturday afternoon after its doors had officially closed: "The judge, the barrister, Col. Hulme, one witness and myself were present. The proceedings lasted five minutes,"[12] recorded James. With those few moments in the panelled courthouse, the uncertainty of the past three years came to an end. He was free to remarry, and he did so—almost at once.

That spring, a few months after he had made the decision to divorce, he had had an encounter that had changed the direction of his thoughts. On May 24, 1920, he was walking into St. Paul's Hospital when a woman emerged whom he thought he recognized, even though it had been 18 years since he last saw her. He spoke to her; she did not remember him at first, but as soon as he reminded her of where they had met and told her his name, it all came vividly back to her—he was the difficult patient she had nursed through typhoid fever in the old Vancouver City Hospital in 1902. It would probably have been hard for her to forget this patient's forceful personality, but she had established a rapport with him and had been his favourite nurse, the only one who could manage him tactfully. Her name was Emily Eliza Edwardes, and she had never married, for she had devoted her life to the demands of an outstanding career in nursing.

After graduating from Vancouver City Hospital in 1905, Emily had done some private nursing to gain experience, but soon decided that she wanted more scope in her work. Ambitiously, she moved to New York, where she was put in charge of the operating room in the Brooklyn Eye, Ear, Nose and Throat Hospital, and before long her exceptional ability gained her a promotion to the position of "Lady Superintendent." Emily was responsible for much of the planning details when a new wing was added to the hospital, but the stress and

EMILY EDWARDES, JAMES'S SECOND WIFE, HOLDING AN UNIDENTIFIED INFANT, 1905. (CVA, PORT P1021.2)

overwork (and probably her own high standards) told on her health severely, and she became gravely ill. A letter by one of the doctors in the hospital indicates that she was operated on for something that might have been an abdominal tumour, but its removal brought with it a "fatal risk," and for some time her life was in danger. He thought that some misdiagnosis might have been involved.[13]

Gradually she improved; however, she was in no condition to go back to work, so she was forced to abandon her excellent prospects in New York and return home to Canada for a prolonged convalescence.

By 1915, with the war in full force, the need for skilled nurses was acute, and Emily—now restored to health—resolved to register for overseas duty. She joined the CEF on July 31, 1915 (even before James), and was on her way to England almost at once. Emily was, in fact, overseas for much longer than James. She served with the No. 5

EMILY AS A NURSING SISTER IN THE FIRST WORLD WAR. (CVA, PORT P190.2)

General Hospital, first in Egypt and later in Salonika (where she once watched a German Zeppelin as it bombed the harbour and then came down in flames in the swamp off the coast). Her worst wartime experience occurred in the Mediterranean on November 23, 1916, when the Red Cross ship she was travelling on (the *Braemar Castle*) was hit by either a torpedo or a mine. At least six of the patients on board were killed outright, and all the survivors had to take to the lifeboats, where they spent several nerve-racking hours on the water before being picked up by other ships. The badly crippled *Braemar Castle* did not sink, as it turned out, but two other hospital ships were destroyed in the same area at about that time, though clearly marked with the red cross.

Undeterred by this experience, Emily stayed on to complete her war service. After further nursing in England, she returned to British Columbia, where she was discharged on October 21, 1919. She had an honourable war record, having been mentioned in dispatches for outstanding service and awarded several decorations—notably the 1914–1915 Star, as well as the General Service and Victory Medals.[14]

Once the war was over, Emily had relocated to Vancouver and had recently started up a clinic for massage therapy when James happened to run into her outside St. Paul's. (Massage was only one of her specialties; she had also acquired skills in dentistry and other aspects of medical care when she worked in New York.) James was delighted to meet her again—he was always very faithful to old friendships and associations—and he immediately experienced that same sense of compatibility he had found so comfortable when Emily was his nurse. They met throughout the summer, became engaged in September and married three weeks after his divorce, on November 16, 1920.

Emily and James had much in common in their early background. Both had spent their early years in a more exotic climate and landscape, Emily in Bermuda and James in New Zealand, and had not arrived in Canada until their late teens—Emily at 17 and James at 19. Emily's father, Captain George Edwardes, had been an officer in the Royal Engineers and spent years abroad before settling in Manitoba. Brought up as a soldier's daughter, Emily had been immersed in the military tradition from childhood and understood the significance that James attached to it. Most importantly, they had in common the special bond of war service, which meant that James was always to hold Emily in very great respect.

They had a military wedding. James asked his former army chaplain, the Reverend Thomas Colwell, to officiate at the ceremony, which took place in Christ Church. James's long-time friend, Charles Rolston, was one of the witnesses. Emily and James each wore their wartime uniforms, as did the chaplain too, and James described it as "a pretty wedding," evidently deriving much pleasure from the effect of the crisp military uniforms and, in a more profound sense, all that the uniforms stood for. The couple honeymooned at Brentwood Bay on Vancouver Island.

There were no children of this marriage. Emily was actually three years older than James, though this was not what she had given him to understand when they were courting. He was quite under the impression that it was the other way round and that she was three years younger than him, and this was the information she had thought suitable to offer when filling in the marriage certificate. He had correctly put his age down as 42, but she—somewhat fancifully—had registered hers as 39. In reality, Emily was 45 years old at the time of their marriage and well beyond normal childbearing age. He was still under the illusion that she was younger when he wrote his family history seven years later, and may not even have discovered the truth until after her death.

Having pursued a demanding career for so many years, Emily was apparently content to give up her clinic and retire from nursing to manage the home for James and Hugh. Although Hugh was extremely attached to his own mother, his generous nature made it possible to for him to accept Emily and to understand that his father needed her affection and support. According to James's perspective, "The relationship between his stepmother and Hughie were [*sic*] most happy and cordial. He was fond of her, and she returned his affection."[15] Undoubtedly, Hugh wanted his father to be happy.

CHAPTER 6

Turmoil and Turning Points

The 1920s were years of major upheavals in James's life. As well as the turmoil of his divorce and remarriage, they included two or three different career moves, a transition from salaried employee to business manager, and finally the complete change of focus that led to his new life as Vancouver's redoubtable archivist.

As 1919 and 1920 went by, he grew more and more embittered over the loss of his managerial position with Imperial Oil after the war. At one time he had been in charge of a hundred outlets, he claimed, but now he felt that the company had let him down and was handing out shabby treatment to an employee who had only wished to serve his country. It was true that they had kept their word and given him back a job, but he had not reckoned on having lost his seniority with the company. After 20 years with Imperial Oil he felt he deserved better. There was also another factor—the typical Matthews' expectation of being in a role of management. It was not in the Matthews family tradition to be in anything other than an administrative position. His father, grandfather and great-grandfather had all been entrepreneurs, owning and operating their own businesses. James himself, having enjoyed a senior rank in the war, was all the more frustrated now with a subordinate position that made so little use of his abilities. Finally, on August 27, 1920, after 21 years with Imperial Oil, he left its employment so that he could go into business for himself.

He started up a tugboat company, which he called J.S. Matthews Tugboats. He had scows and tugboats working for him, he had an office at 470 Granville Street, and business went well, according to his account of it in later years. By the following year he was so satisfied at the way things were going that he decided that it might soon turn into a family business, and so he took the step of making Hugh a nominal partner, changing the name to J.S. Matthews and Son. It was a source of immense pleasure to him that the two of them would continue in their excellent relationship and build up the business together (with Hugh no doubt becoming an active partner at some future date).

His dependence on Hugh's companionship was still as strong as ever. Hugh had been his mainstay during the months that followed Maud's departure, and their mutual affection had developed into a special bonding, which Emily wisely sensed and respected. Hugh had been employed at various jobs since leaving school—he had worked for Imperial Oil at one time, he had gone with John Worden to Saskatchewan in 1921 to help with the harvest, and he had worked on one of the tugs in his father's business. He continued to look for outside employment, even though from 1921 onward he was, in name anyway, a partner in J.S. Matthews and Son.

JAMES'S YOUNGEST SON, HUGH, WAS ON THE KING EDWARD HIGH SCHOOL HOCKEY TEAM. ON THE BACK OF THE PHOTO, JAMES WROTE: "A NOBLE SON." (E. WALSER)

Finally, in August of 1922, he was lucky enough to secure a job he very much wanted—a clerking position with Robertson Godson Co., a firm that sold plumbing equipment. On November 25 he went to work as usual. One of the first things he had to do was go to the basement, collect a customer's order, detach the invoice and leave it behind, then take the order up to the main floor. He got into the freight elevator, but just as it began to move, he realized he was still holding on to the invoice. Hastily he threw it down the elevator shaft for someone below to catch, and without thinking, leaned out of the elevator cage to make sure it had been received. It was a fatal action. His head was caught as the elevator passed a floor and he died instantly of a broken neck.[1]

James's grief can hardly be imagined. "His loss was the greatest I ever suffered, or ever shall suffer," he wrote in in his Matthews family history in 1927, the heartache still as profound as it had been five years earlier. "We had been chums almost from his birth … I think he would have made a bright, clever and good man. God bless his dear memory. Perhaps the Almighty in His infinite goodness had some good reason for taking him. His work perhaps was done. I have expressed gratitude many a time for having him spared to me for so many years—it could have been shorter."[2] Devastated as he was, James understood his rare good fortune in having known this ideal relationship and the privilege of loving and being loved. Years later, his sense of gratitude was all that mitigated his loss.

He and Emily had been building a new home on Arbutus Street that summer, and Hugh had been planning it with him and helping him to construct it. The move had been scheduled to take place on the very day that Hugh died, but instead of a move, James found himself planning a funeral. Their old friend John Worden was one of the pallbearers, along with some of Hugh's friends from work, and many of James's brother Masons attended, for the gravesite was in the Masonic section of Mountain View Cemetery. Maud and the twins were there—the report mentions "the family"—and they placed their own separate card of thanks in the *Province*, acknowledging "the beautiful floral tributes and sympathy."[3]

All winter James was sunk in a dreadful sadness. There was no pleasure to be had in the new house now, and he was simply going through the motions in keeping the tugboat business in operation. His nerves were still raw from the shock of Hugh's death when only a few months later, he was faced with another family crisis. On March 24, 1923, he received a cable from his mother in Wales to say that his father had died that morning.

Herbert Matthews had died of pneumonia at the age of 71. Mary was completely distraught and too much in shock to be able to deal with the immediate future, and James was the one she instinctively turned to. At that time she was not on comfortable terms with Martin. She and Herbert had gone back to New Zealand in 1920 for the sake of Mary's health and had tried living with Martin and his wife, Sadie, but the arrangement hadn't worked and the relationship had turned sour. Back they went across the sea to Prestatyn. Recently they had been persuaded by James to come and live in Vancouver and had been preparing to pack up once again when Herbert fell ill.

Immediately and without a second thought, James dropped everything to be with his mother. He closed down his tugboat business and two days later was on the train to the coast via New York. Travel was slowed down because of winter conditions, and he did not arrive in Britain till April 14. "At last!" exclaimed his mother dramatically, as she clasped him in her arms. Mary was at the end of her emotional strength. She had not stirred from her room since Herbert's death, but had simply shut herself in to wait for James's arrival. Martin was not indifferent to his mother's situation, but took the view that she was not wanting for funds and, in any case, there was nothing he could do to help. Mary, however, was in such a state of shock that she was only too relieved to have someone there to make decisions for her. She willingly agreed to come back and live with James in Vancouver, where he would look after her. Within three weeks they were on their way.

Emily graciously welcomed Mary into her home, but it was a bad, unpromising scenario. Mary had been unable to get on amicably with Maud during the 1908 visit, and the older couple had left to stay in lodgings. The same thing had happened in New Zealand in 1921, when they had attempted to live with Martin and Sadie. Both Mary's daughters-in-law had proved resistant to her egoistic and demanding style, and Emily soon found herself in the same situation, with her mother-in-law as a permanent member of the household. The situation was exacerbated by James's obvious inability to deny his mother anything or go against her wishes. Mary had him in thrall, just as she had had Herbert.

JAMES'S MOTHER, AGED 80, IN AN OIL PAINTING BY SYDNEY MARCH. "THE PRETTIEST OLD LADY IN WALES," JAMES CALLED HER. (GEORGE T. WADDS PHOTO. CVA, PORT P29)

The situation deteriorated as 1923 wore on, and finally by September Emily had had enough: she walked out. James is reticent about this episode, but his insistence on leaving a truthful account of his life compelled him to state briefly: "Family disturbances result in legal separation." The legal separation agreement, which speaks of "unhappy differences," is dated September 14, 1923—confirmation of an event that is surprising, considering their many happy years together afterwards.[4]

Emily must have felt driven to desperation to take such a drastic step as to consult a lawyer and make property arrangements, but perhaps it was the only way to force her husband to take the situation seriously. As a woman who had lived independently for so many years before marriage, she was certainly not about to have her life taken over by the controlling personality of a mother-in-law and be reduced to a non-influential status in her own home. At this point James had to come out of his state of denial and face the fact that he would have to take a stand and support his wife's position. He must have promised to make other arrangements for his mother, for Emily did relent. "Wife returns after one month," he recorded briefly.[5]

Mary had been shocked into some remorse after Emily left and by October 5, she had found herself temporary accommodation in a neighbour's home on Arbutus, and was making plans to live in an upper suite in a house at 2083 Whyte, just around the corner from James. Guilt feelings assailed him; he could not let his elderly mother live like this. He was determined to provide a proper home for her, so his next action was to buy another lot and start to build her a house of her own. The new home was to be at 1306 Arbutus, just a couple of blocks south of his own—just far enough away to be a workable arrangement.

During the winter of 1923 and the spring of 1924 the work of construction went on, but at the last minute Mary began to have second thoughts. As always, she never quite knew what she wanted in the way of accommodation or even which country she wished to live in. The old restlessness set in; she began to have doubts about her relationship with James and had a yearning to see Martin again. Unable to keep these misgivings to herself, she unburdened herself to James and announced, to his dismay, that she was not so enthusiastic after all about staying in Vancouver and was contemplating an immediate return to New Zealand. James could hardly believe she would seriously consider such an act of folly. He begged her not to act hastily—she was nearing 80, he pointed out, and had had a serious illness just a few years before. Besides, he protested, he had put a great deal of effort into her new house, and now it was just on the point of completion.

But neither reasoning nor protests had any effect on Mary, and all that James could do was to keep a careful watch to make sure that she did nothing impulsive. In the end Mary did exactly as she pleased. Eluding his dominating presence, she walked out of the house one day carrying nothing but a handbag and an umbrella, and secretly boarded the *Aorangi* to travel alone to New Zealand.

"Poor dear Mother had lost none of her courage nor determination,"[6] wrote James indulgently. He knew his mother too well to be totally surprised by her behaviour. She left all her belongings behind when she left the house on April 4, but her stubborn fighting spirit, which James had inherited, was equal to any difficulties. She arrived in New Zealand with no adverse effect—in fact, probably feeling rather pleased with herself. She arranged to stay with a widow in Palmerston North, near Martin, and was still living there when she died two years later with Martin by her side. For some time, she had been living with cancer of the breast, perhaps a recurrence of the unnamed illness that had prompted the return to New Zealand in 1920. She died on November 23, 1926, at the age of 81.

When the contents of her will were revealed, it was yet another shock for James: she had left everything to Martin, except for a token amount of £200 to James, a sum that was less than the expenses he had incurred on her behalf.

The disposition of family money had been a source of contention ever since Herbert's death in 1923. Their original arrangement had still favoured Martin to exactly the same degree as Mary's last will: firstly they had each left everything to each other, but in the event of their simultaneous deaths it was Martin who would receive all but £200. Herbert was known as an exceedingly fair-minded individual, so the explanation may very well have been that he was attempting to equalize past expenditures on his sons. But when Herbert died, Mary was plunged into such emotional turmoil that, only six days after James's arrival, she made a new will that reversed the old one—more than reversed it, for it disinherited Martin altogether.

Mary had been terribly hurt by the fact that Martin had not even cabled her after his father's death, whereas James had rushed to her side the moment he heard the news.[7] She found Martin's omission hard to forgive. James had never got on particularly well with his older brother, but even so, he could not accept the inequity of Mary's will. He had started a running argument with his mother, and by October 1923 had persuaded her to relent to the extent of leaving £200 to Martin. A month later, he had induced her to raise it to £600. Then he told her that, in any case, when the time came, he was going to share his inheritance equally with Martin. By the following January he had succeeded in drawing up a new will for her, in which she had agreed to do as he wished and divide her estate in equal proportions between each son. This was what he had expected to find when the final will was opened.

It was a most hurtful turn of events. He had dropped everything to be with her at a time when she was in a state of shock and grief, and he had done it gladly for the mother he idolized—but now, where was the evidence of her love for him? Financially it hit him hard as well, for when his mother had given him cheques to cover the cost of his passage to Britain, he had never brought himself to cash them. There was also the current expense of building the new house for her on Arbutus. But it was the emotional injustice that hurt the most. "Why cast an irretrievable slur on one's own child?" he agonized. The will is the last symbol of parental affection, and James felt he had lost out to Martin. This view of things was not helped by the fact that Martin felt justified in keeping his full share of the inheritance.[8]

James's older brother Martin, aged 32. Theirs was an uneasy relationship. (CVA, Add. MSS 54, 508-D-1, file 5, #5)

After Mary's death there was to be no more struggling with divided loyalties, and James gave Emily his complete devotion. From then on Emily reigned supreme in his life, his ideal of womanhood, invested in his mind with every saintly quality imaginable—courageous and resolute, loving and supportive. The need for a feminine influence had been ingrained in James's psyche ever since childhood, and he had become greatly dependent on Emily's encouragement and her faith in him. He respected her friends, and some of these women, like Ruth Woodward and Rosalynde Latimer, remained his friends for life. He would listen to Emily's advice as he listened to few others'—and he would sorely need this advice and encouragement during the next 20 years.

CHAPTER 7

A New Career

During the 1920s James's career was in turmoil. The towing business had been successful enough, but after Hugh's death he had lost enthusiasm for it. He never cancelled Hugh's partnership in it, and carried on under the name J.S. Matthews and Son; in fact, he kept his bank account in the name of J.S. Matthews and Son for the rest of his life and continued to sign his cheques that way. But he had little motivation to carry on with the business, and when a new position presented itself around 1923, he took it on.

He was probably attracted by the challenge of the new job. His mandate was to revive the fortunes of a failing business, a rope factory called Canada Western Cordage.[1] This was a government-operated concern that had been set up with the object of giving employment to needy war veterans, but it was failing to make a profit and was due for a change of management. James was appointed a director. His energy and common sense were evidently just what the firm needed; he threw himself into the work, and according to James, they made a profit of $10,000 in his first year. On September 12, 1925, he became manager, creating a profit of $30,000 that year. Then something went wrong. "Politics enter," he states cryptically, and the upshot was that in July of the following year he resigned.[2]

Now he had no paid occupation, and for the next two or three years he drifted uncertainly. He missed the handsome salary he had been receiving from Canada Western Cordage, yet he was beginning to realize that the world of commerce would never give him any real fulfilment, and he felt an increasing reluctance to continue in it. He later explained: "I could do it again, but I have lost heart for business, I don't like it. But I must do something."[3]

Over the next two years, James filled the time with a vast number of community activities. He was in command of No. 4 Company of Veterans from 1927 until it disbanded; he went off to various army camps as quartermaster; he was historian and archivist for his regiment, as well as being archivist for the BC Rifle Association; and from time to time he gave rousing lectures on soldierly topics. A keen sportsman, he acted as judge at certain track events, and was an honorary director of the Meraloma Athletic Club at Kitsilano Beach in 1929. He was also still a member of the Western Gate Lodge, and their representative to the Masonic Cemetery Association.

James Matthews, aged 49. (Steffens Colmer photo. CVA, Port P1713)

But all this was not enough. He needed a broader scope for his ideas, and he began to take an active part in civic affairs. He was an early member of the Kitsilano Ratepayers Association, and no doubt a very vocal one, for in 1927 his friends started urging him to stand for election as one of the three parks commissioners. One of the chief issues in Kitsilano was the need to acquire parkland while it was still available, and James made this the centre of his campaign when he ran for election in December 1927. Two particular pieces of waterfront were at stake. One was the popular Greer's Beach, leased from the CPR; the other was the 80-acre Squamish Reserve, which was threatened by the prospect of industrial use—some of its age-old trees had already been felled simply as a make-work project for veterans. James wrote letters to the newspapers promoting his ideas and engendered a fair amount of publicity, but unfortunately, he failed to win a seat. Nor was he any more successful in 1928: the electorate still preferred the incumbents.

James was frequently to state that he retired from other work in the year 1929 with the object of establishing the Archives of Vancouver. This, however, is only a half-truth. In fact, he was still looking around for some kind of employment, and there is evidence that he considered applying for at least one paid position in 1929. In the Matthews files in the City Archives is a letter of recommendation, dated November 21, 1929, that endorses his application for the job of principal clerk in the Vancouver office of the federal Ministry of Marine and Fisheries.[4] The work involved writing publicity pieces for newspapers and journals, a task for which no one could have been better qualified than the Major. But it is difficult to imagine James at 51 in the role of principal clerk in an office, and it is doubtful that he could have adapted himself to the limitations of bureaucracy and petty office routine. He was still looking for work a year later, judging from his correspondence with John Worden, who had been having equally bad luck in finding employment since the war. Worden wrote in 1930: "I am real sorry to hear you have had no luck in re-establishing yourself ... I had a terrible time also, but now have a position of sorts, for which I am thankful."[5]

Since no suitable job presented itself, James occupied some of his time in the late 1920s by compiling a history of the Matthews and Boscawen families. As early as 1921 he had asked his parents to find out all they could and supply him with a family tree, but he had done nothing with this material until 1927, when he turned his full attention to the project of writing it up. While it was his parents' research that formed the basis for it, the account is pungently flavoured with his own memories and observations (very unfavourable in the case of his father-in-law from his first marriage). James took this genealogy project so seriously that in any resumé of his career, he always included it as his principal achievement in 1927.

Heraldry also figured in his interests. After the war he had been seized with a sudden desire for a family coat of arms and a conviction that he was entitled to this on the basis of his war service—for there was no pretence to nobility on the Matthews or Skitt side of the family. "If the spilling of blood in the defence of one's country … does not qualify for bearing arms, then what does qualify?" he argued.[6] He acquired his coat of arms in 1921. Curiously, although he and Maud had divorced so very recently, the design included certain features from the Boscawen family (who really did have claim to aristocratic birth, being descendants of Viscount Falmouth). Not only did he incorporate a "pile" from the Boscawen shield, but he actually adopted the Boscawen motto itself: *Patience Passe Science.*

All this time his collection of documents and relics continued to expand and was by now occupying considerable space in the Matthews' modest-sized home on Arbutus. He had been only 20 when he made his first acquisition, and he had been a resident of Vancouver for less than a month. It was a Christmas promotion advertised in the *Vancouver Daily World*, and it was a new street map entitled "A Bird's-Eye View of Vancouver," which claimed to be "without doubt the handsomest and most artistic work … ever published in the Northwest." He had eagerly expended 50 cents on this map—and without realizing it, had made his first investment in a massive future collection. By 1930 this amounted to as much as a ton of material.

THE BOSCAWEN-MATTHEWS COAT OF ARMS. (END PAPER FOR *EARLY VANCOUVER*, VOL. 1, BY J.S. MATTHEWS)

By the age of 50, James Matthews had become a very knowledgeable self-taught historian, but he still never visualized himself as ever becoming a member of the elite fraternity of the academic or literary world, for which, of course, he had no paper qualifications. His "collection" was still just an interesting hobby for his own enjoyment. He was not a professional.

Seen in retrospect, it is obvious that all James's outside interests—his antiquarian pursuits, his historical writing, his family research, his dabbling in heraldry—were combining to lead him gradually into a sphere of activity far more suited to his tastes than the profit-making hustle of the business world he had so far known. But how did he come to recognize this and what suddenly propelled him into making a career out of this hobby, reinventing his life at a time when many men might have been contemplating retirement?

James himself explained it very simply. Writing to Marion Woodward in 1960, he told her: “It is thirty-one years now since one morning when I was bending down lacing my boots, I suddenly ejaculated to Mrs. Matthews ‘I know what I’m going to do.’ I had been out of a position for two years; a number of positions were open, but did not appeal. So I started.”[7]

An Unrivalled Publication.

There is now in the press and will be published in a few days, a Bird's-Eye View of the city of Vancouver. The size of the sheet is 24 by 43 inches. This will be in every respect a first-class, up-to-date publication. Every street in the city will be shown, as well as every building—public, business and residential. There will appear on the sheet a key, or index, to a large number of buildings. The harbor will also be shown with the vessels bearing their names lying therein. It will be printed in colors, and will be without doubt the handsomest and most artistic work, as well as the most accurate and valuable for reference and other purposes, ever published in the Northwest. Those who have examined the proof sheets—and they have been quite a few—pronounce it to be by all odds the best work of the kind they have ever seen.

Look out for it.

James bought the map advertised here in his first month in Vancouver. It was his first archival acquisition. (*Vancouver Daily World*, November 15, 1898)

The encouragement of his friends in the Art, Historical and Scientific Association may well have been a considerable factor in bringing him to this decision. The AHSA was a prestigious group connected with several cultural interests, but most prominently the museum and art gallery. James had been a member for some years, and had, in fact, sent most of his collection on loan to the museum in a fit of depression after Hugh’s death. (The museum claimed that it was a gift, and displayed great reluctance to hand it back to James later.) In August 1929 the AHSA voted to send him a special letter of thanks in appreciation of “the great amount of work you have done, and interest shown in military records for this city and general interest in the advancement of the Vancouver City Museum and Art Gallery.”[8] James was greatly uplifted by this letter and read it as encouragement of the highest order.

Few people understood James’s need for appreciation, but for all his bluster, he was touchingly dependent on encouragement and praise. The smallest shred of approval was apt to have an effect on his volatile temperament out of all proportion to the context, and the smallest encouragement acted as a powerful stimulant. Many times in the future he was to seize on some brief sentence in a letter of this kind and quote it repeatedly as a means of influencing public officials. He may well have begun to think of it as official sanction to take his archival work to a more professional level.

And so in the winter of 1929–1930, James hauled his boxes of records out of the attic and began the serious business of sorting them into some kind of order. It was a period of initiation into the work of the trained archivist, as opposed to the casual collector. He was very much in need of technical advice, but at this stage he had no friendly contacts whom he could call upon for help, and he had to rely on his own theories and solutions. He was later to describe himself as having worked as "a semi-professional" in this period of transition.

All through 1930 he laboured to organize the collection that filled his home, working long hours just as if it had been a paid occupation. But this was only one aspect of what he believed the work should entail. James's great virtue as an archivist was his tremendous initiative in seeking out history. Every day he was out and about in the community, engaging in the proactive work of the archivist—requesting interviews, striking up conversations and listening to the memories of Vancouver's older citizens. Even a casual conversation in a pub would be enthusiastically transcribed by James that same evening, and the record placed in his files. His sociable personality allowed him to engage easily with people, and he would later say that no one had ever turned him down for an interview.

Then, in the late summer of 1930, he made one of the most significant contacts of his life: it was his great good fortune to be befriended by Victoria's charismatic archivist, John Hosie. Hosie had been appointed Provincial Librarian and Archivist four years earlier, but James had never actually met him in person. He had ventured to send Hosie a letter, enclosing a transcript of one of his interviews, and had received such a kindly reply that from September onward, the two men were in regular correspondence.

John Hosie was as great a contrast to James Matthews as it was possible to be. Two years younger than James, he was a Scot who had come to British Columbia in 1912. He had never married, but lived with his sister and wrote poetry for pleasure. (A collection of his poems, *The Arbutus Tree and Other Poems,* was published in 1929.) He was a sensitive man of more subtle perceptions than James, but with less physical vitality—"I marvel at your dynamic energy," he wrote on June 26, 1933, after exposure to the blast of James's personality. James replied: "I have been blessed all my life with such good health that I cannot understand illness properly. I know something about grief, but poor health is sort of foreign to me."[9] Yet underneath, the two men understood each other very well. Both had come under the spell of British Columbia in their early youth and were passionate about the province's history. Both shared a romantic vision of the world about them. If John Hosie was moved to poetry, James Matthews too displayed a gift for poetic expression in his vivid, picturesque prose.

John Hosie, British Columbia's Provincial Archivist, became James's dear friend and mentor. (BC Archives, I-78523)

As their exchange of correspondence developed and James found his work being taken seriously by the province's principal archivist, his confidence grew rapidly and by early 1931, he was acknowledging his future goal quite openly: it was indeed his ambition to establish an archives for Vancouver. The suggestion he made was a simple but nervy one—that Hosie should accept him and his collection as a branch of the Provincial Archives itself, but based in Vancouver.

Remarkably, he gained Hosie's instant support. By now the two men had met, and with great acuity Hosie understood that he was dealing with an individual of exceptional qualities, and he went to great lengths to put James's case before Deputy Provincial Secretary Royal L. Maitland, who in turn took it to Provincial Secretary S.L. Howe. But early 1930, only months after the Wall Street stock exchange disaster, was the worst possible moment to be making suggestions for setting up a new department. Although Maitland was genuinely receptive to the idea in principle, he could do nothing to implement their proposals. Far from expansions, drastic cuts would be the order of the day, he told Hosie.[10]

Hosie attempted to cheer James. He assured him that he was "exceedingly sorry" not to have the use of his services, but the matter could be reconsidered the following year. He added: "The outline you give me of your work during the last few weeks convinces me beyond all shade of doubt you have in rich measure the archivist instinct and that you are an indefatigable worker."[11] Such a compliment must have thrilled James beyond measure, but the idea of waiting until the next fiscal year was completely outside his way of thinking. He briefly contemplated working for nothing under Hosie's direction; even more briefly, he thought he might "drop the whole thing." Then in April he announced a new idea to Hosie: "Suppose I forgot the provincial idea and went after the city instead? Would that be wise? I don't think so."[12]

But although James was speaking of a City-operated archives merely in terms of a possibility (and not a very likely one at that), in reality this was indeed his new objective, and he had already been galvanized into action on this new front. Only four days after hearing from Hosie, he had started to redirect his campaign and initiate an approach to the Vancouver City Council—the first onslaught in the love-hate relationship that was to endure over the next four decades. He began lobbying members of Council, addressing himself to one in particular, William Lembke, whom he perceived as being sympathetic to the cause.[13]

On March 17, 1931, he wrote to Lembke: "Since some twelve months ago, the matter of the records of Vancouver has taken up the whole of my effort. The work appeared urgent, and precious few hours have been lost ... Lack of an office and official authority renders efforts partially futile. To keep on without assistance is impossible; to stop would be tragedy."[14] In spite of the dramatic tone of the letter, his request was deceptively mild: he merely asked permission to appear before Council and explain the nature of his work during the past year.

Harmless as the request appeared, anyone who knew James could have predicted that his presentation would certainly not stop short at a mere account of his activities. There would be demands—and demands would involve money. He could hardly have picked a worse moment. City Council was retrenching rather than creating new expenses. Its finance committee was planning overall cost reductions, and Council was being forced to consider saving money by such measures as closing down the Kitsilano branch of the library. Relief for the unemployed stood out as one of the major topics of discussion at the 1931 Council meetings and would do so for several years to come. The majority of hard-pressed citizens, struggling to pay their bills, would have regarded the funding of a department purely concerned with heritage as an unthinkable extravagance, and the word "frill" would have come readily to the lips of several Council members.

It was not that British Columbia was indifferent to its history. The province already had its historians, to whom the existence of archival institutions was of vital importance. Writers like Judge Frederick Howay, Dr. Robie Reid and Bruce McKelvie had all been putting out works of historical narrative during the 1920s and contributing to the flow of scholarly information. However, it was one thing for academics and journalists to study history, and quite another for the down-to-earth men on City Council to juggle their finances in such a way as to distribute funds fairly and cause the least deprivation possible.

James did not have any official standing to support his case, and was still regarded by many people merely as a private collector. Besides this, it was argued that the history of Vancouver was already covered by the Provincial Archives. James had an answer to that. In his view, Vancouver was a city with such a splendid future that it was already surpassing Victoria in size and importance, so that the archives of Vancouver were potentially of even more value than those of the capital city.

He was determined not to let the matter drop, and he launched into a tidal wave of activity. He spent March and April harrying his friends at City Hall and stirring up support. One of his chief advantages was his long-time friendship with the mayor, his old acquaintance, Louis Taylor of the *Vancouver Daily World*. Taylor was on his side all along and appreciated the value of what James was attempting, and others such as Lembke were also sympathetic to his objectives. Nobody could deny their support in principle without appearing ignorant and crass, but to effect what James wanted without incurring extra cost seemed an insoluble problem.

Few people could resist Matthews' powers of oratory, nor yet his touching sincerity, and against all the odds, his eloquence had an effect. Perhaps grudgingly, yet not wishing to be considered cultural illiterates, Council came up with a plan. If all that Matthews wanted was an office and some official standing, perhaps they could find him some small corner inside the city library—the basement perhaps, or some out-of-the-way nook that nobody else wanted. Naturally he was not to expect any remuneration—after all, it was just his hobby, wasn't it?

Unexpectedly, however, the library board graciously allotted Matthews a small sum out of its own regular library grant, not as a salary but for buying archival material. The chief librarian, Edgar Robinson, was to issue the grant, and James was to work under his direction. The thought of James Matthews working under someone else's direction must have given rise to serious doubts on the part of anyone who knew him at all well, but in theory the arrangement seemed workable. James thankfully seized on Council's offer, already disregarding in his mind any restrictions that might have been officially imposed. He was in, and that was all that counted.

He was fortunate to have received any consideration at all, and doubly fortunate to have been provided with any sort of grant. Considering Council's problems in the Depression years—and most of their time was occupied by discussion of these problems—this was a huge concession. It was an even more significant decision than they realized at the time, for once the Major's foot was in the door, there would be no dislodging him. Any attempt to influence his style of management would be warded off with ease; any hint that he might retire would prove futile. However many battles would be fought over the next 40 years, Major Matthews would always emerge victorious, the protector of his beloved Archives.

CHAPTER 8

The Archives in the Attic

His admission into the precincts of the Vancouver City Library represented only the most tenuous of footholds, but James Matthews greeted it with unbounded enthusiasm. He was archivist! He had an office! Neither Council nor the library board had any idea what forces they had unleashed when they allowed him in the door, for nothing could stop the Major now. The library had allotted him only the most miserable and uninviting of quarters—not even in the main library building itself, but in an obscure part of the adjacent annex. No one would be paying him for his work. He would have no official authority. He was only there on sufferance. None of this mattered to him, however, on Monday, June 15, 1931, the day when he stepped into his garret office and knew that his real working life had begun.

The annex stood immediately south of the Carnegie Library on Main Street and had only just come into use as an overflow of the library. A castle-like, red-brick edifice with twin turrets and a high central tower, it was originally designed for a surprisingly workaday purpose—the city market of Vancouver. But only a decade later, it was taken over as Vancouver's city hall, and remained so for the next 30 years until the City's ever-expanding departments made it necessary to look for a larger building. In 1929 the city hall had therefore vacated these quarters and moved into the Holden Building (today's Tellier Building) on Hastings Street. The empty city building on Main was then eagerly taken over by the library and used as a library annex and reading room.

JAMES'S FIRST ARCHIVES OFFICE WAS IN THE TURRETED ANNEX (LEFT) OF THE VANCOUVER PUBLIC LIBRARY (RIGHT) ON MAIN STREET. (PACIFIC NOVELTY CO. POSTCARD. AUTHOR'S COLLECTION)

The chief librarian, Edgar Robinson, had been very helpful in offering accommodation to James just at the critical moment in his negotiations with Council. The two men had known each other for some time, since James was often in and out of the library visiting the museum, which was on an upper floor. One day he happened to meet Robinson coming up the stairs. "I said, 'I suppose you have no place you could put me.' Robinson said there was. We looked first in the basement of the Library, then in the basement of the Hall, where records were kept in a wooden box beside the furnace. Finally we looked at the caretaker's room in the tower. It was dirty, empty, with cobwebs and peeling wallpaper, the plaster largely fallen."[1] Robinson phoned James the following evening and confirmed that he could have this attic space if he wished.

It was hardly the most suitable spot to house the future city archives of Vancouver. For years to come, Major Matthews loved to tell the story of the slummy conditions in this long-neglected space at the top of the building, and was to repeat the tale frequently for its dramatic effect. He would dwell enjoyably on the flaking ceiling plaster, the festoons of drooping wallpaper, the bones of the dead pigeon in a corner of the room. The window was propped up with a stick, he said; the table was just a board on four legs, the wastepaper basket had no bottom, and the desk broke as it was being carried upstairs. The bookshelves consisted of some planks placed between blocks of wood. As for the floor, it was "a thick mass of dried paint of every hue." He put on some overalls and scrubbed it clean himself, bringing a brush and pail from home.[2]

But on his first working day in the office he was pleased enough with what he had acquired: "A start was made this morning ... in the room beneath the tower in the 'Old City Hall.' Our office equipment at present consists of two old chairs, and a table without drawers; that is all. The documents are 'the document,' we have one only in a cardboard box."[3] On the back of an old envelope he roughly printed the word "Archives" and stuck it on the door for a sign.

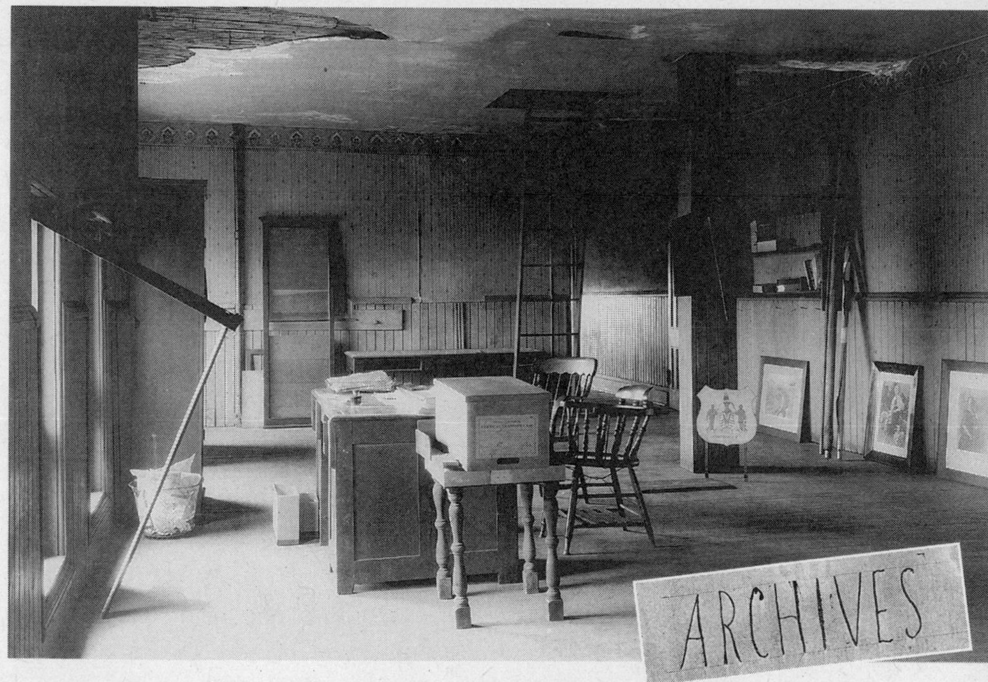

Interior view of the archives in the library annex, "the dirtiest room in Vancouver." (CVA, City N11) (Right) The sign that James improvised and stuck on the office door on his first day as an archivist in 1931. (CVA, Series 437, 37-A-1, file 1, page 28)

Edgar Robinson was well disposed toward the archives project and had even made a brief presentation to the library board on Matthews' behalf. Referring to him a little condescendingly as "a local collector"—and certainly not giving him the status of "archivist"—Robinson had nevertheless spoken favourably about the project, for he was genuinely enthusiastic about history and may also have thought that it would enhance the library's reputation to house the collection there. Nothing very grand was conceived of in Robinson's mind, since on his part it would simply be a gracious concession to indulge an amateur hobbyist.

But Robinson's view of the arrangement was radically different from James's. According to Robinson's report, the Major "was anxious to work under the auspices of the library," inferring that James and his collection would come under Robinson's authority. James did not see it that way at all. It was his own personal collection he was bringing in, and therefore not subject to any outside interference. Fortunately, no one analyzed the situation too closely at the time, and in a spirit of goodwill the library board even granted James $100 for the remainder of the year "to acquire material." The proviso was that it was "to be spent under the direction of the librarian," but this appeared to James to be a mere formality, as did any other scrutiny of the chain of command. It was the kind of official language that really did not register. In a state of high excitement, he began to set up his first archives office.[4]

Day after day, morning and afternoon, he transported his boxes of material to the library annex and began—apparently for the first time—to set up a filing system (alphabetically under subject headings). In addition to a mass of documents, he had accumulated as many as 300 or so photos over the years, and all these needed extensive historical notes, as well as classification. But James was not a man to sit at a desk all day long, and he did not see the job in those terms either. His concept of an archivist's mandate included taking on a vast number of other roles—interviewer, researcher, public speaker, writer and publicist. Obviously he was setting himself an impossible task. In his imagination he could see himself as having the generalship of some large ambitious department, but the fact was that just now he had no assistant, no telephone and not even a typewriter, unless he carried his own machine from home each day.

With James's impatient temperament, it was not long before the reality of the situation sank in and he lapsed into moods of heavy discouragement. Forgetting his success in receiving any funding at all, he gloomily deplored the lack of money to carry out his visionary program for developing the collection. At times, the frustration of seeing opportunities go to waste for lack of money was unbearable, and only a month after he started at the library he was confiding to the ever-sympathetic John Hosie: "No money to buy [archives]. I have started something, but I don't quite see how I can finish it. What's the use? It merely amounts to this, that I am having a whale of a time amusing myself. The sane thing to do, of course, is to abandon it. No one but a madman would do what I am doing. Spending my time and effort and money on a nice little hobby which some rich merchant ought to take up." The office is "a dump," he has no money, his taxes are due. He has had an offer to run a tugboat business, but has stubbornly turned it down. He tells Hosie: "Drop this in the wastepaper basket. I don't want this document preserved." (Hosie did not do so.) In need of reassurance—to an extent that would have amazed many people—he pleads with Hosie to come over for the day and talk. At this stage the two men have still only met once.[5]

For the whole of his first month, James must have been working like a maniac. As well as getting the office cleaned up and organized for work, he was already taking active steps toward *creating* archives—as opposed to merely receiving them. Disregarding cost, he commissioned a photographer from the *Province* to take pictures of some of the old buildings, and with even bolder initiative he contacted a well-known artist, John Innes, to create a painting of a historic scene that no one thought of photographing at the time—the inaugural meeting of Vancouver's first City Council. And at the same time as starting up an archives—as if that was not a huge project in itself—he also decided he should publish a history book, and he was staying up night after night writing up 50 or more of his interviews with pioneers. It would take the form of a historical anthology, and would be called *Early Vancouver*.

He was naive enough to believe that after he had reported to the library board on all these activities, the board would be so impressed that they might produce further funding. This he badly needed, for as well as all the photos he was ordering, he was desperately anxious to spend money on acquisitions. Today it is rare for an archives to purchase an item, and most institutions depend almost entirely on having material donated, but James clearly expected to have to pay for much of it. Time after time he would hear of records that had become available (from an estate, for instance) and lamented in his letters to John Hosie that he couldn't even make an offer on these. But the library board had no extra funds to spare for the Major's archives. "They thought that it was good work, were glad it was being done, said some nice things about me, and finally decided to pass on to other business. All came to nothing."[6]

James was well aware of the value of publicity, and was in fact longing to proclaim his work, so he lost little time in suggesting to Robinson that they engineer some sort of press coverage to make the public aware of the new archives facility. "Our endeavours so far have been almost secret, and it is thought that a public announcement of what is being attempted would lead to considerable activity."[7] Though generally supportive, Robinson was dubious about this idea, fearing that the archives' rather insignificant setting might create a poor impression that would take some time to overcome.[8] But nothing could repress the Major for long, and it was only a matter of time before he found a way of bringing the archives into the public eye.

Just a few weeks later came a perfect opportunity. It happened that two eminent visitors from Britain were touring the country to study Canadian museums on behalf of the Carnegie Corporation. One was a Member of Parliament, and the other was the president of the British Museums Association. It was arranged that on August 4 they should fit in two British Columbian museums on the same day, the Provincial Archives in Victoria and the "Matthews Archives" in Vancouver. The contrast was extreme. The former were appropriately housed in the provincial library in the stately legislative buildings; the latter in a dingy, ill-equipped attic. His eminent visitors were truly shocked by what they saw in Vancouver and could hardly believe their eyes—an archives stored in a dark, cobwebby tower without heat or electric light, and an archivist working without typewriter or telephone. What disturbed them as much as anything, they said, was the apparent lack of public support while he was labouring under such appalling difficulties.[9]

Nothing could have delighted James more, and he quoted their remarks that night in a forthright address to the Pioneers Association. This produced gratifying headlines in the *Vancouver Star* and the *Province* the next day: "Archives Branch urged for City," and "Major Matthews Deplores Lack of Authority in Record Preservation."[10] Better yet, it produced a whole editorial a week later: "Major Matthews is, of course, right. We have been careless of the story of our past, and it is an interesting and honourable and romantic story. It should be preserved, and the sooner steps are taken to preserve it the better it can, of course, be done."[11]

But this brief flare of public recognition was not enough to cheer him for long, and the euphoria of his first two months in office was quickly wearing off. James had been rapidly disenchanted with his dingy office and his unpaid status, and the need for financial support became his principal theme, and remained so for the next 40 years. For the rest of 1931 and on into 1932, he directed most of his efforts into a determined campaign for money—funding for the archives and a salary for himself. He leaned upon his entire Vancouver network of influential allies and convinced several associations to write letters to Council on his behalf. The Canadian Club did so, as did the Native Daughters of BC and the Native Sons, and his friends in the Pioneers Association did likewise. He himself continued to pressure Council members—and a few of them, like Lembke, were genuinely sympathetic, but were faced with the problem of deciding just where to allocate the sparse amount of money available.

James's great ally throughout this stressful period was the Provincial Archivist, John Hosie. James had his second meeting with him in July 1931, when Hosie had reason to come over to the mainland. For two and a half hours the two men talked, and by the time the morning ended, they were sympathetic friends and allies. Hosie discerned the warm, generous spirit that lay behind the aggressive bluster that was all that some people saw in the Major, and when James allowed himself to lower his guard and expose his most dearly held values, it was impossible not to be moved by his sincerity. This encounter cemented an understanding that developed into a true friendship.

The encouragement Hosie offered him did much to restore James's self-confidence and was a major factor in keeping him optimistic, though at the same time it had the rather wearing effect (on Hosie) of giving James full licence to unburden himself and demand further sympathy. Only four days after the meeting, he was penning another tale of woe, complaining histrionically that the Archives were "functioning feebly" and "must soon cease unless aided." This was not to be taken at face value: James was highly unlikely to quit. It was more of an unconscious pressure tactic, for he still hoped he might be taken on as a branch of the Provincial Archives. All Hosie could do—and it was a great mark of faith—was to offer him a grant out of the Provincial Archives budget if Cabinet would approve it.[12]

Amazingly, considering the economic constraints of the times, the Major's persistence paid off, for in 1932 City Council relented. Council was making no move to create an archives department at this point, but James was now to receive a salary of $30 a month out of the library budget, and his annual operating fund was being raised to $390. His status would improve considerably too, for the collection was now to be named the Archives, and he was to enjoy the title of Archivist. In addition, the library would spend up to $100 on redecorating his shabby workspace. All this was good, wonderful news indeed, even though half of his budget would immediately have to be used to pay off bills, since he had recklessly overspent in 1931. The only downside was the written proviso that the Archives would still come under the jurisdiction of the library board. Once again, the implications of this failed to make any real impression on his mind.

The months of June and July were taken up with the preparations for upgrading his office to more habitable conditions. Workers repapered the room for him—"last done probably forty years ago by appearances,"[13] huffed the Major—and in a fit of generosity the City actually installed a telephone. He planned to buy a new typewriter and began a search for a part-time typist (who would have to be paid out of his own $30 a month, however). The mood was a positive one and he basked in rare approval on all sides. The *Province* was giving him good publicity and printing his articles, and he was about to publish his first book, *Early Vancouver*, Vol. 1. Edgar Robinson, who had always assured him, "You have my personal interest and support,"[14] was still on his side.

It was ironic that just as everything was falling into place and he was riding high on a wave of appreciation, Matthews overreached himself. It all arose from the minor question of stationery. His clearly stated instructions were to use library stationery, to which Robinson planned to have the name "Archives" added. But when it came to issuing an invitation to a baronet, Sir Henry Burrard, James was so inflated by the importance of this that he decided that the Archives needed the prestige of having stationery of its own—crested stationery, nothing less. The library's stationery was "not suitable," he insisted. To Robinson, this was a dispute on a point of principle, and he was not about to have the Major setting a precedent for disregarding the terms of his employment. Robinson would not give way. But most opportunely for James, Robinson was due to leave for his holiday in August, and while he was away, James coolly designed and ordered the crested stationery that he desired so much.

A sheet of this controversial notepaper still survives in the files of the Vancouver City Archives. "The Archives" stands out at the top in large, bold Gothic lettering, while over to one side, in the tiniest of fonts, may be discerned with difficulty the words "Vancouver Public Library." The page is impressively embellished with the coat of arms of the City of Vancouver. (The library's own stationery was unpretentious and without any coat of arms.) John Hosie loved the design: "Let me congratulate you on your striking letterhead. This gives you an immediate standing, which you did not hitherto have."[15] However, when Edgar Robinson returned from his holiday at the end of August and not only viewed James's creation but received an invoice for 250 letterheads, he was beside himself with indignation. He swiftly wrote a withering note to James on one of the offending sheets of paper: "Dear Major Matthews, Please do not use this letter head until further notice from me. I am also returning the invoice."[16] From now on it was unspoken war between the two men.

The situation deteriorated rapidly, and within a week James sent a letter to the board, suggesting that it would be best for all concerned if the Archives and the library were to separate. Incensed by this continued refusal to acknowledge his authority, Robinson suspended James from his duties and demanded a return of the office key. James responded by closing the place up for three weeks. However, when faced with the threat of having a successor appointed, he could not stand such a horrifying thought and was forced to go back.

As winter approached, the room got so cold that he and any callers were obliged to keep their coats on, and as the attic was without light as well as heat, they had to talk in the dark if it grew late. By now, rain was leaking into the room from the failing roof above—the dilapidated central tower above his office had already needed to be removed in Christmas week the previous year.[17]

The next salvo from Robinson came in November in the form of a note to James informing him that his work with the Archives would terminate at the end of the year, as the funds would all be used up. James retaliated briskly by removing the whole collection back to his own home. Each day throughout the month of December saw him laboriously carting box after box of his precious material away to his overflowing basement once again—no doubt to Emily's secret dismay.

This latest show of independence provoked Robinson still further, and now the battle lines were drawn in earnest. Robinson's next move came in the form of an outright order—James was to hand over his material and return it to the Archives room, on the grounds that it was the property of the City.

Predictably, the Major exploded with fury. That any outside authority should have the gall to claim possession of his own personal collection, lovingly amassed over the course of 30 years, was the most outrageous affront he could imagine. Had he not rescued much of it from rotting in pools of water or from some damp vault or a waste pile that was about to be burned? Withholding his invective from all but Hosie, he assured the library board that the material was all in safekeeping in his care, but Robinson was on the warpath now and the dispute escalated into a personal vendetta. Using sledgehammer tactics for a rather ignoble purpose, Robinson began to threaten James through the City Solicitor, though he now reduced his demands to claim merely the new material acquired in the past year. James was not about to give in on any point at all and refused to surrender any part of his hard-won collection.

Robinson, who appears to have had an ego similar in size to James's, was convinced that all the board members were in agreement with him. He wrote arrogantly to Hosie (of all people): "Our board has decided to let the Major out, though we are fearful of the effect on him. He does not seem to realise that he is through. In order to rid ourselves of him we told him his grant was discontinued."[18] Robinson certainly misjudged his support in this quarter, for the disgusted Hosie promptly sent a copy of the letter on to James, with the comment that Robinson was "invading the provincial field with his archival purchases."[19] It was quite an intrigue, for Robinson was completely unaware that Hosie had already been in touch with one of the committee members, Robie L. Reid, telling him that his sympathies were entirely with James.

Very luckily for the Major—or he might have been in serious trouble—it turned out that City Solicitor Barney Williams was also secretly on his side. Unknown to Robinson, John Hosie and Barney Williams were exchanging letters and engaged in an active collaboration to bring some of James's supporters together to save his job. "Barney is all for you," Hosie assured James.[20] From January 1933 onward, Williams had been obliged to write letters to James, instructing him to return the material he had removed. But when Robinson demanded that Williams should draw up an affidavit "declaring certain goods stolen," it was too much for him to stomach. He delayed and delayed, in spite of instructions each month (in February, March and April) that he should get on with it, and he put it off so satisfactorily that by May, striking new developments were obviously about to make it redundant.[21]

James's supporters had been working hard behind the scenes to avert disaster, and there was about to be a happy outcome. It had been a very critical situation, and John Hosie recognized it as such. From January to May 1933 he had used all his influence and diplomatic skills to try to secure James's position. Much of his time had to be spent in calming the Major and cheering him with encouraging letters. "I must say I do admire, and friend Barney also admires, the way in which you are facing the situation," he wrote. "You have risen above your difficulties, perplexities and disappointments in a manner that is praiseworthy indeed." He ended his letter, "Cheerio Old Scout."[22] His letters of good cheer kept coming. James was so grateful for this flow of encouragement that he sent off one of his most touching and heartfelt letters of appreciation, which drew a beautiful response from Hosie: "I thank you from the bottom of my heart for the most unusual and finely worded epistle ... and the wonderful letter addressed to myself."[23]

All this time Hosie was contacting his inner circle of friends on James's behalf, and making full use of his high-ranking status as Provincial Archivist to intercede with members of the library board and officials in Victoria. One of the many people Hosie was in touch with was the previous mayor of Vancouver, William Malkin, and in the end it was Malkin who turned out to be the key to the solution.[24] A wealthy and extremely public-spirited individual, Malkin was involved in many aspects of Vancouver's civic life, including education and culture, and he appears to have supported the idea of a city archives department right from the start. Already in 1932, he and Hosie had devised a plan. Their aim would be to get results by diplomatic means, not confrontation, and to do this they would bring together a body of the most influential citizens they could find. It would be done in a civilized manner and in the informal setting of a luncheon party.

Malkin had held the first luncheon back in November of 1932. The atmosphere had been one of general goodwill, but the most practical suggestion to come out of it was that the Archives should have the use of the former Point Grey municipal hall in Kerrisdale. Then the Christmas season supervened. In early 1933 Malkin was away on a trip, but finally he held a second luncheon on May 2, 1933. This time it included three supportive aldermen and it had a definite agenda: "To discuss the Archives and find the best way of getting a resolution through." The need for an archives was almost taken for granted by now, and the outcome of the meeting was a general agreement that it was the duty of the city to preserve historic records and that the Major was the man to do it. Unspoken may have been the feeling that a man like James Matthews might not come their way again, and they would be culpable if they let the moment go by.

From then on there was no turning the tide of progressive thinking. Thanks to Hosie and Malkin, and backed by the approval of Mayor Louis Taylor, the city started to work out a plan for an archives department, and by the time the next council meeting came up on June 12, the subject of the Archives was more of a formality than a debate, especially as the finance committee had already approved a budget. James was told afterward that there was no opposition to his case or any kind of contentious debate. Moved by Alderman George Miller and seconded by James's friend William Twiss, the motion ran: "That the Library Board be advised that the Council has appointed Major Matthews as City Archivist and therefore the Library Board will be absolved from any responsibility in respect to Archives material. Carried."[25]

It was a great victory. At last the city had established an archives department, and at last James Matthews had the official title of City Archivist. He would no longer be thought of merely as a collector (as he had been in 1931), and no longer merely as the archivist in the library (as he had been in 1932), but would receive full recognition as the City Archivist.

The library board thankfully ordered its correspondence filed, and Robinson no doubt heaved a sigh of relief. The problem all along had been that Edgar Robinson and James Matthews were too much alike in temperament. Robinson is described by one biographer as touchy and hasty-tempered, and another comments on his autocratic style, which makes it easy to understand why clashes between the two men were inevitable. Ironically, they did also share the more admirable qualities of drive and enthusiasm for their work, and Robinson's tactics for promoting the library and pressing for more funding and a better building were exactly similar to those of the Major in the cause of the Archives. History held a real attraction for Robinson also—so much so that he was inclined to spend a disproportionate amount of money on archival acquisitions for the library. But, like James, he had to have complete control.

After the decision by Council, everything now fell easily into place. James was happy to see his friend Twiss appointed chair of the committee that was to deal with the Archives, and he was delighted when they were able to find space for the Archives department within the city hall building itself. The Archives, to James, represented the very essence of the city—"the soul of Vancouver," he would say—and he felt very strongly that it carried a great deal more meaning and prestige for them to be housed in the city hall rather than any shared premises elsewhere. His office was to be on the 10th floor of what was known as "the temporary city hall" in the Holden Building. His honorarium would be slender, only $25 a month, out of which he would have to pay any stenographer he hired. However, the generosity of the BC Electric Railway was some compensation, for they presented him with a pass for the streetcar that he rode daily, and they renewed this pass for him year after year. James entered his tenure of office in an atmosphere of great goodwill and public support.

Back in Victoria, Hosie was full of congratulations, immediately writing to Matthews to tell him how "greatly elated" he felt. His pleasure was on James's behalf, but he would have had every reason to feel gratified by the effect of his own intervention, for without it, the outcome might easily have been very different. Hosie had given him credibility. A protagonist of equal or greater rank than Robinson was needed to speak out for James and champion his cause, and John Hosie took it upon himself to be that person. As the Provincial Archivist, with high-level contacts in the cultural and political worlds, his words carried more weight than anyone else's could have done at that time, and when he went out of his way to lend his support, it gave James a standing that he could never have counted on otherwise. It was a great act of friendship, and it was an act that went beyond friendship too, for Hosie's words carried a genuine ring of concern for the future of Vancouver's history. They carried an implicit message to the conscience of Vancouverites that they must act now to save their history before it was too late, and that James Matthews was the right person to do it for them.

CHAPTER 9

Who Owns the Archives?

One of the less pleasing aspects of Major Matthews' personality was that he was an inveterate grumbler, and this trait did not take long to manifest itself in his new, official position.

He should have been profoundly thankful to find himself where he now was, for his success was beyond all logical expectations. To have pressured Council into setting up a new department in the threadbare days of the 1930s was an extraordinary achievement—all the more so, in that Vancouver was the only city in Canada to found its own archives at such an early date. All the other archival institutions in Canada at that point were national or provincial archives, not city archives. (One might speculate that if City Council had realized this at the time, they might not have been so accommodating.) Toronto's city archives opened to the public in 1965; Victoria's, 1967; Edmonton's, 1971; Calgary's, 1981; and Regina's, 1985. Vancouver was 30 to 50 years ahead of its time.

Very adequately installed in Room 1016 in the "temporary city hall" in the Holden Building, the Major now had far more space, more independence of action, and a suitable official status—in all, a vast improvement over his quarters in the library annex. At first he was full of enthusiasm, making plans for a reception and a formal opening at the end of his first month, and Malkin was obliged to calm him down, suggesting, "Get in the saddle properly and wait till September."[1] But already by August James began to sound the familiar litany of complaints. He was worried about money, not surprisingly, for he had overspent his allotment on wildly ambitious projects, had resorted to his own private funds to pay for what he wanted and had been forced to sell his stock in Imperial Oil at an unfavourable rate. Disenchantment quickly set in.

As usual, he turned to John Hosie for encouragement, and as usual Hosie was ready with words of sympathy, but he could do nothing more, for he was now a very sick man. He took a month's leave, but was no better for it—"as weak as a kitten"—and when he entered hospital in October for exploratory surgery, it revealed cancer of the stomach. He recovered so slowly from the operation that he couldn't return to his desk until the beginning of January 1934, but when he did so, he immediately took steps to offer James some practical help. Hosie agreed with James that the funding and set-up were insufficient for a city archives, and more pressure was needed. They came to the conclusion that the only way to make any impression on City Council might be to present them with recommendations issuing from some outside authority. It was obvious that Hosie himself, as the top professional in the province, was the logical person, and he was willing to do this for James, in spite of his own very tenuous state of health.

It was fortunate that Mayor Taylor was still in office and that James had some supporters on Council, for with an unsympathetic Council the request for a professional report might have been dismissed outright. As it was, they agreed that it would be helpful to have an outside assessment, and they commissioned and funded the report, paying for Hosie to stay three days in Vancouver while he looked at the situation.

This report was the last great act of kindness that John Hosie was able to perform for his friend. He didn't feel strong enough to make his survey of the Archives for James until mid-February, and even then he was feeling poorly when he visited James and Emily at their Kitsilano home. Fatigued by travel, he was obliged to leave Vancouver without seeing every contact he wanted to.

One can only imagine the sheer willpower and generosity of mind that enabled John Hosie to complete his survey at a time when he was entering the final stages of his illness. He worked on the report during March, assisted (and probably overwhelmed) by long verbose drafts

Interior of the Archives office in the temporary city hall on Hastings Street, with James's youthful assistant, Margaret Giles, at the desk. (CVA, City N20)

from the Major. Hosie reassured James, "I will prepare your report and make it gloomy re the present and glowing re the future."[2] In spite of his own worsening health, he continued to buoy up James's spirits, telling him how disturbed he was by the sound of his recent letters: "You are almost at the breaking point. The tension is too much ... Your financial situation is deplorable."[3]

The report came out at the end of March in the form of a small booklet, and by mid-May 150 copies had been sent out. It did not perform the miracles that James was hoping for, but unquestionably it lent a note of official authority to his complaints and made his demands sound more reasonable. At the very least, it started up a dialogue, since the Provincial Archivist's report carried weight and could hardly be ignored. No immediate result ensued, but John Hosie had set in train a new appreciation of the standard required of an archival institution.

Hosie's strength was failing fast. By May he was having fainting spells and could not travel, so James went over to visit him in the home that Hosie and his sister Marian shared in View Royal, near Esquimalt. By June he had to abandon his office at the Provincial Library and Archives, and in July was reported to be very ill. Emily Matthews, who had previously given him some helpful medical books, volunteered to come over and nurse him, but his sister thanked her for her kindness and said that she herself was looking after him. "He can't last a week now,"[4] she warned Emily. John Hosie died on August 8, 1934, five days after Marian's letter, at the age of 53.

His staff at the Archives was heartbroken. One of his assistants, Madge Wolfenden, spoke of him as "our beloved chief," and even a year later, another assistant was still telling James how much she missed her former head: "It isn't the same now." At the foot of her letter James noted, "Hosie's attraction, common to us all."[5] Obituaries in the newspaper dwelt on his sympathetic personality, his generosity of spirit and his love of nature and poetry, and quoted from some of the lyrical verse that he wrote at his wilderness cabin on the Cowichan River.

When a new Provincial Archivist in Victoria was appointed, James made a point of establishing contact, but the relationship could not possibly be the same as it had been with Hosie, and so he found himself without the friendly guidance of a fellow archivist who could instruct him in the basics of setting up a collection as well as listen to his problems. W. Kaye Lamb, who followed Hosie, was only in charge for six years and no strong relationship seems to have grown up between him and James. "Dr. Lamb has many good qualities, but he is not Mr. Hosie," noted James sadly.[6] Early on, Lamb established a firm note on the subject of money, but did relent so far as to send James $150 worth of supplies shortly afterward and allow him custody of some of Victoria's records relating to Vancouver.

In the case of Lamb's successor, Willard Ireland, the interaction between him and James was actually quite negative and fraught with tension. Ireland was by no means disposed to bear with the Major's lengthy epistles or rate his abilities very highly. No longer could James bombard the Provincial Archivist with letters every two or three days, as he had with Hosie (who had only had the time to answer about one in three), nor could the correspondence be conducted on the same familiar terms. "We must be patient, Major, old chap,"[7] Hosie would say, or, he would end affectionately: "Best regards to Mrs. Matthews and your good, kind, generous-hearted self." Unfortunately for James, Willard Ireland's spell as the province's archivist was of a length to rival his own—a period of 34 years, as compared with James's 37 years—so they were obliged to be civil to each other, but their correspondence was cool and distant, with a barely concealed note of impatience detectable at times on Ireland's part. On one occasion he told James quite openly that he entirely disagreed with some of the statements James had made and did not think they were true of the situation. The Major retorted: "No one will ever be able to accuse you of lack of candor or frankness. Others criticised, but not to my face."[8] He was to pronounce later: "Ireland has never been friendly to the City Archives, quite the opposite. Why I don't know. We have been more than generous to him."[9]

Bereft of his friend and confidant, John Hosie, James lapsed once again into a state of discouragement as winter set in. He began to be more and more conscious of the negatives in his situation and still persisted in looking at the gloomier side of things. Added to this, he fell ill with some serious but unspecified complaint that landed him in Shaughnessey Hospital for most of December and January.

Apart from his illness, however, he did not actually have too much to complain of. Contrary to the downtrodden impression that James liked to create, he was in reality quite fortunate to be backed by a council that included some positive supporters. Aldermen Twiss,

Bennett, McRae and Miller had a real appreciation of all that he was doing, and above all, James had the sympathy of the mayor himself. Louis Taylor told him years later: "I should have liked to have done more, but these Aldermen; they're only a lot of ignorami; they never read."[10] He no doubt did these gentlemen an injustice, but as the former publisher of the *Daily World*, Taylor believed he took a more enlightened view of life than some of his municipal colleagues. James was forever grateful to him for his support of the Archives at a critical moment, and rated this as unquestionably Taylor's greatest civic achievement. He once told Taylor's sons: "If he [Taylor] had done nothing else during his eleven years as chief magistrate … and had done merely one thing, i.e. establish the City Archives, or enable me to do it, it would have been of sufficient importance to justify his eleven years in office."[11] (James would have been indignant to discover that in a biography of L.D. Taylor published in 2004, the establishment of the Archives rates no mention whatsoever.)

Things were looking up at the office too by 1934, when a young woman named Elsie White came to work for him as a stenographer on a volunteer basis, as she wanted to gain office experience. (He did eventually start paying her out of his own pocket.) Her help in the office relieved him of much of the routine work and freed him to pursue more creative areas of endeavour. He was indeed working day and night on all his various projects—compiling albums of clippings, writing further volumes of Vancouver history, seeking out acquisitions, giving lectures and slide shows and penning vast numbers of letters. How he found the time to write these long screeds full of complaints about money and full of descriptions of his own labours at the Archives is hard to imagine, but in the course of his life he wrote literally hundreds of these letters.

Throughout 1934 and 1935 he carried on his campaign for better funding—a campaign that would drone on for the rest of his career—and he continued to pester the city comptroller and anyone else who would listen. It was not only money, but space he was running out of, and he clamoured for more receptacles and more storage room for his latest acquisitions. To his surprise, his endless complaints did pay off, for at the end of 1935 the City gave him the good news that it would double his salary to $50, and would give him another $50 to cover the expenses of supplies and stenographic services. It would even create some extra space for him by allowing him the use of an adjacent room in the Building Department.

This was a particularly surprising development in view of the fact that City Hall was now dominated by a new and very different mayor, the brash, flamboyant figure of Gerry McGeer—and McGeer made archives a very low priority on his list.

Gerald Grattan McGeer was a showman who liked objectives that had a high visibility, plenty of colourful display and an aura of prestige. The unspectacular work of the archivist, delving into past history, held little interest for him compared with his own objectives for the contemporary, living city. Overflowing with confidence and enthusiasm (just as James was himself), McGeer had colourful ideas for boosting Vancouver's morale during the grim days of the Depression.

He began by implementing lavish and costly preparations for Vancouver's Jubilee year of 1936 (it was the 50th anniversary of incorporation). The celebrations were launched on June 30 with a big fireworks display and bonfires along the river. The festival continued all through the summer with a brilliant series of events—a grand military spectacle, the opening of a rainbow-hued fountain at Lost Lagoon, a special Jubilee train and a First Nations presentation of regalia. There were outdoor concerts and shows of all kinds. The climax was the visit of the Lord Mayor of London, who presented Vancouver with a replica mace from the City of London. McGeer made a grand ceremony out of this event, ordering himself a cocked hat and an expensive new robe with trimmings of purple and gold, and devising an elaborate ritual for the presentation, which took place in the Crystal Ballroom of the Hotel Vancouver. It was followed by a procession through the streets of Vancouver. Apparently all this was just what was needed to cheer up the drabness of the Depression, for most people in Vancouver were exhilarated by these events—contrary to more conservative predictions—and were ready to celebrate and enjoy the holiday mood.

But all this was only the precursor to an even greater orgy of spending. The grand finale of the year was the opening of the monumental new city hall at 12th and Cambie. No expense had been spared in the finishes of this fine heritage-quality building. Ceilings of the main areas gleamed with a lustre of gold leaf; the walls and stairs shone with marble; the woodwork featured marquetry of beautiful workmanship; even the door handles were engraved with the City's coat of arms. It was an Art Deco masterpiece by McGeer's personally chosen architects, his friends Fred Townley and Robert Matheson.[12]

McGeer was criticized in some quarters for his reckless commitment to such huge expenditures, but in fact he managed to raise a large proportion of the funding by his own energetic efforts. Much of the cost of the Jubilee was borne by his wealthy friends back east, whom he pressured to contribute, and he raised money for the hall by arranging for Council to issue low-rate serial bonds, which were bought by some of Vancouver's well-to-do businessmen. Nevertheless, his detractors were many. Librarian Edgar Robinson was especially bitter, contrasting the new "gold-plated city hall" with his own cramped quarters at the aging Carnegie building.

WHEN THE NEW CITY HALL ON 12TH AVENUE WAS BUILT IN 1936, JAMES WAS GIVEN A FINE NEW OFFICE ON THE 9TH FLOOR WITH A SUPERB VIEW OF THE CITY. (COAST PUBLISHING CO. POSTCARD. AUTHOR'S COLLECTION)

Major Matthews was no friend of McGeer's either. At first James may well have been enthused by these new projects, for he always had a weakness for pageantry and ceremony, and he was full of suggestions for the Jubilee, even though he was not invited to be on the committee. Certainly he could not have failed to approve of the plan for a new city hall, for surely he must have been overjoyed at the prospect of the spacious new quarters he would occupy once the Archives moved into the prestigious new building.

But only a couple of weeks after the grand opening of the hall, Matthews' dignity received a crushing blow. Mayor McGeer, sounding off at a Council meeting on December 16, 1936, turned on James and his collection in language that drew glaring newspaper headlines the next day: "City's Archives Are Just 'A Lot of Junk'—Says Mayor."[13] The words that the mayor had so intemperately spoken were in classic McGeer style: "When you come to collect a lot of junk that will be worth nothing in five years, you are going to step into foolish expenditures of the people's money. We should condemn this departure in civic affairs." He continued in full spate: "It's a frill of accumulated wealth. If somebody wants to set up a fund for it, well and good. I understand Matthews was doing this work as a hobby, and now it has reached a point where he has been 'oozed in' on the payroll." To McGeer, archives were nothing but a dilettante dabble that should be relegated to a library or art gallery and privately funded.

This flare-up had arisen partly out of a report prepared for Council by a financial consultant, W.J. Barrett-Lennard, on the subject of civic administration. Barrett-Lennard, who was being paid handsomely himself for this report, had been shocked by the minimal pay Major Matthews was receiving, and had had the nerve to declare it "a public disgrace."

On the issue of money, it is understandable that many officials at City Hall should have been unsympathetic, since James had laid himself open to criticism for his unorthodox use of the funds at his disposal. Unarguably, he overspent, and, as many thought, he spent unwisely. He was certainly not the most prudent of money managers, and simply forgot the existence of a budget when something he badly wanted was involved. McGeer was no timid spender himself. He had committed the City to the costly projects of 1936 before ever establishing the financial backing to do so. But when James coolly presented a bill for Jubilee photos at double the agreed price, McGeer exploded and gave voice to the famous remark about "junk."

James's financial critics certainly had a point, for his priorities were distinctly unorthodox, not to say luxurious in scope. The Vancouver Archives he envisaged was intended to have a stately, Old-World atmosphere. Its rooms would be hung with paintings of historical events; its furnishings would be of oak, not common fir; the books and albums on its shelves would be handsomely bound in rich colours of blue and crimson and gold. He often decried the idea that an archivist lived in an ivory tower, removed from the everyday world, but his preferred taste in design certainly inclined to the grandiose. Consequently, he commissioned pictures, furniture and bindings that lived up to this concept, regardless of how he was going to pay for them.

To be commissioning paintings at all was beyond the scope of his mandate. During his first year in office, in an act of incredible recklessness, James had ordered six paintings of historical events from the noted painter John Innes, which had elicited from Hosie the horrified comment: "I admire your temerity. How will you get it paid for?"[14] Vaguely James hoped that patrons of the arts would contribute, and to some extent they did. His friend Louis Taylor and others made donations toward a painting of Vancouver's first council, "The Builders of Vancouver," and Imperial Oil later bought Innes's painting of Captain Vancouver's ships and presented it to the City in 1955. James continued to spend money on artists, picture framers, embossers, bookbinders and brass moulders.

Another criticism related to his selection of archival acquisitions, and here James was also on very shaky ground, for many of these were not archival at all, but came more into the category of "relics." His passion for antiquities was not limited to documents and photographs, and so he found it impossible to resist the allure of old, broken-down, discarded pioneer items, which certainly did not belong in the category of archives, and were really artifacts and better suited to a museum. This was where the complaints about "junk" came in.

JAMES STANDS BESIDE ONE OF JOHN INNES'S PAINTINGS, "THE BUILDERS OF VANCOUVER." JAMES GREATLY ADMIRED INNES'S WORK AND COMMISSIONED HISTORICAL PAINTINGS FROM HIM WITHOUT ANY IDEA HOW HE WOULD RAISE THE MONEY FOR THEM. (CVA, CITY N22.1)

City lawyer Donald McTaggart, wandering into James's office one day in 1942, was startled to find the floor littered with a miscellany of ancient objects, which he, like McGeer before him, could only describe as "junk."[15] A yoke for carrying pails, an old iron kettle, chains from a chain gang, a piece of steel rail from the BCER, some cannon shot and other bulky pieces formed a clutter in the limited space around the filing cabinets. A couple of glass cases housed a medley of smaller things—objects like gold jewellery melted in the Great Fire of Vancouver. James was thoroughly offended by McTaggart's suggestion that relics did not constitute archives, and came up with the rather weak argument that each one of them was directly connected to some document in his keeping. However, as McTaggart reasonably pointed out, "This would throw the door wide open to anything."[16] The truth was that to James each one of his relics was a precious piece of history that crystallized some bygone way of life, some unique event, some special personality, and by looking at it or touching it you could summon up the aura of those times. James's attachment to his relics was a powerful one, and not without a rational base, for archives and artifacts are inextricably linked. The separation of the two—usually in different buildings—is necessarily difficult and arbitrary.

At times the collector's frenzy overtook him if there was the risk of some choice object vanishing from the country, and he lost all sense of reason in his desperation to save it for Vancouver. The most notable example of this was the Annandale incident in 1936. Captain Thomas Annandale of New Westminster was the owner of a document that the Major greatly coveted. It was the certificate of the young George Vancouver's commission to the rank of lieutenant in the British Navy in 1779, and for James this was a very great treasure indeed. He had been aware of its existence for some time and had repeatedly urged Annandale to donate it to the Archives. Annandale was now willing to part with it, but far from donating it, he was expecting it to fetch a figure of $1,000, which he then upped to $1,500, and he was even in the process of looking for a competing offer from the government of Washington State. He left the document in the Major's care while City Council was considering his proposal, but when he came to the office reclaim it, to his utter outrage, James adamantly refused to hand it back.

A three-hour verbal battle ensued, in which Annandale was bested. He was obliged to leave without his property, with only James's promise that he would either receive a cheque or else have his document back by the following Thursday. Frantic at the thought of losing such a treasure, James instantly sent Annandale's parchment away to Victoria to the safekeeping of the Provincial Archivist (who may not have heard the whole story). As far as City Council was concerned, the matter ended when it received a valuation from Maggs Brothers Ltd. in London, England, informing them that without any autograph it was only worth £30 at the most.[17] Evidently Annandale got his document back safely, for next the Native Sons of BC, Post 2, weighed in to try to raise funds, and by March 1937 donations were starting to arrive. Annandale said he would give them only until April 10 to come up with the money, but there the story peters out—there is no more in the file.[18] As it turned out, Captain Annandale did not dispose of the famous parchment after all, for 20 years later (in May 1956) his son, K.F. Annandale, donated it to the City on behalf of his late father. "It was a moment of triumph for Maj. J.S. Matthews," reported the *Province* with great restraint.[19]

City Council could tolerate a certain amount of nonconformity—and Vancouver has always rather prided itself on the eccentrics it has fostered—but after watching James in action for a few years, City officials began to feel uneasy that the limits of his role were so vague and ill-defined. The City had a degree of authority over the management of the Archives, but how much? The City owned the Archives, or did it really do so? With his high-handed ways and autocratic behaviour, the Major seemed to regard the collection as his own personal property still. Officialdom decided it was time to regularize the existing lax and nebulous arrangement and draw up a legal agreement.

James himself, totally absorbed in his work, did not really mind about the vagueness of the situation. It would be a great deal of trouble to sort out who owned what—perhaps even impossible, he said—and what did it matter, in any case, who owned the Archives other than the people of Vancouver? This attitude of philanthropy did not prevent him from displaying the utmost degree of possessiveness over the collection, and the enormity of parting with it and handing over legal control to a group of ignorant officials was too much to contemplate, however much he wished it to be secured for posterity. This was his great dilemma throughout his career, and one that was never fully resolved until after his death.

From the City's point of view, however, the matter was permanently settled in the notorious agreement that they forced on him at the end of 1938. As a start, the City insisted on having an inventory taken, and then ordered James to bring in all the items that were still stored at his home. After much resistance and many excuses, he did so, chiefly because he would have forfeited a grant of $500 if he had not. Fifty cartons of photographs and numerous artworks, books and newspapers arrived by truck, crowding out the office and remaining unpacked for sheer lack of cabinets. "Little remains at home now,"[20] he told Council, not very truthfully. In fact, he had still not handed over his most valuable items, which would amount to about another ton of material when eventually surrendered some years later.

Now came the crucial question of the legal agreement. At this point James and Emily thought that they themselves ought to seize the initiative, and in mid-1937 they drafted an agreement of their own: "We request the corporation of Vancouver to accept, on behalf of the citizens, all that collection of historical records formerly in our home, now in the City Archives."[21] They valued it at $25,000. The reason for this apparent change of heart was the alarming suggestion of their executors (the Royal Trust Company) that should James and Emily die, the beneficiaries named in their wills would have the power to sell everything if they wished and invest the proceeds for themselves. But even to protect himself against this eventuality, James could not quite bring himself to go through with his proposal, and once again he put off the moment of decision. He refused to finalize the offer without learning what sort of administration the City proposed for the Archives, and as this had not been settled, he and Emily never sent a final version of their proposal. (However, James always maintained that the signed draft he originally sent to the City Clerk counted as a valid statement of intent.)

It was another 18 months before the contentious final agreement was signed on December 30, 1938. One of the subsidiary goals of the agreement was to set up a formal structure for the Archives and make it a requirement to have a group of seven trustees to administer its affairs. The names of the seven trustees met with James's entire approval and, in fact, most of them had been approached by him in the first place. There was only one woman—Aldyen Hamber, wife of the current lieutenant-governor. The others were Ramsay Armitage, Dean of Christ Church Cathedral; Royal Lethington Maitland, MLA; Alderman John Bennett; Walter J. Barrett-Lennard, financial consultant and good friend of James's; William Ditmars of the Pioneers Association and the Freemasons; and Arthur English, James's executor and manager of the Royal Trust. In this document, James and Emily sombrely agreed to "assign, transfer and set over unto the said trustees

James and Emily reluctantly sign the Archives ownership agreement with the City of Vancouver in December 1938. Standing, left, City Clerk Fred Howlett; right, Mayor George Miller. (CVA, Port P352.3)

all the right, title and interest"[22] of the collection in the city hall building and anything that might be added to it. No attempt was made to differentiate James's own personal collection from items collected subsequent to 1933, since it was thought that placing everything in trust would solve this problem. The trustees had authority to sell or dispose of any item, but only with the consent of the City and the Archivist (and one can imagine how difficult this would have been to extract).

As might have been foreseen, it was not a trouble-free signing. James wanted his own wording and objected to the official version—"too legal"[23]—and was persuaded to sign it only with great difficulty—"to save a desperate situation,"[24] he afterwards claimed. In the end it was Emily, the realist, who saw that they had no other choice. She put her finger on the real weakness of James' position, for she knew his worst fear: "'Jimmy, mark my words. If we do not sign, they will close it up.' Next morning she put on her fur coat, we went to City Hall and signed."[25]

It was an episode that rankled bitterly in his memory and preyed on him more and more as time went by. In his mind he more or less disowned the whole agreement, feeling that he had been forced to sign it against his better judgement and had no moral obligation to adhere to it very strictly. "A vicious document"[26] was his description of it. Predictably, this was by no means the end of the controversy and the plotting, and further battles lay ahead.

CHAPTER 10

The Major Takes Command

The new city hall on 12th Avenue had its official opening on December 4, 1936, and Major Matthews moved into his new accommodation there shortly afterward. Until the novelty of his princely new quarters in the new city hall had time to wear off, James allowed himself to enjoy an unusually contented frame of mind. After his limited quarters in the city hall in the Holden Building, he was genuinely delighted with the luxury of his new office space—the whole of the ninth floor to call his own, and with it a magnificent sweeping view of the city below and blue sea and mountains beyond. In one of his more buoyant moments, he wrote to W. Kaye Lamb: "I started with the dirtiest room in British Columbia in the tower of the old City Hall, unused for forty years ... Today I have the ninth floor and fourteen filing cabinets. I lecture, and I have given a radio address over western Canada."[1]

In his early years in the new hall, he had to deal with a constant stream of visitors ascending to the ninth floor just to admire the view and take photos. Once up there, they would stop in at the Archives out of curiosity and engage in conversation, wasting a great deal of James's time. When he complained about this, the elevator operators were instructed to use their discretion and admit only important visitors. However, as the numbers began to drop, this did not please him either, for fear that the Council would no longer regard the Archives as a necessary department, so he was obliged to withdraw his objections and make the best of it.

From 1937 to 1959, this was where the Archives were housed. It was his domain, his own kingdom, where his best years as an archivist were spent. In spite of the ownership dispute that lay uneasily in the background, his enthusiasm for the work itself remained as high as ever. His energy was phenomenal, and when he claimed that his working hours were from nine in the morning until late at night, every day of the week, it was probably not far from the truth. He had not had a holiday since 1929, he told people—and this state of affairs seems to have continued throughout his whole archival career; James's descendants cannot remember him taking a vacation, and in all his years of archival correspondence, there is never any mention of his absence from the office, except for two spells in the hospital. His work was simultaneously his pleasure and his passion.

Every year or two he was producing a new volume of *Early Vancouver*, though the issues subsequent to Volume 1 were issued only in typewritten form and in limited quantities—no more money was available to pay a printer. He continued to conduct interviews, collect stories, write articles for the newspapers and deliver countless lectures to local societies. He produced a compilation of the street names of Vancouver and their history; he drew up a map of Native villages around Vancouver, and another map depicting Vancouver at the time of the Great Fire. He created handsome albums of special events, and he put together thousands of what he called "dockets," which consisted of press clippings and cards, contained in brown envelopes and filed under subject headings (these are now on microfiche and in constant use today). "His zeal for research outruns the terms of his arrangement with the City," observed the City Comptroller in 1938, when denying Matthews yet another request for money.[2]

It was impossible now for him to devote time to his former military interests. His affection for his old regiment remained constant, even though he was critical of the way in which it had been reorganized after the war, but in 1929 he had resigned as president of the 102nd Battalion Veterans Association. In 1935 he withdrew from the BC Rifle Association also, though he remained custodian of their records, since these were now transferred to the City Archives. His last active service with the military had been in 1930, when he was secretary of the Officers' Mess of the BC Regiment and also quartermaster of a camp at Maple Bay on Vancouver Island, but he was not put on the retired list until September 1, 1937. He was then nearly 59 and had served for what his record describes as "34 yrs, 5 mos and 15 days of continuous service in one Vancouver regiment."[3]

In 1939 came the outbreak of the Second World War. Unbelievably, at the age of 61, James offered himself as a volunteer. Fired up with patriotic spirit, he proudly put on his uniform on the very day that Britain declared war, September 3, 1939, and went down to headquarters to enlist in any capacity he could. "But," he discovered, "they didn't want me." He volunteered a further two or three times during the year that followed, but each time the answer was the same. Emily Matthews was more successful in contributing to the war effort, for as a former nurse she was soon involved in volunteer sessions of rolling bandages and first-aid dressings.[4] James's twin sons, now 40, each volunteered for home defence duties, Lyn as a sergeant in the Army Service Corps and Merle as a member of the First Searchlight Regiment of the Royal Canadian Artillery. Neither went overseas.

Money troubles had continued to haunt him during the 1930s and early 1940s. His salary still stood at $50, and now he had used up all his sources of credit. He had borrowed from the bank and had exhausted his three life insurances. He hadn't paid the taxes on his home for several years and lived in constant fear of a tax sale. He was not even earning any money from his newspaper articles, since he thought this would be unethical in his position as Archivist. At last, in 1942, he had the welcome news that he would be receiving a cost-of-living bonus and a salary raise that would bring his monthly income up to $90, and although prudence was not his major virtue, he made it a priority to direct some of this windfall toward the outstanding taxes on his home.[5]

With his money problems temporarily shelved, James had little reason to be dissatisfied with progress as the 1940s wore on. By 1943 he had a staff of two, and an increased budget for archival expenditure. Throughout the war years, the governance of the Archives had proceeded uneventfully. The 1938 agreement had called for trustees to be appointed, and most of them James depended on as good friends whom he found highly supportive, though limited in their ability to extract more money for the Archives. Emily Matthews had joined the

James in his office in the city hall on 12th Avenue, 1941. (B.W. Leeson photo. CVA, Port P567)

governing body in 1943, as well as James's good friend Captain Twiss, both as "co-optative" members. Another good friend, W.A. McAdam, the agent general in London, was brought in as an honorary member. The collective body (known as the Senate) numbered as many as 22, and was supposed to meet quarterly.

But in 1947 the situation changed, and City Council came out with a second legal document for James and Emily to sign, the purpose of which was to reformulate the objectionable agreement of 1938, for Council was now insisting that the governing body of the Archives should be incorporated. They described this as "finalising the structure of the Archives Department at long last."[6]

Incorporation meant that a new agreement had to be drawn up, and once again James was busy drafting his own version of what it should be. He consulted closely with a sympathetic lawyer, Major Reginald Tupper (grandson of Sir Charles Tupper), who was the trustees' honorary legal advisor. Tupper worked extremely hard to draw up an agreement that would be satisfactory to all parties, but it proved to be an impossible task to satisfy James. Council approved Tupper's recommendations, and on March 6, 1948, the body of trustees was incorporated as the Vancouver Archives Society. Now all that had to be done was for the former trustees to sign a document handing over their authority, but this was where James Matthews drew the line. As in 1938, he and Emily refused to sign.

He invented a whole series of objections. He objected to the inclusion of one of the trustees, John Bennett, who he said had "betrayed him" by signing. He alleged that the document had been altered. He was also upset on Emily's behalf, letting them know that she was "indignant at the discourtesies shown her."[7] The real truth was, of course, that at the last minute, he found the act of signing over the collection again too terrible to face. He announced that the whole project of incorporation should be cancelled, but that—in what he considered a gracious gesture—he himself would "continue, mournfully, as archivist."

At this, the once-patient Reginald Tupper lost his composure. Like many others before him, he made up his mind he would have no more to do with this impossible man. Almost by return mail, he fired off an angry letter resigning his position and accusing James of having wasted everybody's time and effort.[8] Other trustees, more diplomatically inclined (such as Barrett-Lennard), hastily rallied round to persuade James and Emily to think better of their refusal, if only for the sake of Vancouver and the general good. This was a powerful argument that carried more weight than almost any other. With a heavy heart James withdrew his objections and reluctantly signed, along with the ever-loyal Emily. (Tupper soon relented after this episode, and by June was once again receiving James's continual flow of correspondence and complaints in the normal way.)

The only positive note that was struck at this distressing time issued from Chief Justice W.B. Farris's address to the Supreme Court on May 18, 1948, when the incorporation process was ratified. Farris made it an opportunity for giving public recognition to James and Emily and was unstinting in his praise: "Vancouver, British Columbia and Canada owe a great debt to Major Matthews and his wife for their splendid work ... They have worked tirelessly and ceaselessly in spite of the tremendous difficulties and odds they have had to surmount [and] have succeeded in establishing an archives which ranks with any in Canada."[9] James was present in Supreme Court chambers when these words were spoken, though his deafness prevented him from hearing them, and they had to be relayed to him afterward by friends. As always, he was profoundly touched and gratified by words of appreciation, and seemed to find in them some kind of consolation.

The postwar years brought a death that severed early connections in James's life and emotional ties with the past—it was the death of his first wife, Maud. On February 4, 1947, she had died of a stroke in Vancouver General Hospital at the age of 69. She was not, of course, buried in the Matthews family plot in Mountain View Cemetery, but in Ocean View Burial Park. She left all her possessions and any money she had to her son Merle to share with his brother, and her wishes were carried out amicably. Michael Barry survived her for four years, dying suddenly at the age of 92 on August 9, 1951.

James also lost another link with the past in the person of his old friend Charles Merle Rolston, who passed away at the age of 74 in the same month as Maud.

But in 1948 came a far more terrible event. During the late fall of 1947, Emily had experienced some disturbing physical symptoms, and as a nurse she could not fail to recognize them for what they were—the early stages of breast cancer. Her condition deteriorated rapidly, and by February it had got to the point that she was relying on James to look after the greater part of the household chores. During all the stressful negotiations over the Archives agreement she must have been a very sick woman, summoning up her last reserves of energy to see James through that crisis. By June she was so weak that her widowed sister, Mabel Willis, came to stay with them to nurse Emily and run the household. At some point Emily was operated on, but the cancer was spreading, and she died in Shaughnessy Hospital on November 2, 1948. She had just turned 73.

The blow to James was appalling—"the blackest day of my life," he wrote. He had used similar words when Hughie had died, 26 years earlier. His letters to friends in the years to come would make constant reference to his dependence on Emily and her love: "That heroine, my dear wife, Mrs. Matthews ... My dear wife, my aid, my counsellor and support ... Her influence is ever present night and day."[10] Many times over, he would repeat that it was only her constant affection and encouragement that had enabled him to persist in the face of criticism and indifference. Without Emily, he always maintained, the Archives of Vancouver would never have existed. This statement hardly does justice to his own tenacity, but there is no doubt that her belief in him eased his life, encouraged him and freed him to pursue his goals. Emily loved him, and understood him too. Eighteen days before her death, she gathered up her strength to write a four-line will, leaving everything to her husband, and in a few loving words telling him what he had meant to her: "My dearest Jimmie, This is a small donation towards all your kindness to me. Don't fret for me, dear. We have had many happy days together. All my love, darling. Emily Eliza Matthews."[11]

Emily's funeral took place in Christ Church Cathedral on November 4, 1948. James never ceased to miss her, and for the rest of his life he was constantly alluding to her and idealizing her in his letters to his closest friends, as if he drew a little comfort from writing her name and recalling old memories. He wore her wedding ring on his little finger as long as he lived.

After her death he was racked by guilt that she had given up so much in order that all their disposable income—and more—should be lavished on their joint mission for Vancouver's history. He thought of the dresses she might have had, the pleasure trips they might have made, and his conscience troubled him. They had not had holidays together since 1929, nor had they spent money on some of the little amenities of life. "How she endured those dreary years of adversity is hard to comprehend," he told Emily's friend Ruth Woodward years later.[12]

Determined to do everything he could to make up for all that she had sacrificed, he spent his money on a series of artistic tributes to his dead wife. (Ironically, his salary had improved a year or two after her death.) His first action was to have a stained glass window placed in Christ Church Cathedral in memory of Emily as a nurse.

It is called the "Nurse Window," and it depicts the figure of a nurse kneeling before Christ, who is placing a golden crown on her head. James designed it himself and inserted the Matthews family coat of arms in the lower corner. Ruth Woodward unveiled the window on June 25, 1950, and told James, "Dear Matty will be there too; smiling at us. I am sure she will be very close. She loved Christ Church, and loved her nursing. A very great woman."[13]

Next he commissioned a bronze bust of Emily, contacting the finest sculptor he knew of, Sydney March, even though his studio was in England. March was one of a talented family of artists—seven brothers and a sister, who ran the studio jointly and were accomplished painters as well as sculptors. (They were best known in Canada for having designed the Canadian War Memorial in Ottawa.) Sydney March's bust of Emily, completed in 1952, remained always in James's office, comfortingly close to him, right up to the time of his death.

The Nurse Window and the bust had both represented Emily in the idealized role of nurse. But now James wanted something more, an image of Emily the woman. He commissioned March to create yet another likeness of Emily, but this time it was to be an oil painting and it was to show her looking gorgeous in evening dress. The painting was based on photographs from the late 1930s and it resulted in a portrait which reveals a different Emily—a poised and handsome woman, stylishly dressed in a low-cut black gown, with a sparkling necklace and drop earrings, and a gauzy black wrap. A muted crimson background sets off the dark dress, on which are pinned her three colourful war medals. James evidently admired her looks, just as he had his own mother's. The portrait gave him some degree of consolation and he wrote to his friend R. Rowe Holland: "I have done what little I can to compensate after her death for what I failed to do in her lifetime."[14]

There was one more memorial of a different kind that he created in the 1950s, and it was for Hughie as much as for Emily. When Emily willed James all her money, he did nothing with it for five years while he cast about in his mind for a use that would be truly worthy of her. Then, in early 1953, a real estate advertisement caught his eye: it was for a scenic waterfront property on Bowen Island, and it was almost at

EMILY, LOOKING DISTINGUISHED IN EVENING DRESS. (GEORGE T. WADDS PHOTO. CVA, PORT P949.1)

the very spot near Cowan Point where Hugh and he had started off on their desperate journey across the island to seek aid for the stranded boat party. Instantly he knew he had to have this land, and within a month it was his. At that moment he had no idea what he was going to do with it, but soon an idea came to him: this 20 acres on the bluff would make a most beautiful wilderness park where boaters could come ashore and picnic and enjoy the forest trails, and because of its associations it would be the perfect memorial to his lost son Hugh. He had the cove officially named Apodaca Cove, to commemorate the name "Isla de Apodaca," which the Spanish explorer José Maria Narvaez had given to Bowen Island in 1791. When the land was accepted for a park in 1954, it took the name of Apodaca Provincial Park, which it still goes by today.[15] It is now considered an ecological reserve.

No one could replace Emily, but James was not without family and friends who cared about him. At home he was well looked after, for Emily's sister Mabel stayed on after Emily's death to keep house for him. Besides this, he was often in touch with the grandchildren, as his personal papers reveal. He was good to them and their families, and they enjoyed his company and his exciting war stories. The youngest grandchild, Evelyn, felt close to her grandfather and has fond memories of James taking her to the Hotel Vancouver as a special treat to have a fancy tea in an elegant setting. His oldest grandchild, Hazel Valentia, sometimes helped him with office work.

James was always fortunate with his office staff. His assistants were all female (except for one ill-fated experiment, described in chapter 11), and all of them seem to have been devoted to him, for in his relations with women he shed his defensiveness and allowed himself to relax his militant approach. They stayed with him for years, and he grew to depend on them heavily. When his first regular stenographer, Margaret Giles, started at the Archives in 1934, she was still in her teens and he regarded her benevolently as "just a little schoolgirl," but she turned out to have a natural aptitude for the work. She stayed with him for over a decade until she married. (Eager to give her a generous wedding present, James impulsively went down to Birks, bought a gold purse, and crammed it full of $5 and $10 bills.) He relied just as heavily on her successor, Mrs. Jean Gibbs (a former teacher), who, like Miss Giles, understood the foibles of her difficult chief and looked on his eccentricities with a tolerant eye. "She chides her boss into keeping his medical appointments and lays out his noon meal of sandwiches, cake and tea," observed journalist Wilton Hyde.[16] True, no doubt—but she was also a knowledgeable and competent deputy archivist who remained with him from 1951 to 1965, assuming full responsibility whenever he was absent from the office.

Many of his supporters within the Vancouver community had become dear friends as the years went by. Captain William Twiss, one of the aldermen who had pushed hard for an archives department was one of these; Walter Barrett-Lennard was another. Both had been pallbearers at Emily's funeral. Reginald Tupper remained well disposed in spite of his earlier annoyance, and another trustee, barrister R. Rowe Holland, had also become a good friend. He told James once: "I wish I had the happy faculty that is yours of saying just exactly what is in my heart."[17] The trustees in general respected and liked their outspoken archivist, for James's passionate sincerity was hard to resist, and as sorely as he tried their patience at times, they made allowances for his moods to a greater degree than he may have realized.

Unfortunately, he could not help making life difficult for himself by taking offence so quickly at the slightest hint of criticism or dissent, when no insult was actually intended. Friends warned him about this. Royal Maitland once told him: "That's a good letter, but I wouldn't mail it."[18] The City's lawyer, Donald McTaggart, pointed out that James's aggressive tactics were not exactly calculated to endear him to City Council and achieve results; he could not insult people and then immediately ask for money—he should use diplomacy. Barrett-Lennard too urged James in a tactful letter to soften his approach and tone down his need for argument. James was greatly moved by what he termed a "superb epistle," but still seemed to believe that everybody was against him: "You advise me, my dear good friend, to lower my guard. My advice to you is to RAISE YOUR GUARD ... When the foe is the puppet, the false witness, the business degenerate, and the charlatan, their cold clammy palm is not for my hand, and to such the guard will not be lowered."[19]

It has to be acknowledged that the Major did positively relish a good fight and derived an immense amount of satisfaction from routing his adversaries. Not that James would have admitted this, even to himself. He once made the laughable statement: "I don't like rows."[20] And again: "They [the rows] don't achieve anything." But practice was different from theory, and he appeared to thrive on controversy. It is obvious that he thoroughly enjoyed one of his altercations with McTaggart: "I arose from my seat and leaning across my desk, pointing my finger very close to Mr. McTaggart's features, said, as I snapped my fingers together: 'I don't care two raps about the Council firing me ... I don't care what the Council thinks.' Mr. McTaggart made a hurried departure."[21]

Reporters too came in for scathing comments, usually being accused of inaccuracy or superficiality. As for any journalist who ventured to present the goings-on at the City Archives in a less than favourable light, he would be speedily pulverized with a verbal blast from the Major. Even in his dealings with the general public he could be difficult and contradictory. He managed to offend many visitors with his gruff manner and impatient tone, and was apt to display an extremely suspicious attitude, even toward serious academic researchers.

His feelings were to some extent understandable. Certainly he had plenty of his time wasted by casual visitors who merely wanted to tour the building, or by senior citizens who thought they would while away an afternoon reminiscing about the past; and at times the frustration of all this became too much for him. On at least one occasion he said that he had to lock the Archives door "to fend off tourists who want a guide."[22]

He found himself in a lot of trouble, however, when he was accused of physically pushing an elderly man out of the Archives. It happened on a day when James was having to devote all his time to three different parties studying in the reading room, and so he had shut the door to deter any other visitors. But this new caller, a Mr. Grimmett from a pioneer family, had knocked insistently at the door, and when the stenographer answered it, he had attempted to push his way past her. James hurried over and gave the door a mighty heave, "ejecting the old gentleman with such force that, had it not been for a supporting cane, he would have fallen in the hallway"—or so the newspapers claimed. The Major was unrepentant."I didn't know him from a bale of hay,"[23] he grunted afterward. (Ten years later, on July 15, 1959, he insisted on making a sworn declaration that this incident had never happened, but it is noticeable that his memory had convenient lapses at times.[24])

Another time he abruptly turned away some important visitors who were being shown round by a sergeant-at-arms, James's only reason being that it was one of the periods when he had arbitrarily limited the opening hours to two a day. An outraged Mayor Cornett felt so strongly about this insulting behaviour that James narrowly missed having the Archives shut down for good. Incidents like these soon became enshrined in the number of quotable stories that grew up around the Major's combustible personality.

Difficult personality or not, James Matthews had won an enormous amount of popular acclaim by the beginning of the 1950s. Twenty years in office, with a huge body of work to show for it, had given him considerable standing with the public at large, who were inclined to make allowances for his fiery outbursts and even derive some entertainment from them. His forthright style came as a refreshing change from the smooth utterances of officialdom. He was now regarded as one of Vancouver's notable eccentrics, to be admired for the cause he represented, and certainly not to be trifled with. The irritation that he caused each city council in turn began to subside into a sort of amused resignation, tempered by a respect for the Major's formidable personality.

Life became far easier for James in the new decade, and this had much to do with the arrival of a new mayor, the genial millionaire Fred Hume, who was elected at the end of 1951 and managed the changing postwar city for the greater part of the confident 1950s. Hume and the Major obviously got on well together—James said he was on the phone to Hume almost every day, and one has the impression that Hume rather enjoyed his contact with a personality as robust as his own. Hume liked to spend money, and he was shocked to discover the low rate of pay for the Archivist and the minimal funding of the Archives itself. It was surely no coincidence that in early 1952, just after Hume's arrival, James saw an immediate raise—to his amazement everything was doubled, both his own salary and his allowance for the Archives. It was a sudden jump from a total of $6,000 to $12,000. "And the odd thing was that I did not apply for anything at all,"[25] he exclaimed in wonder.

It was during Hume's period of office that James received the first in a series of awards that brightened the 1950s for him. The moment was certainly right for some public acknowledgement of his achievements. His crusade to make Vancouverites aware of their history had resonated with success, and many people felt that it was time he was offered some form of recognition. He was, after all, in his 70s now, and any award was long overdue. The Kitsilano Ratepayers Association carried out a determined campaign on James's behalf, and on November 16, 1953, City Council voted to award James their top honour, the Freedom of the City of Vancouver.

It was an honour he would be sharing with very distinguished predecessors—Prime Minister Mackenzie King, the Lord Mayor of London, and lieutenant-governors W.C. Woodward and Eric Hamber among them. James was awarded his gilded scroll the following year. Normally the ceremony was held in council chambers, but at

James's special request the venue was changed so that the award could be presented at the annual Pioneers Dinner, held in the pavilion in Stanley Park. This was an event very dear to his heart and it meant more to James to receive this honour in the company of old friends than in a more impersonal ceremony.

As the 1950s went on, further recognition came his way. James had been involved with the Native Sons of BC, Post No. 2, for 20 years or more, but it was only in 1957 that they grudgingly decided at last to award him their annual Good Citizen medal. It was an award that was shamefully overdue, for his name had been put forward regularly from as far back as 1939. Each year he had been denied the medal. In 1949, one supporter put his finger on the problem: "He has, I suspect, antagonised a few influential Native Sons, as he has dozens of others. So what? A handful of disaffected ones should not outweigh many many thousands. Must Major Matthews await posthumous distinction?"[26] Nevertheless, even after this frankly worded plea, Matthews had to wait another eight years, by which time he was going on 79, and it could easily have been a posthumous award. However, all acrimony was forgotten on June 18, 1957, when a friendly crowd filled the BC Building at the PNE grounds for the Native Sons' annual Appreciation Day. Old friends gathered to congratulate James—even his old war comrade, Sergeant Taylor, who had saved his life on the Somme. "It was one of those occasions ineffaceable from memory," James recorded with deep feeling.

The honours of the '50s were rounded off in 1959 by one other presentation, the Kitsilano Citizen of the Year Award. "We thought it was time his own district recognized him,"[27] said a spokesman for the Kitsilano Ratepayers. It was a beautiful July evening on one of the hottest days of the summer when they made the presentation at the Kitsilano Showboat Festival at English Bay. Thousands of people packed the beaches, fireworks lit up the sky, and James beamed with pleasure as MLA Mrs. Buda Brown presented him with his award, the Don Brown trophy cup. It was another occasion to remember.

CHAPTER 11

Banishment to the Library

The year 1957, when Matthews received his Citizen of the Year award in a blaze of glory—almost literally, as fireworks tinselled the waters of English Bay—may well have represented the peak of his career. The enormously productive years of the past quarter-century were behind him. He had just brought out the latest volume of his *Early Vancouver* series (Volume 7) and he had to acknowledge, "It was a long weary task. I shall never do another, it is too exacting work."[1] The day-to-day work of running the department was devolving more and more on Jean Gibbs and a part-time stenographer. "My two lady assistants do most of the archival work. I am increasingly administrative," he told another correspondent in 1956. "I have reached a point where I don't care as keenly as formerly I did. I do the best I can and let it go at that."[2]

James was approaching 80 when he wrote those words, and the problem of selecting a successor had been increasingly on his mind since the beginning of the 1950s. He felt extremely ambivalent on this question. On one hand he knew that a successor was necessary; on the other hand he showed no inclination to actually retire. He appeared to find it difficult to visualize the Archives without himself at the helm, and he openly declared that it was his intention to carry on as long as health and strength permitted. In effect, his unstated plan seems to have been that he himself should select and train the person of his choice, but at the same time hold a position of complete authority for as long as it suited him. Although he welcomed the prospect of having shorter days at the office once he had an assistant, he by no means considered that this should involve giving up his position as Archivist.

Back in the late 1940s, when he had just turned 70, there had been some talk at City Hall of putting him on a pension and finding a replacement, but James had swept aside the suggestion of retirement in horror, grandly stating that this "would be depriving Vancouver of the best informed man on this particular task."[3] At that stage he was not looking for a deputy archivist at all; what he wanted was more office help, not a rival. In any case, the question was academic, as the City had no money for extra positions.

Even when it came to clerical help he was extremely choosy, turning down one applicant because he had lived in British Columbia for only three years—you had to have been in the province for at least 30 years to have enough background, he maintained. Another applicant was a female graduate from Britain with excellent training in archival and library work, but she too was excluded on the grounds that she had no local knowledge. (The reason was more likely that he felt threatened by her degree status; he always maintained that graduate training was not necessary, but even a disadvantage, and that a practical, down-to-earth mentality was more useful in the job.)

By 1955 James began to realize he must take the problem seriously and he started to cast around for suitable candidates. Predictably, he was so exacting in his standards that it was impossible for anyone to measure up to the criteria he set. "I am looking for a successor but can't find one,"[4] he lamented. As the months went by, he became slightly less rigid, and approached a succession of people whom he thought might possess the qualities he thought essential—energy and passion for the work.

The first possibility whose name appears in James's correspondence was W.T. Ward, who was at that time the editor of *Wildlife Review*. One wonders what personal qualities Ward possessed that suggested him as a future archivist, since his specialty was clearly not in the realm of history. At James's urging, Ward visited the Archives and was given the full tour and every courtesy, but he felt no more than an appreciative interest, and was wise enough to recognize that any spirit of detachment would be fatal to the work. He wrote back to James: "I do not feel I could do justice to the archives; one must love the subject passionately. I thank you and Mrs. Gibbs for showing me glimpses of these treasures."[5]

The question assumed an added urgency during the winter of 1955 to 1956, when James was hospitalized for a couple of months with a serious illness requiring an operation. "It frightened me," he admitted. "My age 78. My assistant—a lady—58." Thoughts of mortality began to weigh on him more heavily, yet still he could find no one he considered equal to the high calling of Vancouver's custodian, and even if he were to, would the City offer a good enough, competitive salary? "I had a man in mind," he told Victor Odlum, "but he was getting $400, and we have not got $400."[6]

For several months in the summer of 1956 he was in touch with a man named Lloyd J. Hills, who had applied for the position, but when he asked Hills to take some photographs for him, it turned out that Hills' equipment was not up to it (and perhaps neither were his skills), so this possibility too petered out. In October James rejected an otherwise well-qualified applicant from Britain on the grounds that he would be completely lacking in local knowledge: "His whole value might be in his knowledge of how to arrange records, but nought else."[7]

James was beginning to lose hope of ever finding the successor of his choice, and more especially because he maintained it would take him a full five years to train this person. He sighed despairingly, "What we want is some man akin to Mr. Rose, our Secretary of Trade, or Mr. McAdam, Agent-General; a live wire with a sense of duty and propriety."[8]

Then suddenly in early 1957, an inspired thought came to his mind. It occurred to him that all this time, within his own circle of acquaintance, there existed the ideal person for the job, someone he already knew through his literary contacts, someone who was fired by a sense of excitement about history—the writer Bruce Ramsey. Ramsey appeared to satisfy all James's idiosyncratic requirements. Born in the West Kootenays, he was a native son of British Columbia; he did not have the academic background Matthews objected to, but was an ex-newspaperman; he was engaged in historical research (for a book on BC place names); and he displayed an enterprising spirit.

Immediately James began to train the full force of his persuasive powers on a doubtless surprised Ramsey, who was actually quite content with his current job as librarian for the *Vancouver Province*. James's initial suggestion was that the *Province* should "lend" Ramsey to him just for a limited period to help him catch up on a backlog of work, but it may have been more of an invitation to see how much aptitude Ramsey had for archival work and how the two men would get along together. Ramsey was indecisive. As he pointed out to James, he was "extremely happy" where he was, he would soon be up to $100 a week, and he also had to think about his pension. Moreover, he had serious doubts about taking on a role that would have to be regarded as "a lifetime commitment." Hedging his bets, however, he did not rule out the idea and still said he would like to be considered for the position.[9]

From May to July there were other applicants, including the writer and historian Reginald H. Roy, who applied for the job but then had second thoughts and withdrew.[10] Roy eventually had an academic career and became a professor of history at the University of Victoria. As for Ramsey, he went on to produce a series of books on British Columbian history, and was no doubt much happier in a creative role than in the disciplined life of the archivist.

But all these job interviews turned out to be irrelevant, for City Council began to register some unease at James's display of initiative on the question of hiring. They announced that they themselves would place an advertisement for the position. Although Mayor Hume agreed that they should "appoint an understudy as soon as possible,"[11] it was clear that he intended the City to make the choice.

Regardless of Council's new ploy, the irrepressible Major still carried on with his search for a successor. By September he had found a candidate and was confident enough to announce the name of this person. Two weeks later, Council acknowledged defeat once again and ratified the Major's choice. Curiously, after years of search, he had found his potential successor close to home—within the walls of the city hall itself—in the person of one of their long-time employees, the current Registrar of Voters, a man of 38 named Ronald D'Altroy.

Both James and D'Altroy were extremely hopeful for the success of the arrangement. James pronounced his new assistant to have "the necessary ability, energy, courage and spirit,"[12] while D'Altroy, who had applied directly to the Major for the job, agreed bravely: "I'm willing to gamble on success."[13] It was indeed a courageous statement, coming from one who had been in a position to observe Major Matthews in action at city hall over the previous 14 years.

It was, of course, a partnership that was fated not to succeed, though it staggered on for a period of two difficult years. Ronald D'Altroy is said by those who knew him to have been a diplomatic and patient man, and he needed both these qualities in his association with the Major, who was notably lacking in either. The Archives correspondence files give no hint of a troubled relationship, but problems were slowly building up. Possibly James was unaware of the effect his angry moods might have on a less armoured personality than his own, or the frustration of working for a superior who was so incapable of listening to another viewpoint. It turned out later that there had indeed been several "blow-ups," as D'Altroy described them to the press, but that he and his chief "always came together again."[14] James appears to have been in the habit of firing D'Altroy from time to time without seriously meaning what he said. But when Matthews uttered this threat in August 1959, it was for the last time, declared D'Altroy—he was quitting. He could take these eruptions no longer, and this was the final breakup. It was commonly believed that James really had fired D'Altroy, though he vehemently denied having dismissed him at all and preferred to give the impression that it was the City that had done so. "To add to the confusion," noted the *Sun* on September 11, "the Major put in a last word to D'Altroy: 'It's a terrible thing they're doing to you, my boy.'"

In actual fact, D'Altroy was not dismissed from the service of the City at all. Even though he and James could never work together again, he was too valuable an employee for the City to lose, especially without cause, as City Hall saw it. Inured to the Major's ways over long years of argument, City officials were hardly surprised by the way things had turned out and, far from dismissing D'Altroy, they merely transferred him to another department, the Northwest History Room in the main branch of the Vancouver Public Library. Public sympathy was all on D'Altroy's side, which James resented deeply. In a private note to himself, he scribbled: "I wonder if the truth should not be told. Why permit a recalcitrant clerk to be regarded by the public as an ill-treated hero?"[15]

Ronald D'Altroy took the situation philosophically, announcing blandly that he "had no quarrel with the Major," and went on to enjoy a distinguished career in the library until his retirement in 1980. It was D'Altroy who founded the library's massive collection of historical photographs (still regularly consulted by historians and writers and other researchers today), and who put a great deal of energy unto unearthing new collections. The Major's passion for history must have communicated itself to D'Altroy during their time together, fortuitously adding a new dimension to his life.

After James's plan for training a successor unravelled, there was no talk of repeating the experiment. James's immediate reaction after his run-in with D'Altroy was to issue a press announcement saying that he had decided to give Jean Gibbs the title of Assistant Archivist. As an afterthought, he made a formal application to Mayor Tom Alsbury to sanction this. Alsbury was not going to let the Major get away with such high-handed behaviour, as the more tolerant Hume might have done, but flatly contradicted James's announcement and informed reporters that Major Matthews had no authority to appoint staff. Ignoring this, James proceeded to add Jean Gibbs's name to his official stationery as Assistant Archivist. It was a position she must have been well qualified to fill, for she was in effect already carrying out most of the responsibilities attached to it, and she enjoyed James's complete trust. Council let the matter slide—it was no doubt easier that way. Whatever alternative Alsbury might have considered, the upshot was that Mrs. Gibbs was still functioning as James's Assistant Archivist until her retirement in 1965 and continued to be described as such on the stationery.

The angry explosion that had ended his relationship with D'Altroy was probably induced by the extreme stress James was undergoing at that particular time, a stress that had nothing to do with D'Altroy at all. It was the culmination of two years of tension, resentment, anger and extreme lowness of spirits, for he had just been overtaken by a terrible calamity—he and his Archives had been forced to relinquish their very desirable quarters in the city hall building and move into the new Vancouver Public Library building on Burrard Street. The move had taken place on August 8, 1959, and the row with D'Altroy had occurred just a month later.

The threat of being moved out of city hall into the library had been hanging over James's head throughout the 1950s, for already the large new city hall was running out of space and needed to expand several of its departments. Contrary to James's fears, City councillors, who had no wish to be regarded as a crude bunch of philistines, made no draconian suggestion of closing down the Archives—they merely wanted it out of the way in another building and thought of the modern new library building as a perfectly suitable solution.

James was horrified at the very thought of sharing accommodation with the library again. "Goodbye to the City Archives if ever they do," he fulminated. "They are opposed to each other; one or the other must predominate, in which case the other disappears."[16] Besides this, Edgar Robinson was still the head librarian, and James's memories of their feud in the early 1930s remained fresh in his mind.

It was not only the prospect of having to work in a building dominated by Robinson that so appalled him, but he also had the belief that it would be extremely demeaning to the reputation of the Archives. In his mind, the care of an archives represented a sacred trust, and the building that was its repository should be invested with dignity and prestige. "It is shattering to any confidence in us," he protested to the City comptroller. "The City Archives is a sanctuary … The suggestion that we shall be identified with a PUBLIC LENDING Library cannot fail to be disturbing to those who entrusted treasures to our care and may prevent others from depositing theirs."[17]

At first he completely refused to consider the move at all. "Move Me, Just Try It, Says Major,"[18] ran one headline. "Once more unto the breach goes the bristling major,"[19] proclaimed another. For two years he successfully resisted Council's wishes, dragging his feet as long as possible, but for once he was forced to admit defeat. Even General

Victor Odlum's spirited, last-minute plea to Council on February 10, 1959, had no influence on the outcome.

Victor Odlum had been one of James's commanding officers in the Battle of the Somme, and as old war comrades they shared special memories and a mutual respect. For a time after the war James had been critical of Odlum, holding him partly responsible for breaking up the DCOR into other units, but when they renewed their acquaintance in the early 1950s, James forgot his resentment. He said that Odlum had "relaxed his former stiffness,"[20] and James grew to depend on him touchingly as a friend and confidant, just as he had with John Hosie.

Odlum now did his best to relieve James's gloom, writing wonderful, warm letters to "my dear old friend and colleague," and encouraging him to take the long view and look forward to a better prospect ahead: "I am glad you are cooperating—we need goodwill for our future plans. I think the sun is about to shine and brightness is on the horizon." And again: "We cannot allow you to give way to exhaustion. You are on the verge of a splendid triumph and you must carry through."[21] The kindly influence of Victor Odlum was an important factor in easing the negotiations through and buoying up James's spirits in this intensely depressing period.

Since he had reacted so violently to the idea of space in the library, Council offered him the alternative of the upper floor of the Bicycle Registry Building at Broadway and Yukon—a suggestion he repudiated with scorn as unworthy of a city's archives. The library therefore it had to be. James had to agree that the new library being fireproof was a point in its favour—probably the only point—but nothing could really reconcile him to the loss of his privileged situation within the city hall. This was the building that symbolized Vancouver itself and the heart of city governance, and the Archives was a fundamental part of this entity. Its records were more than just mouldering scraps of paper; they were precious fragments of history that represented the identity of Vancouver and were inseparable from City Hall itself. His uppermost feeling remained that the Archives had been sadly diminished in stature by the enforced move.

Another source of great dismay was the realization that he would have to downsize the holdings of the Archives in order to accommodate it to the space available in the library. This could only be done by parting with some of the "relics." Some may have been given or loaned to the Vancouver Museum, but he preferred to stash many items away in his home or a private vault. Mayor Alsbury assured him that he would have 3,000 square feet of space, and that the city would provide him with architectural advice on the layout and his requirements. Nevertheless, it was a sad day for him when he walked into his new premises for his first day at work there on Saturday, August 8, 1959: "I called at the new place today, picked up the mail, and left. It was a very painful experience, and my attitude frigid."[22]

As it turned out, he never did have to contend with Edgar Robinson after all, for his old adversary had died unexpectedly two years earlier. Robinson had never enjoyed one moment of time as head of the modern new library he had fought for so hard: only a week before it had opened in 1957, he had collapsed with a heart attack and died in hospital shortly after. He had never lived to benefit from the result of his 30-year campaign for a new building. Ironically, a similar fate was to befall James Matthews.

James's spirits remained low for some time to come. "I was once full of hope," he wrote despondently, "but today that hope has gone; much of the once proud City Archives … has disintegrated, and much of the most valuable records are no longer within its walls. It looks as though it is no use trying any more. Evil has been too strong to overcome. I keep on mechanically, because, daily, some useful service to someone is open to us to perform."[23] He was still troubled by his belief that the Archives had lost prestige as a result of being separated from the city hall. So demeaning did he consider it to use the library's address for his correspondence that he continued to use the City Hall heading on his stationery, and successfully insisted that all his mail should be sent over daily to the library from there.

He never lost his sense of profound injury over the move to the library. There now seemed to him only one way out of the situation and this was to work toward having a separate archives building, designed expressly for the city's records. It was a remarkable ambition at that time. No other city in Canada then had a building specially designed for such a use. Some of Canada's provincial capitals had erected buildings for their provincial archives, but none had yet put up a building for its city archives. Nevertheless, James regarded this as his only hope of getting independence from the library.

He had first begun to dream of this back in 1952, immediately after his first big increase in funding. Barely had he registered surprise and satisfaction with his improved grant than he was exclaiming: "What I am after now is a separate building."[24] It was hardly a serious goal at that point, as he well knew. He would sometimes joke with the architect Fred Townley, "When are you going to build me a new archives and museum building?"[25] but it was not a suggestion that was ever considered in earnest until James forced the issue with his persistent refusal to move into the library. He had racked his brains to think of some way out of the hateful prospect of the library building, and in sheer desperation had told Victor Odlum that he was willing to make an extraordinary offer to the City—he himself would donate $25,000 of real estate for the erection of an archives building. His proposal would cover only the construction of a concrete shell, he said, but he expected the City to pay for the interior finishes, spending the equivalent of what they would be spending on his proposed quarters in the library. His offer, however, was contingent on one very doubtful condition—that the City should buy his collection for a figure of $75,000.

Nothing more seems to have been heard of this quixotic idea, but the idea of a new building took a firm hold of Matthews' imagination. At one point James told the Archives Society that he would show them his plans for a $1 million building. He also seems to have contacted architect J.Y. McCarter and was enthusiastically recommending possible building sites. Interestingly, both sites were close to where the Archives stands today. One was at the south end of Burrard Bridge opposite the Seaforth Armoury, and the other was in Hadden Park beside the Maritime Museum, which had just been built the previous year. Another possibility was one of the concrete RCAF buildings in Vanier Park, and this remained under discussion for several years, but although the building committee of the Archives Society thought it suitable in every way, Council could not be induced to act on it.

At this point things suddenly took an unbelievable turn for the better: a very wealthy sponsor entered the scene. P.A. Woodward, of the iconic Woodward family of Vancouver, was about to take an interest in the Major's cause.

Percival Archibald Woodward was one of the two sons who had taken over the management of Woodward's department stores after the death of their father, Charles (the original founder). Percival, usually known as "Puggy," had dissociated himself from the company in 1954 and was devoting his time in retirement to giving away large quantities of his fortune to deserving causes. To administer this project he had formed the Woodward Foundation in 1951, changing the name in 1953 to record his wife Marion's involvement and calling it the Mr. and Mrs. P.A. Woodward's Foundation. He and Marion are particularly remembered for their magnificent gifts to the University of British Columbia in the form of the Health Sciences Centre and the Woodward Library, but they also provided the funds for many other philanthropic projects. Education was a cause very much in the forefront of Woodward's thinking, and this was perhaps what influenced him to turn his attention to the need for an archives building.

He first met with James some time around June of 1960. The initiative seems to have come from Woodward rather than James (though the Major was not shy about approaching prominent people), and it must have come as one of the most stunning moments in his life when Woodward announced his desire to fund a new building for the city archives. There is no evidence to show that the two men had met previously, though James had been acquainted with Percival's late brother, W.C. ("Billy") Woodward, who had been an honorary governor of the Archives in the 1940s and whose wife Ruth had been on very friendly terms with Emily. P.A. Woodward's interest in an archives building was more likely due to all the newspaper publicity that the Major had generated. At the same time, Woodward could hardly have failed to be impressed by the high opinion held of James by people like General Odlum and other well-known citizens. But Woodward was a cautious businessman, and however strongly he believed in a need for an archives building, he was not about to plunge into such a project without exploring every angle.

"Mum's the word,"[26] he told James at this first meeting. He made it very plain that he was not to have his name brought into it until their plans were rock solid, but he outlined his broad intentions. He was offering the Major a building worth a quarter of a million dollars and the services of one of the top architectural firms in town—McCarter, Nairne. It was James Matthews' dream come true.

During the early summer of 1960, no obvious action was being taken, but James was evidently in close touch with the Woodwards throughout this time, for by July his letters to both Percival and Marion had taken on a warm and intimate tone. He was clearly feeling confident enough of their friendship for his writing to assume the self-revelatory style he so easily adopted with those whom he trusted. Percival may have taken alarm slightly at this, for he warned James once again not to mention his name till their plans matured. (Discretion was not James's strong point, and eventually he could not resist a word or two to trusted contacts such as Howard Green.)

At last, in August, something definite was brewing. John McCarter called to see James, bringing with him his associate, William Leithead, who, along with Ronald Nairne, was now heading the firm of McCarter, Nairne. The two men had excellent news for James. Since P.A. Woodward was determined on nothing less than a high-quality, well-designed building, Leithead was to visit Britain early in 1961 and make a study of archives buildings, old and new, and report on them on his return. James's hopes soared once more. He sent Woodward his own plan of what the archives should be, and at Christmas he enthusiastically sent Leithead a card designed by his good friend Gerry Andrews (BC's beloved surveyor-general), which pictured the kind of building he would like to have.

Leithead made his tour and issued his report, dated March 20, 1961. As one might have guessed, with the international style of architecture coming into full swing and historic buildings in Vancouver falling regularly to the bulldozer, his choice strongly favoured a modern style of design. "It is the author's conviction that the building should be contemporary in design ... No attempt should be made to achieve a design which is monumental in appearance ... Exterior ornamentation should be kept to a minimum, relying more on quality of material rather than extraneous ornamentation." In an apparent contradiction, he did, however, suggest that sculpture or murals would be a highly desirable addition at some later date. One unusual item on his list—at Woodward's special wish—was a chapel in memory of veterans, a feature never incorporated into the present archives building.[27]

In view of his love of the traditional, James might have been expected to balk at the idea of such a plain and functional building, but on the contrary he seems to have been delighted with the concept. He announced to Leithead: "You are the best man to be my successor. Build your building, and then take charge of it. Then give me a rest; after thirty years I'm tired, but I can help for many years yet. You are the best qualified man in BC."[28] But carried away in this mood of exuberance, James was beginning to take too much for granted and was about to make the error of overreaching himself yet again.

Only two weeks after Leithead's report, the press got hold of the news and the *Province* quickly made it known. Before long P.A. Woodward's anonymity was breached, and his name appeared in April as the mysterious benefactor who was about to fund the building. Along with Woodward's name came his revelation to the press that the site he had in mind was on the UBC campus on the Point Grey peninsula.

James was appalled. Because he himself had always been attracted by the Kitsilano area, it had been his understanding all along that this was the general area that Percival Woodward also favoured as a site for the Archives. He had never considered the likelihood that a sponsor of Woodward's standing would have his own vision for the building and its site. In Woodward's mind an archives building on the UBC campus would link up perfectly with the Woodward Library that already stood there, but to James the Archives was a resource that tied in so closely with the life of the city that it ought to be available to the public in a much more central location. At UBC, he complained, it would be "five miles out in the country—a mere adjunct to an institution already overflowing."[29] He feared too that a university site would invest the Archives with an academic tone too far removed from the affairs of everyday life. Although he thought of the Archives as a place of dignity and prestige, he did not view it as an academic, ivory-tower type of institution, but as a "people place" that represented the heartbeat of the city, and he knew that as the City's archivist, he would certainly never have felt comfortable in a university atmosphere.

All too hastily, James set down his thoughts on paper. In a letter to trustee George Buscombe, he poured out his angry reactions in a way that might have been cathartic for him, but betrayed a devastatingly rigid frame of mind. Regardless of the fact that he was hardly in a position to dictate to his would-be benefactor, he was utterly uncompromising in repudiating Woodward's choice of site. No diplomatic language here. It was "a colossal mistake," he insisted, "and one which I shall oppose with all my might." Rashly, he concluded his letter: "I request you to be so good as to intimate the nature of my opinion to Mr. Woodward."[30]

A month later, James was wondering what had happened to the project. There had been a strange silence, he complained, and no one would tell him anything. Seemingly he still had not absorbed the damage he had done to himself, nor had it occurred to him that in his single-minded enthusiasm for his own particular vision, he might have inflicted a death blow to it. He had not regarded his letter as an ungracious response, but merely the frank expression of what he thought to be the best interests of the Archives. But there had already been too many sensational headlines about the Major, and as a successful administrator himself, Woodward may have begun to entertain misgivings about James and his relationships with others. On the other hand, the chief stumbling block may well have been the fiscal caution of the City itself. According to a later statement by Leithead, City Council killed the project by deciding that they could not afford the operating costs involved in maintaining a separate archives institution.[31]

Three years later, James was still in a state of denial over his part in the affair. He opted to put the blame on the City. "A millionaire offered a quarter of a million to build an archives building, but someone at City Hall offended him and he withdrew it"[32] was the way James chose to remember it by 1964, and by this time he was too heavily involved in promoting other ventures to dwell on it unduly. The only tangible consequence of the Woodward–Matthews–Leithead episode was that it was Bill Leithead who did ultimately design the archives building a decade later.

JAMES WOULD HAVE LIKED A GRANDIOSE ARCHIVES BUILDING, AND HE THOUGHT THAT THIS 1936 DESIGN BY SHARP AND THOMPSON FOR A PROPOSED STADIUM COULD BE VERY SUITABLY ADAPTED FOR THE PURPOSE OF AN ARCHIVES. (CVA, PHO P134, N198)

Briefly, in 1963, James seems to have contemplated the possibility of asking the firm of Sharp and Thompson to adapt one of their designs for use as an archives building. It was a 1936 drawing for an auditorium, stadium and drill hall, to be built on the former Squamish Reserve at the south end of Burrard Bridge. It was an imposing edifice with pediments, portico and cornice in a simplified Art Deco version of the classical manner, and would have appealed to James's concept of a dignified repository for historic records, but again it was an idea that came to nothing.

As the 1960s unfolded, James was left without the prospect of a building to call his own, yet still the despotic ruler of his own domain on the third floor of the library. He continued to ignore the wishes of City officials and evade their orders as far as he possibly could, dispensing with much of the paperwork and making up the rules as he went along. "We do not bother very much about rules and regulations and minutes of the last meeting … Mrs. Gibbs and I do what we like [with the grant] and set our own salaries. All I can say about the 'set-up' is that it works."[33]

He felt entitled to adopt this attitude, because—like many another leader—he believed himself to be divinely inspired. "Sometimes I think the hand of The Lord is on my shoulder,"[34] he confided to a friend in a moment of deep emotion. It was his conviction that he had been led by a divine hand to a particular mission in life, and he said as much to Victor Odlum: "I thank God for the good fortune which has been mine, and offer thanks to Him who directed it. It makes me wonder why, from among the host, the Great Architect chose me for this especial task."[35]

CHAPTER 12

Activist or Troublemaker?

More battles lay ahead for James during the 1960s, all of them revolving around the same questions: how much of the archival collection was his own personal property, and how much authority did he legally have over it?

Because of misgivings on both these points, in 1957 the City had made one last attempt to increase its control of the Archives and had had a third legal agreement drawn up for him to sign. The problem was that the trustee system had not been working as effectively as expected, for James was dominating the meetings and had gradually assumed a position of control in which his decisions were going almost unquestioned. Sometimes the board did not meet for months or even years—possibly because they had faith in his management (for he commanded great loyalty among them), but possibly because they felt they were merely rubber-stamping actions that the Major had already taken. James said they were "squabbling among themselves." Mrs. Hamber did not attend the meetings, because she felt uncomfortable about being the only woman on the board.

The City was determined to assert its rights and exert complete control over its unruly Archives, and the way they planned to do it was to bypass the existing management system of trustees and assume sole legal authority. The matter went to the Supreme Court and the City's petition was granted. On September 17, 1957, Justice Norman Whittaker ruled that the City of Vancouver was appointed sole trustee of the Archives, under the trust agreement of December 30, 1938 (an agreement considered invalid by James).[1] The new ruling also involved a change of name for the Archives—and a kind of demotion. Until now it had enjoyed a special status as the City Archives, but in future it was to be merely another department, termed the Archives Department of the City of Vancouver, and its affairs would be handled by a special committee of council.

All this did not mean that the Archives Society of volunteers and patrons would have to disband—which was fortunate, as it was still needed for nominal support and a basis of goodwill. In practice, James carried on much as before, though nursing an even stronger state of grievance toward the City and a distrust of their intentions.

Whatever the troubles of his professional life, James Matthews was at very few periods in his life devoid of the comfort and reassurance of a stable, well-run home. With the exception of the two years following Maud's departure, he was always able to depend on some kindly, sympathetic presence to see to his well-being. His 20-year marriage to Maud had given him a home life which had been completely agreeable to him, if not to her. Even in the difficult two years after the break-up, he had had Hughie to listen to his troubles and help him to keep up the home. Then had come Emily, who became the embodiment of the perfect wife and counsellor, just as Mary Matthews had represented the perfect mother.

Since Emily's death, her widowed sister Mabel had been looking after the home for him. This was an arrangement very satisfactory to them both. Mabel told everybody she regarded 1158 Arbutus as her home now, and James declared that "no one could make me more comfortable or well fed."[2] James loved his home and surroundings, the clear, translucent views of sea and mountains, and the fire-streaked sunsets across the water. He and Mabel kept up an old-time flower garden copious with roses, lilacs, bluebells, dahlias and hydrangeas, and here and there some ornamental bird baths set in the shade of the laburnums and laurel. James had installed an iron flagpole in the garden and took pride in flying the Union Jack on Sundays and holidays.

Before Emily died, she had made James promise to look after her sister, and he kept his word. He advised Mabel financially and bought her an annuity. Twice a year he took her for a trip to the Empress Hotel, Victoria's finest. When she had a lengthy illness between July

Above: This house at 1158 Arbutus Street was James's home for nearly 50 years. (CVA, Add. MSS 54, 508-D-1, file 5, #10)
Left: Bessie Bolton and James raise the flag at 1158 Arbutus Street in honour of James's 88th birthday. He flew the Union Jack on Sundays and holidays. (CVA, Mon P138)

1962 and March 1963, he brought in a nurse for her, and afterward gave her what care he could himself, fetching her hot water bottles and cups of hot milk at night. She was still feeling rundown and depressed when in 1964 she took such offence at one of James's sharp remarks that she immediately packed her bags and left. They had a reconciliation, but she did not return, and a year later, on March 22, 1965, she died of cancer in Vancouver General Hospital at the age of 77.

Now he was on his own again, so he engaged a housekeeper, a Mrs. Tucker. This arrangement did not last long. Mrs. Tucker had little patience with James's difficult temperament, told him roundly that he was "a crabby old man" and left. Next came a Scottish lady, Mrs. Bessie Bolton, and now once more he was fortunate in his home life, for Mrs. Bolton looked after his domestic affairs in a way that was completely to his liking, and she had no trouble in getting along with her plain-spoken employer. A visiting friend wrote: "It was a great joy to me to see your comfort in such capable and kind hands," and commented on the pretty flower arrangement Mrs. Bolton had created for the occasion.[3] James, in fact, felt so grateful to his housekeeper for her care and friendship that he made generous provision for her in his will, increasing his bequest as the years went by.

It is evident that James found it a great deal easier to achieve compatibility with women than with men. His misunderstandings with anyone of the female sex were rare; his aggressive behaviour was almost always directed toward men. Even in the case of his break with Maud, it was she who had initiated it, yet he who wanted her back. His unquestioning love of his mother had instilled in him an image of womanhood as the sweetly guiding complement of man, and the effect of this conditioning was to predispose him to be sympathetic to and uncritical of the female sex. His views were very traditional. He did not approve of flirtatious women, and was said to have been rather shocked by any hint of sexy behaviour. An old-fashioned courtesy toward "the fair sex" was more his style and attitude. One who remembers him from his days in the library describes him as gallant, even courtly, in his manner, tipping his hat politely to the ladies at the desk as he entered each morning. Even though he *had* made Mrs. Gibbs his official assistant, it would never have occurred to him to consider the possibility of a woman succeeding him as the head of the Archives.

His female assistants in the Archives stayed with him for years, tactfully accommodating themselves to his ways, managing his moods and generally looking after him. Certainly he respected them for their judgement and efficiency, as he frequently noted, and he depended on their professional ability, but he also appreciated their feminine touch, entertaining his visitors and bringing him his tea and cake every afternoon. Even the female staff of the Provincial Archives in Victoria in the 1930s seemed to regard him with great affection, and would answer his letters in a most sympathetic vein, as if to a friend.

His most self-revealing letters are, with few exceptions, the ones written to the women he regarded as personal friends. Ruth Woodward, who always sent him a Christmas card, was the recipient of long intimate screeds in which he would freely expose his continued sense of loss since Emily's death. Rosalynde Latimer, who knew him for nearly 40 years, wrote in 1971 that she felt privileged to have been his friend: "I use the word 'privilege' to convey the rapport and mutual respect which characterised our friendship over the years … The Major was one of the few personalities to be able to strike the fire of enthusiasm in others."[4] And although James may have conducted a running battle with many male journalists, a female reporter named Edith Murray made a habit of sending him an effusive valentine card each year with inscriptions such as "To the nicest man in Vancouver, my good and indispensable friend, who is never too busy to bother with a perpetual nuisance."[5]

Children liked him too. He would sometimes take parties of schoolchildren on bus trips around Stanley Park, telling them in his own lively style about the forest and the Native people and the early explorers. If a school party visited the Archives, candy would be handed out all round, or if a child came in to study for a homework assignment, then tea and cookies would be hospitably dispensed. Mrs. Gibbs told a reporter that the children all loved his exciting stories, and there was always fun and laughter. He was a great entertainer.

Although James had a soft, sentimental side to his character, it would be a mistake to assume that this quality became more marked as he moved into his 80s. He did not lapse into a stereotypical, benevolent old age, but became even more opinionated and fiery than ever, though "fiery" was a word he repudiated when it was used of him by the affable columnist Himie Koshevoy. "You hurt my feelings,"[6] he told Koshevoy; nevertheless "fiery" remained his public image. Victor Odlum gently remonstrated with him. "Your friends know that you are a very kindly person, and that you do many gentle things,"[7] he assured James in 1961, urging him to put quarrels behind him, as he had found best in his own life.

His advice was in vain, for James's altercations with City Council not only continued to rumble away in the background, but in the mid-1960s developed into outright war. The essential problem lay in Matthews' conviction that he himself was the supreme authority and guardian of Vancouver's history—a position far beyond the status of city officials who only came and went—and that this being so, his priorities had precedence over the policies of the latest newcomers on Council. As always, Matthews was superbly confident that he was right. And so, when his views clashed with Council's, it was not so much a case of his opposing them as of simply disregarding them as if they did not exist.

This was the situation with two of James's dearest projects: the statues of Canada's Governor General, Lord Stanley, and Captain Henry Larsen of the schooner *St. Roch.* James was a historian who placed enormous importance on the recognition of great events in a tangible form—scrolls, plaques, cairns, paintings, statues and monuments. History interpreted through art had always appealed greatly to the romantic in him. He believed too that a great city deserved the dignity of great monuments—and Vancouver was somewhat lacking in major works. There were ornate drinking fountains; there were bas-reliefs; there was sculptural decoration on buildings; but with few exceptions, little free-standing sculptural work adorned the city in the 1950s.

The familiar statue of Lord Stanley near the entrance to Stanley Park, extending his arms in joyous greeting, would never have been thought of, let alone built, had it not been for the daring imagination of James Matthews. The idea of the statue came to Matthews in 1952, when he first viewed a copy of one of Vancouver's most historic documents—the illuminated scroll that Mayor Oppenheimer had presented to Lord Stanley when Stanley Park was dedicated in 1889.[8] The City had promised to put up an artistic stone cairn, but it had not been there in time for the dedication ceremony. Eventually they had kept their word and built a cairn in the park, but over the years it had disappeared, probably lost in the long grass and unknowingly knocked down during road work. The revelation of this piece of history immediately inspired James with the idea of making good the City's promise and putting up a worthy memorial—not an insignificant cairn, but a large impressive statue. It would be the figure of Lord Stanley himself, created by the most prestigious sculptor James knew: Sydney March.

James immediately sprang into action and commissioned the statue with a blithe indifference to the problem of raising the money—an intimidating sum of $4,500. He did not look for a sponsor; in fact, he spurned the idea of some wealthy citizen "buying into" the project, but insisted that the money must come from the average citizen in small donations of perhaps $1 each. "It's the common people who use it [i.e., the park], and it is those people I want to share in the job of erecting the statue."[9] He had hoped for 5,000 donors, but four years later had acquired only 220 backers. However, their donations were sufficient to pay the costs up to that point, and he was lucky in raising further large donations to cover the rest.

The big advantage (and perhaps ulterior motive) of doing it by private donation was that it gave James complete control of the design process. Ignoring demands for a public competition, he dealt directly with Sydney March himself, setting out his requirements, explaining his own concept of the work and the pose of the figure, and authorizing March to carry it out. James paid $200 for a bronze model of the statue, which he proudly exhibited to the parks board as a fait accompli. Parks board members, no doubt too much taken aback to protest, could do nothing but murmur unconvincing words of approval.

It was only when the completed statue arrived in April 1956 that the real problems began. It seemed as if James could do nothing without creating controversy, but this time his protests were fully justified, for he had discovered that the parks board were not planning to display his statue in a position of high visibility. On the contrary, they intended to relegate this fine work of art to some obscure woodland corner of the park where few people would ever see it. Feeling as he did, that the statue of Stanley, with arms outstretched in welcome, embodied the whole spirit and intention of the park—a place for "the use and enjoyment of all colours, creeds and customs," Lord Stanley had said—James was adamant that it must stand prominently near the entrance and catch the eye of every visitor. Besides this, he actively disliked the plain style of the granite base the parks board intended to mount it on.

THE LORD STANLEY STATUE, COMMISSIONED BY JAMES FROM SYDNEY MARCH, OVERLOOKS THE ENTRANCE TO THE PARK AND WELCOMES ALL VISITORS. (D. SLEIGH)

Unable to convince the parks board, James resorted to desperate measures: he decided to hide the statue. He spirited it away into a downtown Vancouver warehouse, its whereabouts unknown to Council or anyone else, and announced that he was prepared to leave it there for years if need be. He was as good as his word. It remained hidden for several years while the arguments went on, but, as usual, the Major ended up by getting his own way. When the statue emerged in 1959, it was placed on an expensive architect-designed pedestal costing over twice as much as the parks board had originally budgeted, and it was erected close to the Georgia Street entrance to Stanley Park, where no eye could fail to see it. Then, at the last minute, one more problem arose. The Major learned to his disgust that no unveiling ceremony was planned. At this he threw another tantrum, with the satisfactory result that the unveiling took place with great ceremony on May 29, 1960, and Governor General Georges Vanier himself stood on the platform to do the honours.

The satisfaction of this personal triumph encouraged James to carry on a campaign for another statue. This time it was to commemorate one of the outstanding figures of Canadian seafaring history, Captain Henry Larsen, of Northwest Passage fame. In his RCMP patrol boat, the *St. Roch*, Larsen had forced a passage through the massive ice floes of the Northwest Passage in 1940–1941, not just once, but twice—first from west to east, then from east to west. Larsen was the first man to conquer the Northwest Passage since Roald Amundsen in 1906, and the first ever to accomplish this feat from west to east. He also circumnavigated North America in 1950 by sailing from Vancouver to Halifax via the Panama Canal—a full circuit that was another first in maritime records. Today, sadly, his name is no longer universally recognized by the public at large, but in the 1950s and 1960s Henry Larsen enjoyed huge acclaim for his record-breaking voyages.

All this was exactly the sort of historic adventure to set James's imagination racing. He contacted Larsen soon after the voyage to offer congratulations, and the Matthews and Larsen families exchanged Christmas cards from at least 1947 onward. When Larsen returned to the west coast on periodic visits and they met in person, he was deeply touched by James's support and came to regard him as his greatest friend in Vancouver.

Matthews' first thought in the early 1950s was to get the *St. Roch* brought back to Vancouver. The idea of the statue came later. The ship had been retired from Arctic patrol duties since 1947 and was sitting idle in Halifax, in danger of demolition. James and others campaigned hard to have the *St. Roch* brought back to Vancouver, and under the leadership of Fred Hume, City Council voted to put out the money and buy the *St. Roch* from the RCMP for display in Vancouver. (Hume felt so strongly about this that he told James he would have been willing to put out the money himself.) In 1954 the rather worn-out vessel limped back to Vancouver harbour, where Larsen was greeted with what he described as "a royal reception." James himself delivered an address at a ceremony in Council Chambers, declaiming,

"The name of the *St. Roch* and Superintendent Larsen will reign in history with those of Columbus, Captain Cook, Captain Vancouver and Amundsen."[10]

It was obvious that the *St. Roch* would require a great deal of restoration, and at first James concerned himself purely with this. On the day following the *St. Roch*'s grand arrival, he and Mabel Willis opened their own personal *St. Roch* Preservation Fund, of which he was the sole trustee. Shortly afterwards, Mayor Hume set up a special charitable fund, registered in December 1954 as "The *St. Roch* Preservation Society, the Mayor's Fund, under the patronage of City Council," and James became a trustee of this also. It was soon after this that he had the idea of the Captain Larsen statue.

His first act was to open yet another trust fund, which he called the Larsen Statue Fund, and now people were confused as to which fund they should donate their money to. However, a few contributions started to come in, and once again, James asked the sculptor Sydney March to produce a design and create a small-scale version of it for his approval. This arrived in August of 1957. March had done full justice to the inspirational nature of Larsen's achievement, and had executed a lively study of the dauntless explorer, posed in his heavy Arctic furs. It was no mere clay maquette, but a well-finished figure in bronze, which was a work of art in itself. The final statue was intended to be a large-scale figure, eight and a half feet high, but to pay for this James would have some serious fundraising to do, for he needed the same sort of sum as he had for Lord Stanley's—about $4,500. Having only $1,500 in his fund, even James, with all his financial insouciance, hesitated to place the order, in spite of one of the aldermen's urging him to "get that statue ordered."[11] The Major's formidable energy was flagging at last as he approached his 90th year, but this was not the only reason for his hesitation. By now he was so disgusted with what he called the "*St. Roch* debacle" that he sadly admitted, "I almost dislike pronouncing the word '*St. Roch.*' "[12]

The reason for such despondency was the shockingly long delay in starting the preservation project, in spite of the many trust funds that had been set up in the first flush of enthusiasm. With the 1958 centennial coming up, the City chose to channel all available funding into the more visible project of building a maritime museum at Hadden Park, but while the planning went on, the *St. Roch* continued to lie rotting in the water at the Gore Street wharf. James grew more and more dismayed, so much so that when they finally did haul the schooner into dry dock beside the new museum in 1958, he refused to attend the ceremony.

Another eight years went by before the City finally protected the ship from the weather by building an A-frame shelter—a Van Norman design that James did not like at all; nor did Larsen, who saw the plans before his death in 1964. The ship rested in the shelter, still more or less untouched, for six more years before the Maritime Museum gained federal funding for an intensive restoration in 1971.

James was still maintaining a trust fund for the Larsen statue when in 1968 Sydney March suddenly passed away. He was the last remaining brother in that talented family of sculptors, and his artist sister then closed down the studio, thus precluding any chance of creating the full-sized version of the Larsen statue. At 90 years old, James was beyond the effort of looking for another sculptor, and so his Larsen statue project never did come to fruition. A copy of James's statuette is sometimes on display at the Maritime Museum, but the main focus has turned to a new, large statue of Captain Larsen, which was unveiled there in June 2006. Designed by Canadian sculptor Simon Morris, the figure of Larsen stands on the deck of the *St. Roch*, looking out to sea, as in life.

One would like to think that James would have been gratified that his ambition for a Larsen statue had been realized at last, but it is doubtful. He had already disapproved of the site for the Maritime Museum, and after this he had arbitrarily taken an independent attitude over a site for his Larsen statue. "Anywhere but the Maritime" seemed to be his feeling. He considered North Vancouver, where the ship had been built, and asked Mayor Carrie Cates about a site on a bluff overlooking the harbour in Moodyville Park.[13] Later he had even toyed with the idea of placing it in Oslo, where Larsen was born, as "a gift with the goodwill of the people of Canada to the people of Norway."[14] All that is sure is that James would certainly have found fault with whatever site any government authority had in mind.

Left: This statuette of Henry Larsen, captain of the *St. Roch*, was commissioned by James from sculptor Sydney March. (D. Sleigh)

Right: A different concept of Henry Larsen is embodied in this new statue by Saltspring Island sculptor Simon Morris. It was unveiled at the Vancouver Maritime Museum in 2006 and stands on the deck of the *St. Roch*. (D. Sleigh)

These two statue projects were by no means all that occupied James's time outside his regular archival work; in fact, they represented only a fraction of the concerns that occupied his thoughts. Throughout his 70s and up till his late 80s, his mind continued to teem with ideas and projects; they did not just remain in the conceptual stage, either. Usually they required money, and he cheerfully threw funds of his own into these schemes, whose fulfilment gave him more pleasure than any other personal indulgence.

Artworks had always been one of his extravagances, and he continued to put out money for paintings as well as statues. Often he found sponsors for these artworks, but sometimes he shouldered the whole cost himself. In 1960, for instance, he lavishly commissioned

Sydney March to paint him not one, but two oil portraits of Captain Larsen—one for Larsen himself (who was given the choice of picture), and the other for the National Maritime Museum at Greenwich.

Many of the memorials around Vancouver were either initiated by James or strongly supported by him. On a building at the corner of Hastings and Hamilton, for instance, an artistic bronze plaque and bas-relief marks the spot where the early surveyor Lauchlan Hamilton drove the first stake when he laid out the streets of Vancouver. This was one of James's projects, and his influence is very obvious in the choice of Sydney March as the sculptor, and in the poetic wording of the plaque: "In the silent solitude of the primeval forest he drove a wooden stake in the earth and commenced to measure an empty land into the streets of Vancouver."

Stanley Park is liberally strewn with plaques, cairns, bas-reliefs and statuary, and James took a concerned interest in all of these. The brass plaque dedicated to the early mill owner Captain Edward Stamp owes its existence to Bruce McKelvie and Major Matthews, who persuaded the provincial government to install it. The Major also had a direct influence over the location of the Lions' Gate Bridge when it was still in the planning stage, since it was his map of First Nations sites that led the engineers to make a slight change in order to avoid harm to the Sunz Rock (a Native figure).

THIS PLAQUE COMMEMORATES THE SPOT WHERE SURVEYOR LAUCHLAN HAMILTON DROVE HIS FIRST STAKE IN HIS PROJECT TO LAY OUT VANCOUVER'S STREETS.

It was also due to James's influence that the City of Richmond received the donation of two historic oil paintings—portraits of the first reeve of Richmond, Hugh Boyd, and his wife, Mary. James was one of the principal speakers at the presentation ceremony on June 11, 1947. One of the most interesting aspects of this event is that it is one of the few occasions when he was recorded on tape, and it is a rare example of James's speaking voice in rich oratorical mode. To this author, who once lived only a few miles from the Matthews home in Wales, overtones of his native Welsh accent can be clearly heard in the sonorous rise and fall of his speech, though it has largely adapted to his Canadian environment.[15] As for the paintings, since there was no suitable place to hang them at the time, James took them off to his own private vault, where several other special artworks were stashed away and where they were found after his death. They are now housed in the Richmond City Archives.

Many of James's initiatives led to noisy arguments with Council and more headlines in the press. One of the most newsworthy of these disputes concerned the grave of Captain Vancouver. George Vancouver, dead at 40, had been buried in the quiet country churchyard of Petersham outside London. For many years the Native Sons of BC, Post No. 2, had held a wreath-laying ceremony on the anniversary of Vancouver's burial and at one time had also paid for some improvements to the grave. However, in 1961, James was distressed to hear from the agent-general in London that the grave had become neglected and was "in poor shape, weeds, long grass." Immediately he dispatched $60 out of his own pocket for the head gardener of a local estate to tidy the grave up and make repairs. He then presented the bill to Council, telling them that they could reimburse him if they thought fit.

The aldermen strongly resented the fact that he had never consulted them before his highhanded action. "He put the gun to our heads," snorted Bill Rathie. "It seems he does what he likes and we accept it."[16] Council paid up. Even so, James despised their reluctant attitude and what he thought of as mean-spiritedness to such an extent that he decided that in future he would pay the maintenance costs of the grave himself. He provided substantial funding through the purchase of a War Stock certificate under the name of 'Perpetual Care and Maintenance of Captain Vancouver's grave,' and this arrangement continued until the time of James's death. The Matthews family then declined the responsibility and wished to redeem the certificate, so this was done, and Council took over the maintenance as of December 1, 1970.[17]

Another controversy, and one that caused him great anguish, arose out of the demolition of the historic McCleery farmhouse, the earliest residence surviving in Vancouver in the 1950s. The descendants of the McCleery family had been forced to sell the farm to the City in 1954 because of rising taxes, and a golf course had gone in soon afterwards. James entered vigorously into a campaign to save the farmhouse itself, but this was one battle he lost, for the house was bulldozed in December 1956. He was disgusted by the parks board's plan to put up a cairn on the site—a pitiful and insulting gesture, as he saw it. In August 1957 he strode into their boardroom, seething with anger. "Don't do it. You are dealing with angry men," he boomed. "If you do, the retribution demanded will be terrible."[18] This cryptic threat had no effect, for the board did put up some kind of cairn, though, according to the Major, it was not built out of the foundations of the old house as they had promised, but out of stones trucked in from North Vancouver.

The friction between the Major and the City grew worse and worse as the 1960s went on. Increasingly, James chose to think of himself as the sole champion of Vancouver's history, heroically fighting the forces of ignorance—and by this he frequently meant City officials. In fact, they were not unsympathetic, nor were they ignorant, but the question of preserving heritage was not at the forefront of their minds. The aldermen were mostly successful businessmen with a practical approach to the job. James's own view of his work as a noble and sacred trust was so completely out of tune with the prosaic outlook of City Hall that it was little wonder that James had fallen into a mindset in which he saw himself as the sole arbiter of anything to do with heritage.

All these factors had resulted in a continued hardening of James's attitude in his dealings with City Hall. He expected opposition by now, and often invited it with his contemptuous pronouncements. Often he was seen as difficult, rude and obstructive. Nevertheless any threats to his position temporarily tapered off as he reached the age of 80, since everyone assumed he was on the point of retiring.

The problem became, however, that he did *not* retire. Any questions on the date of his retirement were cheerily passed off with

James with Parks Superintendent Stuart Lefeaux in front of a Native canoe shelter, 1963. (Eric Lindsay photo. CVA, CVA 392-604)

assertions that his health was fine and he had no intention whatsoever of quitting. "No council is going to tell me when to go. I'll decide that myself."[19] But when he reached the age of 83, still laying down the law to all around him, one Council member lost patience and made a strong and deliberate attempt to subvert James's authority. Alderman Bill Rathie, unencumbered by any long-time associations with the Major or any false ideas of deference for his age, decided to meet aggression with aggression. When he arrived at the council meeting of December 28, 1961, he came armed with a long list of the Major's infractions—and a hostile motion all ready to present. It was really a declaration of war, for what he wanted was James out of the way. "The board of administration should take immediate action to retrieve care and control of the Archives from the Major," he declared. At last the retirement issue was out in the open.[20]

Mayor Alsbury, though he subsequently proved to be thinking along the same lines as Rathie, sensed that not all of his council would go along with these draconian measures. He stalled and asked Rathie to produce a formal written report. But when it came to the crunch, the majority of aldermen could not bring themselves to take such a ruthless and hurtful action. Mostly they were used to James's ways and had grown to entertain a genuine liking for his gruff personality. Nothing came of Rathie's challenge, and for the moment James's position was saved.

A couple of years went by and Rathie was now mayor. Alsbury was still on council as alderman, and was frequently in an adversarial position against Rathie, but the two of them were as one on the question of Major Matthews. He should certainly be retired, agreed Alsbury, when budget time came round in January 1964. At the age of 86, Matthews was 21 years beyond the city's compulsory retirement age, Alsbury pointed out. After a palpably insincere statement of concern for James's health and a wish for him to enjoy some leisure time, Alsbury went on to make his real point: that James must step down and that some chief must be appointed who would have the responsibility for three operations—the Archives, the City Museum and the Maritime Museum. Nobody seemed to have much faith that anything would come of this proposed review. As Alderman Halford Wilson said, "We might as well try to blow up the nine o' clock gun or Siwash Rock" (and he knew the Major better than any of them, having served as an alderman since 1930, even before James was appointed).

Rathie tried again the following year. The scenario he proposed went as follows: first Council would put the Archives under the control of the library board and make James an employee of the library (the same hated situation that he was in during 1931 when Robinson was librarian); then, when James did retire, they would put the Archives collection into storage until a proper facility was built, and give the third floor space to the library. This was clearly an intolerable suggestion. James continued to insist that he would be the one who decided when to retire, but in truth his position was becoming more and more precarious with his advancing age.

Theoretically, Council agreed on some of Rathie's proposals, but still no one had the heart to enforce them. It was not until another year had gone by that Council decided to make another attempt to dissuade James from carrying on. At an in-camera meeting on May 31, 1966, Alsbury referred to "a certain action taken in conjunction with Alderman Bell-Irving" to try to solve the problem of Council's relationship with the Major.[21] No explanation was given, but from the context it seems that this time they adopted a more diplomatic approach. This was an approach far more likely to obtain results, for James could often be won over by sympathy and kindliness, whereas confrontation would only make him more difficult. The committee agreed not to impose any official sanctions, but instead, the inference is that they may have asked James's good friends Victor Odlum and John Buchanan to try to use their influence with him. But niceness did not work either: the Major stood fast, and now it was a stalemate again.

This marked the end of Council's attempts to unseat him. Rathie's term finished at the end of 1966, and incoming Mayor Tom Campbell had other priorities to establish. As usual, James had come off victorious. As one columnist put it: "He has bested the brightest boys who ever passed through city hall over four decades."[22]

But the fact was that James dare not retire: it was clear to him that once he did abandon office, Council would certainly close down the Archives, perhaps for years. He unequivocally had to remain in charge in order to protect the work that had been his raison d'être, the essential core of his life, for half a century or more. To the general public he announced that he would retire once the Archives had been given a building of its own, and once a successor had been found and trained. Since neither of these events seemed likely to occur (especially as he claimed that it took five to 20 years to train an archivist), he simply carried on as before.

What his true estimation of the future might have been is a matter for conjecture; sad to say, his final and realistic appraisal of the prospects for the Archives seems likely to have been of a depressing and cynical nature. But of one thing he was now sure—that, as the City of Vancouver would discover one day, he was making it legally impossible for them ever to lay hands on his own personal collection of archives.

CHAPTER 13

A Long Stewardship Ends

The last five years of James Matthews' life, though occasionally brightened by some form of public appreciation, were years of increasing discouragement, not least from the fact that they coincided with the growing mood of ruthless modernism that took over the city in the late 1960s. They were years that saw a distressing amount of heritage vandalism in Vancouver, all in the name of progress and artistic prestige. The architects who had learned as postwar students to revere the functionalism of Le Corbusier and Mies van der Rohe had now matured into heads of firms or senior team leaders, and many of the designs they were turning out favoured the new aesthetic of architectural "brutalism." The new arbiters of public taste opted for "clean lines" and "purity of design," which favoured symbolism over representationalism, and stark utilitarianism over a wealth of ornament. The 1891 Vancouver Opera House was demolished in 1968 to make way for the Eaton Centre; the Courthouse gardens and its gorgeous magnolias were razed in 1966 (amid protests from the Pioneers Association) to give place to a new Centennial fountain; the Burlington Railway station was pulled down in 1968; and the old Carnegie Library was now at risk, standing empty and boarded up after the museum moved to its prestigious new quarters in 1968.

James must have felt that he had been fighting a useless battle in the face of this growing threat to heritage architecture, and must have felt sick at heart as he witnessed the destruction of so much artistry and tradition. Freeways and urban renewal seemed to be the priorities of the new Council, and the Vancouver whose rise he had watched with such pride began to metamorphose into a different character.

Changes to the old order troubled him greatly. He loathed the new maple leaf flag, which had ousted the Canadian Red Ensign in 1965. For him the time-honoured Union Jack was "a sacred emblem" that represented patriotic feeling and national pride—in fact, he had once written a stirring article titled "Your Flag and Mine—the Union Jack."[1] He disliked the socialist trend of modern politics, and spoke up in favour of a privileged class: "I am a very strong supporter of the system of nobility ... because of the mode of life and ethics which it stimulates, it is something like the teachings of Free Masonry."[2] A great adherent of British tradition, he felt uneasy too about the number of European immigrants who had flooded into Canada since the Second World War, referring to them doubtfully as "displaced persons."[3]

At times he wrote dispirited letters to his friends, conscious of the fact that his vibrant, vigorous years of the 1950s were behind him now—years in which he had felt appreciated by many influential figures and had enjoyed the goodwill and confidence of some of the leading citizens of Vancouver, including the mayor himself. But Frederick Hume had retired from the political scene, and mayors Alsbury and Rathie had had no wish to be lumbered with the baggage of the past, nor with any sentiment of obligation to aging archivists. As for the present mayor, Tom Campbell, James hardly knew this latest arrival. He was out of synchrony with the men he now had to deal with, and was beginning to feel alienated from his own times.

He was lonely too. His sister-in-law Mabel was dead; his grandchildren had lives of their own; and his old friends from the past were almost all gone—John Hosie, John Worden, William Lembke, William Twiss, Louis D. Taylor, Walter Barrett-Lennard. He deeply appreciated the Christmas cards from his friends of more recent times, but said in 1966 that he no longer had the energy to send out any himself. Pearl Steen (one of the trustees), Rosalynde Latimer and Ruth Woodward were among those whose letters and friendship sustained him most. He appeared disappointed in his twin sons: he regarded Lyn as too passive and unenterprising, and he disapproved so completely of Merle and his "dubious associates" that in 1950 he said he hadn't spoken to him for 20 years.[4] This estrangement had never been repaired by the time Merle passed away on November 2, 1967, dead at 68 following an operation for a duodenal ulcer. In spite of his epilepsy, he had held down a job as a steelworker for Dominion Bridge for 30 years till he was obliged to give it up for health reasons in 1950. He had been briefly married at one time (he married in 1952), but is described by one family member as having been basically "a loner."[5]

Often in his later years, James turned to the portrait of his mother and communed with her as if she was still alive. He confessed to his friend Sydney March: "Mother's portrait is in the front room. I have adopted a sort of weird habit; sometimes when no one is near I talk to it. Not in a loud voice; no one could hear me in the next room … Don't think I've gone crazy; I've not."[6] One of his granddaughters witnessed these scenes in her youth and has poignant memories of James standing before his mother's portrait with tears in his eyes and repeating: "Mother, where did I go wrong?"

Nevertheless, James continued to persevere at the Archives, more watchful and more suspicious than ever, since the dangerous attempts of Alsbury and Rathie to unseat him. It had been a near thing, as he must have known at heart, and he felt all the more determined that he must stay on to protect his cherished collection, for otherwise the calamity that he most dreaded would happen—Council would close down the department. The underlying tension resulted in an even greater edginess and irascibility. He strongly disapproved of some of the younger researchers and their casual hippie style of dress and manner, and would withhold material from them if he deemed them unworthy. One librarian recalls seeing the occasional researcher come away "almost weeping with frustration" after this type of encounter with Major Matthews. He despised most reporters on the grounds that they garbled everything, and he gave them short shrift, bellowing angrily and indulging in a great deal of desk thumping—he gesticulated so violently during an interview with Himie Koshevoy that his glasses shot off and flew across the room.

Leonard McCann, later to be curator of the Maritime Museum, had occasion to consult the City Archives at an early point in his career. The Major greeted him with a few snarls of distrust, under the

James Matthews, 1961. (Williams Bros. photo. CVA, Port N941.2)

impression that he was a journalist, but eventually he passed the test and was admitted behind the counter to view some material. "Then there was a complete switch of personality. If you could withstand the first blast, he became completely charming and helpful." McCann records one memorable visit when Matthews actually fell out of his chair with rage. It was not McCann who was the object of his wrath, but the despised new maple leaf flag, which Matthews had noticed fluttering from a nearby building. Launching into a violent harangue, he started to pound the table and toss around in his chair and generally work himself up into such a state of indignation that, with one excitable gesture too many, he suddenly overbalanced and tumbled to the floor. He was a heavy, unwieldy man, and it took the combined efforts of McCann and the unflappable Jean Gibbs to help him back into his chair. Mrs. Gibbs seemed prepared for this, remembered McCann. With the ease of long practice, she drew out a bottle of something restorative from a cupboard and administered it. Then, after a little huffing and puffing, the Major simply carried on the conversation as if nothing had happened.[7]

James was also capable of being extraordinarily kind and generous to unknown visitors, if his heart was touched. This unpredictable man made a profound impression on teenaged Millie King, whose aunt (a granddaughter of the fur trader Henry Moberly) had sent her to call on the Major in the summer of 1965. He looked at her with his customary suspicion and growled: "What do you know about your great-grandfather?" "Nothing," she faltered with trepidation, as she handed him a rose fresh-picked from her aunt's garden. Suddenly his manner softened. "Sit down, and I will tell you all about him," he offered, and in the next hour she enjoyed one of the most wonderful and inspiring conversations of her life. She came away with an inscribed copy of one of James's pamphlets and was later to receive a rare photo—a print of a Sydney March oil painting of Walter Moberly (Henry's famous explorer brother), which James had issued to no other person in Canada. The correspondence with Millie and her aunt continued on an intimate basis for the rest of the year, with James confiding his sorrow at Hughie's death and his affection for John Hosie, as if he had a great need for some sympathetic listener.[8]

"I am often despondent. Sometimes disgusted, sometimes worried to death with my troubles and trials," he told this young girl in one of his letters, and he then characteristically concluded: "But it is no use letting tribulations disturb you; keep on; keep on."[9] And he did keep on, if only for the sake of keeping the Archives alive. It was clear to him that no one else at that time had the same sense of mission or the same degree of motivation, and he thought of himself as the only person who stood between the survival of the Archives and the threat of closure by an adverse City Hall.

By the late 1960s he was no longer demanding a building and no longer looking for a successor, but reserving all his dwindling energy merely to maintain the status quo. After 1966 he wrote no more pamphlets or newspaper articles, nor did he put out any further issues of the *Vancouver Historical Journal.* The final volumes of *Early Vancouver* lay unprinted. Even his correspondence, once voluminous, was reduced to the occasional angry letter of protest against some perceived affront. It was enough for him now just to keep the Archives running, with the invaluable help of a new assistant, Mrs. Mary Isabel Beveridge, who had arrived to replace Jean Gibbs when the latter retired in July 1965. Mrs. Beveridge and James hit it off immediately, and she swiftly became his trusted ally. Historian Patricia Roy remembered her as his "protector-assistant"; to another historian, Michael Halleran, she appeared as "a kind of female Matthews." Courteous but firm, she dealt with the day-to-day demands of the Archives with great efficiency and totally identified herself with the Major's interests.

By the time he reached the age of 90 in 1968, he had grown cynical over the chances of ever having his own building. Even though the City was currently enlarging its own premises by adding a four-storey annex (which opened on October 29, 1968), they still had not included any provision for the Archives in all this new space. Much as he would have preferred to have a separate building, James had actually declared himself willing to move to the annex—anything to get away from the indignity of being included in the library. (His attitude to the library would not have been improved by the fact that Ronald D'Altroy was gradually assembling a library collection of historical photographs of a quality rivalling James's own collection.)

Now came a new threat: Council began to grudge James even the office rooms he occupied on the third floor of the library. The City clerk had long ago made the troubling claim that the Archives was "little used by the general public" and that "the space could be better used for library purposes"—to which the Major had countered, "An astounding report. We work day, night, weekends and holidays."[10] He remembered bitterly how City officials had turned him out of his fine location at the top of the city hall—merely so that they could store their rolls of building plans there, he claimed contemptuously. Now it was the library that wanted him out. By 1965 a new factor had emerged to compound his bitterness. Reluctant as Council was to tolerate the Archives, let alone spend money on it, they were paradoxically about to indulge in a big financial splurge on a heritage project of another kind—the prestigious Vancouver City Museum.

Ironically, at the same time as belittling the importance of historical records, Council was planning to contribute large sums of money toward impressive new quarters for this showpiece of a museum. It seemed that little expense would be spared to equip it. A Gerald Hamilton design, it would stand on a superb site in Vanier Park overlooking the water (just where James had visualized his Archives), and thanks to the generosity of logging magnate H.R. MacMillan, there was also to be an elegant planetarium, which would rise gracefully at the centre of the complex.

But where was there any provision for the Archives? For a while there was indeed some talk of including an archives wing as part of the museum. On July 13, 1965, aldermen Broome and Williams had specifically proposed this as a motion and engendered some discussion, but after much wrangling, Council had tabled the proposal and it had died a quiet death. Another hope dispelled, James was obliged to stand by and watch as the elaborate and imaginative new museum complex took shape—but minus the archives wing that had been half-promised earlier. When the centre opened to much acclaim on October 26, 1968, James had to make do with a nominal role as a guest of honour, though MLA Herb Capozzi spoke for many people when he declared at the ceremony that "Major James Skitt Matthews is largely responsible for what we have today."[11]

Herb Capozzi was not the only representative of the provincial government to turn the spotlight on James that year. In April the premier of British Columbia, the legendary W.A.C. Bennett, heaped lavish praise on the Major in front of a crowd of 2,000 people at New Brighton Park. Bennett was in Vancouver, along with nine cabinet ministers, to unveil a plaque to mark the centenary of the Hastings townsite, the earliest community in Vancouver. Like many other plaques, this one had been entirely Major Matthews' idea. James regarded this spot as one of the most historic sites on Burrard Inlet, and he had been pestering the Historic Sites and Monuments Board of Canada to list it ever since 1961. Even though he had been scathing about the committee's choice of "New Brighton" for the name—"a colossal error," in his view[12]—he was quite ready to stand on the podium and deliver a speech in his own inimitable heroic style. Premier Bennett, beaming cheerily as always, announced, "The pioneers have done a good job, but none better than Major Matthews. He's 90 and he hasn't wasted a single day. He hasn't had a holiday in 33 years, because his mission in life is to look after the archives of Vancouver and British Columbia."[13] James received a standing ovation from the huge crowd and was visibly moved.

It would seem that Council may have experienced some remorse over the imbalance of their objectives, in the light of their negative attitude toward the Archives and their preferential treatment of the museum. For nearly a decade, they had been procrastinating on the question of a permanent home for the Archives—and here was this incredibly dedicated archivist, 90 years old, and still without the archives building this sort of dedication deserved. Two months before the new museum opened, Council suddenly felt some collective need to remedy their neglect of the Archives, belatedly recalling that it was, after all, their other co-existing historical repository. And so, on August 14, 1968, James received an astonishing letter from the City clerk.

It was a letter full of compliments and wonderful promises, almost too good to be true. From it, he learned that Council had passed a resolution noting that whereas they had "moved forward" with the Maritime Museum and the new Centennial Museum, it was equally desirable to house the Archives properly. Besides this, they intended to find some way in which Major Matthews himself would be "permanently honoured."[14] The solution, of course: appoint a committee. They did so—it was to consist of Alderman Marianne Linnell (on record as demanding an archives building) and Alderman Halford Wilson (James's oldest friend on Council). That was good news as far as it went, though James had to be satisfied with the vague promise that some time soon this committee would be studying the future housing of the Archives and "a suitable way of honouring our first archivist, Major Matthews."[15]

Did this communication raise James's spirits at all, one wonders, or did it leave him unconvinced that anything would ever come of a few conscience-salving words and belated compliments? It is doubtful that he allowed himself to place much confidence in Council's assurances, even though they were phrased in much more concrete terms than ever before. It would have been wiser to remain skeptical, and so he probably did, in view of the past record of previous councils. On the other hand, the hostile atmosphere created by Alsbury and Rathie was now a thing of the past, and the current mayor, Tom Campbell, was by no means indifferent to the arts; he liked to commission pieces of sculpture for the high-rise buildings he put up during his career as a developer. There was also the hopeful thought that yet another centennial was coming up in the near future, the 1971 centenary of British Columbia entering Confederation, and Vancouver would soon have to decide what sort of a landmark project it would opt for this time. James continued to hear encouraging hints of a building to be named for him, but now the question was, would he live to see his dream come true?

The records of his final two years are scanty, but all indications point to failing energy and absence of creative drive. His speech at New Brighton Park in April 1968 was his last important public address. His 1966 newspaper article in defence of the CPR was probably his last piece of journalism, and his 1968 pamphlet on Bowen Island his last piece of creative writing. His last signed letter in his business correspondence file is dated May 13, 1969 (he happily tells his correspondent that "Mayor Campbell is advocating permanent quarters for the Archives as a most important feature of the forthcoming 1971 Centennial").[16] From then on all the work of the Archives was carried out by Mary Beveridge, in whom James placed such trust that by December 1967, he had already named her as one of the executors of his will.

Still he maintained his determination to carry on to the end. In March 1969 he wrote to an English archivist, "I have no intention of retiring." He indicated the same thing when they piped in his birthday cake that September at a special luncheon in honour of his 91st birthday laid on by the Kiwanis Club at the Hotel Vancouver. All his old enthusiasm returned as he talked to them about his plans for the future—to put up the Henry Larsen statue, to have the old engine at Kitsilano re-enact the first CPR journey to Vancouver and, above all, to see the Archives appropriately housed in its own building. It was an upbeat audience. The president, Hugh Bird, declared emphatically: "We must have an archives building," and urged his fellow Kiwanis to form a building committee of their own (the Linnell committee had never produced any results). As the guests departed, James saw to it that each man was presented with a copy of the speech he had written."Take it home to your wife and children," he instructed them.[17]

It was a great finish to his career—for it was the last birthday celebration at which he was publicly honoured. Only a few days after his birthday, he was taken ill and admitted to Shaughnessy Hospital with some unspecified complaint, and he remained a patient there for about 10 days before he grew restive and "stomped out ... with his cane and a bouquet of flowers sent to him by the city,"[18] according to Mayor Campbell. But he had not really recovered, and within a week he was reported seriously ill at home and under constant medical care.

James never recovered sufficiently to make even a brief return to the office, and the indications are that he was a permanent patient in Shaughnessy Hospital for veterans from late October 1969 onwards. By January 1970 Mrs. Beveridge was dealing with all his mail and informing his correspondents of his illness. His sudden deterioration is thought by the family to have been due to heart disease, and his death certificate mentions a condition of severe coronary atherosclerosis. He was profoundly deaf now, too deaf to carry on a real conversation, and no amount of amplification could help. He was not in pain, Mrs. Beveridge told his correspondents, but he was in no condition to comment on their letters. In August 1970 she told one correspondent not to send a tape this person had offered, as he would not know what it referred to. After his death, the same correspondent conjectured that "his mind had slipped, because he could not adjust to having to give it all up,"[19] but his granddaughter Evelyn strongly refutes this suggestion and says that he held perfectly lucid conversations with her whenever she visited him in hospital. His friends continued to drop in, and many people sent him flowers. The hospital gave him the best of care. He lived to reach his 92nd birthday, still officially the City Archivist for Vancouver, for—true to his word—he never did retire. One of the best things the City ever did for him was to send flowers for this last birthday of his, for the nurses all noticed how much happier he seemed after this final act of recognition. It made a dramatic change in him, reported his granddaughter Hazel gratefully.[20] Then, a month after his birthday, he was gone. He died on October 1, 1970, following a four-day bout with bronchopneumonia in both lungs.

To Vancouverites he had seemed indestructible, and now he was gone. The man who believed that his archives represented the soul of the city had succumbed to mortality himself, and the city was spiritually the poorer for it.

The funeral service in Christ Church Cathedral on October 7 was all James could have wished for. He was accorded a civic funeral, which was attended by leading citizens and dignitaries. On behalf of the province there was Grace McCarthy, minister without portfolio, who had once worked with James on a Stanley Park committee. The City was strongly represented by Mayor Tom Campbell, eight aldermen and some senior officials from the Hall, all of whom were honorary pallbearers, along with Major Reginald Tupper. The active pallbearers included his grandson Robert Matthews, his grandson-in-law Donald Walser (husband of Evelyn), parks board chair Andy Livingstone, and Brock Webber, the printer of *Early Vancouver*. A crowd of about three hundred people filled the cathedral for the service, which was held according to the rites of the Anglican Church with great dignity and honour. The reading of the Twenty-third

Psalm was a traditional choice, but the hymn that was sung was non-traditional, yet very fitting—a hymn specially written for Vancouver by Dean T.H. O'Driscoll titled "The Winds of Juan de Fuca." And, according to the Major's express wishes, the casket was draped with the Union Jack, one last defiant gesture.

An honour guard accompanied the Major to his final resting place in the Masonic section of Mountain View Cemetery, where a simple graveside service took place. In the guard were men from the armed services, for the military had been so much a part of James's life, but there was also a contingent from the Vancouver police and fire departments. The Major would surely have given it all his approval—the ceremony, the uniforms, the almost military honours and the final plaintive strains of "The Flowers of the Forest" by Pipe-Major Andrew Perrie of the Vancouver Police. It was a grand send-off.

CHAPTER 14

Major Matthews' Legacy

James must have much regretted the fact that he would not be there to witness the reaction of City officials when the contents of his will were made public. At last he was going to have his moment of triumph, posthumous though it might be, for he was about to score heavily over his old adversaries at City Hall.

He must have gloated many times over the cunning strategy he had devised to ensure a successful resolution of the grievances that had obsessed his mind during his final years. His first ambition was to deliver a hearty rebuff to the City of Vancouver and ensure that his own personal archival collection was kept well out of their hands, and therefore he had carried out the threat he had perpetually used throughout the 1960s: he had not bequeathed his collection to the City, but to the Province of British Columbia. His second object was to force the City's hand over the construction of an archives building and ensure that there would be no further delay. And so, in a resounding ultimatum—his master stroke—he had decreed that unless suitable accommodation for the collection was created within the space of one year, his material should be put up for sale and the proceeds awarded to the residuary legatees.

It was a rancorous incident in March 1961 that had decided the terms of the will. At that point the City had become somewhat paranoid about the fact that the Major liked to keep the most valuable acquisitions in his own private vault, so it had issued a restraining order that legally denied him the right to remove any item from the Archives. It was an outrage that he could not forgive, and he would never trust Council again. This was when he resolved never to allow the City to get their hands on his private collection, and he drew up his new will of 1962.

Then, however, another thought struck him—suppose the Province should decline his bequest? Much correspondence went on over the years, conducted through James's lawyers and the Attorney General, until finally Premier W.A.C. Bennett signed the crucial document of acceptance, dated April 26, 1968: "This is to certify that I, James Skitt Matthews, do hereby bestow to the Province of British Columbia, in the name of Her Majesty the Queen, all archival material now in my possession for the use of the citizens of the Province."[1]

The 1962 will had been replaced on December 6, 1966, by another one that clarified and detailed his intent, noting, for example, that he was leaving to the Province his copyrights, as well as the historical records and objects. In a later codicil he remembered to include his artworks too, a fine collection of sculpture, paintings and etchings. In fact, he added no fewer than six codicils between 1967 and 1970, as various ideas occurred to him, chiefly increasing the provision he had made for his housekeeper, Bessie Bolton. Grateful for all her good care and attention, he left her $175 a month for one year and the lifetime use of his Arbutus Street home, as well as a sum of $1,000. The rest of his estate, in bonds and insurance, was to be shared by his four grandchildren.

His executors were his lawyers, Reginald Tupper and his son David, and James's assistant archivist, Mary I. Beveridge (to whom he had left $1,000 even before he made her an executor). Reginald Tupper died in 1972, while many issues relating to the will were still under discussion, and Mary Beveridge, who was also elderly, died in 1976. It was a complicated estate, and the executors took 10 years or more to settle it completely. After James's death the three executors faced an incredibly difficult assignment. Firstly, they had to solve the legal position and the contradictory terms of James's intentions. On the one hand he had refused to let his collection fall into the clutches of the City, yet on the other hand he had specified that the collection was to be housed in Vancouver within one year. Secondly, the executors had to identify all the different components of his collection, which reposed in various caches around Vancouver—some of the artwork adorning every room of his house, some of it hidden away in a private vault, other items in the City Archives mingling inextricably with City-owned material. All this had to be assessed by experts before any decisions could be made, and it would be a major voyage of discovery, since nobody but Matthews himself really knew the exact nature of the collection. The need for a review was considered so urgent that only a week or two after Matthews' death, another special committee (aldermen Marianne Linnell and Walter Hardwick), assisted by several expert authorities, was already considering the nature of the collection and analyzing the rationale behind Matthews' decisions.

In December they made their report, and now came all the criticism. In the days immediately after James's death, an atmosphere of respect and admiration had prevailed, but now his reputation was in the hands of the very academics he had been so wary of. Provincial Archivist Willard Ireland, who had always been rather patronizing in his attitude to James, was one of the chief experts consulted. It was retired Dominion Archivist W. Kaye Lamb, however, who made the detailed memorandum that guided the committee in 1970.

When the special committee reported officially to Council on December 21, 1970, their remarks were by inference most damaging to the Major's reputation. In spite of his magnificent 40 years of preserving history, what emerged from their findings was that he had had little interest in collecting the administrative records of City Hall. Municipal records were entirely outside his sphere of interest and alien to his imaginative concept of Vancouver's history. He had chosen to save whatever he recognized as bringing history to life: personal memoirs, contemporary pictures and photographs, objects connected with great events or outstanding personalities—symbols of humanity without which a later historian can never fully understand the mood of a vanished era. Failing to look at the broad picture of Major Matthews' aims and achievements, one member of the special committee carped unappreciatively that the state of the Archives was "desperate and chaotic," and a former City official even went so far as to say that since the Archives housed no municipal government records (they were stored in the City's vault), "there is no City of Vancouver Archives."[2]

How do you define the function of an archives? This was the first time in its history that the City had had the opportunity to discuss the question in free and open debate. No one had stopped to define the purpose of the City Archives before, but had allowed James complete freedom in his interpretation of its role. Various people had hinted that his interpretation was a fairly loose one, but on the whole it was tacitly accepted that he was collecting material that illustrated the history of Vancouver, and that this material was largely in the form of private records. Nobody criticized the fact that he was making no effort to take charge of municipal records; the City certainly did not seem to care. Most archival institutions today tend to be a combination of the two, if storage permits, but whether public or private records, the word "archives" would apply equally to either. James had concentrated on private records, but these still constituted an archives, and one that specialized in the records of Vancouver, and so it had been fully justified in describing itself as the City Archives.

However, now was the moment to make a change and expand the scope of the Archives to bring it into accordance with current thinking. It was a pivotal decision for the special committee to make, but they did not hesitate to take this step and make it their first recommendation: that the Archives should take on a whole new responsibility and take charge of the huge collection of city records currently stored in the city vaults. It would be a dramatic change of focus that would transform James's old idiosyncratic collection out of all recognition.

The committee's other recommendation was even more momentous, or so James would have thought: it was nothing less than the construction of the archives building. The Major's great dream, never realized in his lifetime, was about to be forced on the City now. The building was to be a memorial to Major Matthews and his work, the committee specified, and they went on to endorse the very site that James had ideally wanted, the waterfront setting of Vanier Park. They added hopefully that it might be a feasible project for the approaching 1971 centennial.

After all the long-drawn-out debate that had dragged on for years, all of a sudden Council agreed to these quite radical commitments with barely the blink of an eye; the change of attitude was incredible. The retention of selected City records was approved the very next day, and a month later an architect for an archives building was appointed. On the question of a centennial project, there was some variety of opinion among the public at large. A downtown coliseum was one popular suggestion; a replica of HMS *Discovery* was another; but the aldermen were unanimous in their decision on January 19, 1971, and the archives project won out.

Unfortunately, the doubts that various experts had cast on the quality of the Major's archives had an unsettling effect on a number of people, and in spite of his prodigious efforts in the cause of Vancouver's history, the greatness of his achievement seemed to be temporarily forgotten in the light of the modern approach to archival management. W. Kaye Lamb's belittling reference to the City Archives as a "non-archival collection" was most injurious, and the damage went further when James himself came under the scrutiny of the narrow academic world of the professionals, who patronizingly rated him as "self-taught" and "self-styled." As for the politicians, a few of them tried quite hard to sink the whole project, even after they had approved it in principle and appointed an architect. Alderman Art Phillips and others were uneasy over the cost of the project, but James's supporters, aldermen Ernie Broome and Hugh Bird, rallied to its defence, and although the arguments went on till as late as April, Council did not change its intent.

In the meantime there was a legal problem to be cleared up, because although James required that his collection should be kept in Vancouver, he had actually given it over to the Province, and the Provincial Archives was in Victoria; so how was all this to be worked out? The eventual arrangement did not take long to determine. The Province would retain ownership, as signed for by W.A.C. Bennett in 1965, but the City of Vancouver would be given the actual custody of all the material relating to its geographic area (other material would be held by the Provincial Archives). The copyrights of all James's writings were bequeathed to the Province, but it was suggested that the City should handle the sales and share the profits with the Province.

As Provincial Archivist, Willard Ireland was now virtually in charge of James' collection and determining its fate. Shortly he would be in the process of assessing, with a cold and critical eye, all the Major's most prized possessions. How James would have disliked the thought of this man passing judgement on his own personal treasures, yet had he thought about it, he ought surely to have guessed that Ireland would be the Province's inevitable choice to evaluate his bequest. By March 1971, Ireland had gone over the contents of James's home and vault, and had decided which material to recommend handing over to the City Archives. The rumour had gone around that James had stashed away countless treasures in hidden vaults, but this was quite unfounded: the number of items in storage was not large, and some of them had little commercial value. James's grandchildren put in a request to keep a few special pieces for themselves, like a statuette of Lord Stanley and the maquette for Henry Larsen, but Mrs. Beveridge was obliged to confirm that James had definitely intended some of these to stay with the rest of the collection.[3]

One more problem arose when Mrs. Beveridge, in the process of compiling the inventory of James's household possessions, was startled to discover that an old trunk in the basement contained some extremely hazardous-looking objects buried under a pile of military uniforms. She noted drily: "I did not disturb, as there were hand grenades with pins, bullets, etc."[4] When Leonard McCann was called in to check this out, he found to his amazement that they were indeed live grenades from the First World War—and situated in a corner immediately beneath the Major's own bedroom. These objects were removed with great caution and sent to the armed forces base in Chilliwack to be detonated by the bomb disposal squad.

As for the house itself, Bessie Bolton had been given a life tenancy, and she continued to make it her home until about 1981, when she is believed to have retired to Scotland. (She is said to have started writing an account of James's life, but no one knows what happened to this material.) Eventually the property was sold to a developer; the house was demolished, and in 1985 the city directory listed the site as "under construction." By 1986 a building with four apartments stood on the site. The Major's cherished garden now lies beneath this structure, and only his laurel hedge remains.

Fresh criticism emerged when James's successor, Robert Watts, took over in May 1971 and started to take stock of the situation at the Archives. Watts was a young man in his mid-20s, a graduate with a master's degree and one year's experience at the Public Archives of Canada—in short, the very type of potential successor whom James had been most suspicious of (too young, an academic and a newcomer from eastern Canada.) As James might have feared, Watts saw the need for many changes. He noticed that there was "no standard archival or subject index to any of the material in the dockets," and he saw an urgent need for superior methods of conservation and storage, for the Major had not kept up with the scientific aspect of archival care. It would take time, but Watts began to pave the way for the huge task of modernizing the Archives: sorting, cataloguing, ordering acid-free containers, analyzing the adhesives used in repair work and generally caring for the collection.[5]

James would not have liked all that was going on. He would have been disappointed to see many of the surplus books in the Archives transferred to the Vancouver Public Library, and he would have been even more distressed to know that Watts was sending a consignment of about 80 artifacts over to the Centennial Museum, where they more appropriately belonged. But what would probably have upset James most of all was the fact that Watts was carefully extracting from the dockets anything that was not an actual document—medals, ribbons, photos, all the small accessories that had been part of the life of the person who featured in the docket. For James, all such trivia had breathed life and animation into the mysteries of the past.

When R. Lynn Ogden succeeded Watts in January 1973, he made the same sort of comments as others like Ireland and Lamb had done: "pretty much a hodge-podge collection" was his description. Like Watts, Ogden was obviously greatly concerned to halt deterioration of the records, for without delay he secured a grant to do paper repair and he began copying documents to microfilm and microfiche, even though he regarded this as "late in the day."[6] (James would not have approved of the microfilming, and had dismissed the idea outright when it was once suggested to him, probably regarding it as a soulless way of viewing a document hallowed by history.)

One other financial question arose in 1974, when the executors discovered the existence of three of the Major's trust funds, which still contained donations for the Larsen and Lord Stanley statues and one other. All this amounted to the sum of $2,500, but these projects were dead issues now, so Lynn Ogden was asked for his ideas on the best use of the money. He suggested such ideas as buying journals or microfilm copies, or spending money on indexing maps, so although James would certainly have preferred plaques or similar memorials, the funds were allocated to the use of the Archives.[7]

But in the most important regard, the Major had won a superlative victory. Almost unbelievably, after waiting 40 years, the Archives actually was about to be promoted to a building of its own. With gleeful guile, James had made it a condition of his bequest that suitable housing for his collection must be provided within the space of a year—and the threat had worked. The stipulation in James's will had an extraordinarily galvanizing effect on Council to make a remarkably speedy decision, and the building was already under construction by the end of 1971. A strike in the summer of 1972 delayed completion, but the building was finished at last in December—the first archives building in Canada to be built especially for that purpose. It was a triumph for Major Matthews—but bittersweet too, for it had taken his death to force City Council's hand at last.

He would have rejoiced to see the archives building completed, but unfortunately, as far as the actual architecture was concerned, he would have been greatly disappointed had he lived to see the result. The site in Vanier Park was certainly the site of his choice, but James had envisaged a fine monumental building, perhaps not in the classical style of the European buildings he admired, but at least a building that would catch the eye, do justice to the setting and form a worthy complement to the museum and planetarium complex across the way. Instead the architect, Bill Leithead, chose to virtually conceal it from view.

This was the same architect whom Matthews had worked with when P.A. Woodward had thought of funding an archives building, and Leithead had favoured a modern style all along, but possibly no one had guessed how extreme his concept would be. The new "brutalism" that was the current trend in architecture would define Leithead's approach and influence him to design a building that was as starkly functional in appearance as it is possible for a building to be—that is, the part of the building that is visible. Most of it is buried under the grassy swell of the park, with the vaults and storage area covering a vast hidden area beneath the ground. Little of the building can be seen except from the parking area or the water. No visitor approaching the impressive entrance to the Centennial Museum and Planetarium would even be aware of the Archives' existence, since all that comes into view from that angle is a hummock of turf surmounted by a box-like concrete structure, which one critic has described as looking like a "better sewage treatment centre."[8] Leithead described it as "an unfinished concrete memorial," and hopefully suggested that "the public will only be conscious of a reflecting pool and green spaces." In his mind it embodied the obscure symbolism of a "defence fortification" that was transformed into "a lantern over the City's collective knowledge," but undoubtedly James himself would have chosen to have his building stand proudly and conspicuously in full view, a monument to the City of Vancouver.[9]

City Council in 1968 had promised James a memorial, and it had been implicit that this memorial would take the form of naming the building for him, but the 1971 council had had their confidence shaken by all the naysayers, and for a long time refused to commit themselves on this. Fortunately, the pressure of public opinion prevailed, and at last in June 1972 they made the announcement that the Archives' new home was to be known as "the Major Matthews Building." It was not opened with the fanfare and glory that James would have desired. No lieutenant-governor or premier was in attendance, the ceremonies were minimal, and the opening date of December 29, 1972, was unlikely to attract a large number of onlookers. Mayor Tom Campbell stood on the steps of the building and cut the ribbon (his last official function as outgoing mayor), and the small gathering of about 30 people listened to an invocation by a chaplain and speeches by Arthur Laing and Laurie Wallace on behalf of the higher levels of government. They

Top: Side view of the present City of Vancouver Archives building, which was erected after James's death. Half-concealed by a grassy mound, it stands near the Centennial Museum in Vanier Park. It was opened by Mayor Tom Campbell in December 1972. (D. Sleigh)
Bottom: Visitors' entrance to the Vancouver City Archives. (D. Sleigh)

toured the building, walked over to a small reception at the museum, and it was all over—a poor substitute for the elaborate ceremonies and noble words that James would have thought only fitting for such an occasion.

Happily, there were some who wished for something more in the way of a remembrance, feeling there was a need for some personal and visible reminder of Major Matthews and his unspoken presence. In 1974 Mrs. Theresa Galloway, a generous patron of the Archives, announced to the newspapers that she would like to commission a bronze bust of the Major—a most appropriate idea, in view of James's own great enthusiasm for statues of people he admired. Her offer caught the eye of sculptor Elek Imredy, and he was selected to carry out the work.[10] The bust, which Mayor Art Phillips unveiled in February 1976, has been given a highly visible position, mounted on a column of travertine marble in the foyer and dominating the scene. The sculptor has caught the Major in an affable mood, apparently soothed by the presence of his own cherished collection, and from his plinth he gazes benignly down on all who enter or leave. A bust of Emily (the one commissioned by James some 25 years earlier) stands in the reading room, a reminder of their wonderful partnership in founding the Archives of Vancouver.

Bust of James Matthews, commissioned by former Archives trustee Theresa Galloway and sculpted by Elek Imredy. It stands in the foyer of the Vancouver City Archives and was unveiled in February 1976 by Mayor Art Phillips. (D. Sleigh)

Epilogue

The legacy left by James Matthews was not merely the legacy in his will, bequeathing the documents, artwork and memorabilia he had preserved—though this in itself was of vast proportions. That was the tangible legacy; the intangible legacy was immeasurable.

Major Matthews' contribution to Vancouver's history was unique. He may not have been a professional or been able to flourish any paper credentials to impress his peers; he did not use the academic jargon or formal language that might have inspired confidence in official circles; but none of this mattered—*he* knew exactly who he was in terms of his vocation, and knowing himself to be an archivist, he acted on his convictions and performed magnificently.

He was an individualist, a one-of-a-kind character in the great catalogue of Vancouver's remarkable personalities and eccentrics. He did not fit the academic mould, or any other, and therefore has been consistently underrated by many of the present generation of archivists. His concept of an archivist was very different from the narrow definition understood today. To James, an archivist was a combination of historian, antiquarian, record keeper, author, publicist and activist, and he flung himself into all these roles with an all-absorbing energy. His self-appointed work as an archivist was therefore of an extremely varied nature.

First, there is the undisputed fact that, single-handed, he established the City of Vancouver Archives. He forced himself on a reluctant Council, and did so in times of an appalling economic depression, when Council had no money for anything at all, let alone an archives. He rescued records that were decaying in damp basements or about to be junked. His cataloguing system may not be approved of by today's archivists, but he catalogued the records according to standards suggested by the Provincial Archivist, his friend John Hosie. All this was the normal work of a conventional archivist.

But James went much farther than this, for he also threw himself into the role of historian and historical writer. He saw Vancouver's history not just as a study of documents, but in terms of life and colour, and he needed to bring these stories alive to a wider audience. Not only did he produce a flow of historical articles for the newspapers, but he produced a major historical work, the seven volumes of *Early Vancouver*, a series built out of unique pioneer interviews. This was followed (when he was in his 80s) by another series, the six issues of the *Vancouver Historical Journal*. His body of historical writing is impressive in itself, considering the number of other projects he involved himself in.

Major Matthews has been faulted for certain inaccuracies in his writings, and perhaps he should have sought out more reference sources than he did—apparently he never once visited the Provincial Archives during the three decades of Willard Ireland's tenure. Neither was he remembered by librarians as ever dropping by the Northwest History Room of the Vancouver Public Library to consult historical references. He may have given more credence to oral accounts than was justified, without checking documentary sources. Many discrepancies in James's spelling of names were noted by author Fred Thirkell when he indexed *Early Vancouver*. However, official documents too are rife with similar discrepancies, as any genealogist quickly discovers, and if one adds to this the problem of variations in spelling in newspaper accounts, there are many possible explanations for James's inconsistencies. The grammarian might also fault him for occasional lapses in syntax, though the quality of his language easily compensates for these. It would be small-minded to place undue importance on such flaws in his techniques when he interpreted so magnificently the grand pageant of Vancouver's history. Even his harshest critics have never disputed that his most important legacy has been to leave us a graphic, atmospheric picture of Vancouver in the late 19th and early 20th centuries that we would not otherwise have had.

The Archives needed no public relations officer while James was around. A gift for words combined with a turbulent, supercharged personality to make him the most brilliant publicist any archives could ever have. Most cities are barely aware that they have an archives in their midst, but with the Major always fighting some battle or promoting some insanely ambitious project, the Vancouver City Archives seemed to be always in the news. His ability to create headlines made him a constant joy to the city's newspaper reporters, who quite enjoyed their frequent skirmishes with him and even his withering put-downs, as they made such excellent copy. News items that would normally never have interested an editor would regularly find their way to the front page: "Fiery Major's Not Quitting; Another Battle Brewing; Court Order Doesn't Faze Archivist"—and even though they usually centred around some quirk of James's personality, at the same time they kept the public aware of the existence of the Archives.

As a public speaker he was very much sought after, and he kept up a tireless schedule of appointments, especially in his early years as an archivist, when he gave innumerable talks and slide shows to local societies like the Pioneers Association; the Native Sons of BC; the Arts, Historical and Scientific Association; the Masons; and various military bodies. He likewise needed little persuasion to hold forth—most eloquently and movingly—at any public gathering. With his vivid turn of speech and stirring delivery, he was a splendid narrator, according to those who knew him, and he had the gift of inspiring others with his own passionate beliefs. It was this star quality that placed him in a class of his own as an archivist.

Archivist, historian, writer, orator and publicist—James Skitt Matthews was all of these and more. But remarkable as all these aspects of his persona may have been, perhaps his most interesting and unique quality was his imaginative vision of Canada's past, which infused all vanished times with a glorious aura of romanticism. He not only read about and studied those bygone times, but he felt and saw them in his mind as part of a heroic age, and he wanted other people to feel and see them in this way too. History for him was not a textbook account, but a real and living panorama, and he thought of it as he would some grand painting in a gallery. When he imagined a scene, it came to him in visual images; and when he wrote a story, he wrote it as if he were a painter, filling it with colour and atmosphere. Everything was invested with a kind of nobility.

In James's imagination, battle scenes were heroic, not murderous. "The picture of those grand men pushing back the frontier of France was a scene that would make a noble subject for a painter"—this was the way he remembered the assault on Regina Trench. The pioneer life was never squalid and toilsome, but full of dignity and worth: "There was something very beautiful about those pioneers' days; the going was rough, the inconveniences many, but there was a sweet wholesomeness to those sincere souls who led the way ... a tender sympathy, a simple faith, which has left memories which grow fonder and fonder as the days pass ... The air was fragrant with purity." But his finest and most lyrical words were always reserved for his own chosen city of Vancouver: "The magic city which grew out of a forest whose trees were taller than our monumental buildings." Always he phrased it in terms of enchantment: "In the short span of a single life it rose like a magic thing, out of a wilderness of forest."[1]

This was his first vision of Vancouver, seen through the eyes of an impressionable youth, and he preserved this image in all its freshness for the rest of his life, recasting it in only slightly varying words, repeating it over and over again throughout his speech-making years. It did not matter that the Vancouver of the 1960s was not the city he had first fallen in love with, for romanticism was a gift of spirit that he never lost. The automobile might have taken over the streets, trucks and heavy machinery might trundle around the dockyards, a freeway might force its way in from the Fraser Valley, but none of this disturbed his romantic vision, for Vancouver had cast its spell upon him.

Appendix

A Simplified Version of James Matthews' Family Tree

John Matthews = Mary Pryce
1785–1846 1786–1864

William Matthews = Ann Owen
1819–1890 1825–1889

Herbert Lewis Matthews = Mary Jane Skitt
1851–1923 1844–1926

Martin Matthews 1873–1941 = Sadie Aldersley

Agnes Owen Matthews 1875–1880

Catherine Valentia Maud Boscawen 1877–1947 = James Skitt Matthews 1878–1970 = Emily Elizabeth Edwardes 1875–1948

Frank Woolrich Matthews 1882–1895

Frank Aldersley Matthews 1914–

James Evelyn Huia Boscawen Matthews 1899–1980 = Florence Vera Beatrice James 1904–1988

Herbert Llewellyn Terua Boscawen Matthews 1899–1967

Edward Hugh Pryce Boscawen Matthews 1900–1922

Hazel Valentia Boscawen Matthews

Hugh Evelyn Robert Boscawen Matthews

Amy Letitia Boscawen Matthews

Margaret Evelyn Boscawen Matthews

Endnotes

JSM James Skitt Matthews
CVA City of Vancouver Archives
BCA British Columbia Archives
NAC National Archives of Canada

Introduction

1. *Province*, Nov. 23, 1956; Oct. 10, 1957; Feb. 11, 1959.
2. Ibid, Feb. 11, 1959.
3. CVA. Matthews Collection, Genealogical Files, Add MSS 54, 508-D-1, File 5.

Chapter 1

1. Maurice Richards. *An Outline of the Newtown Woollen Industry.* Newtown, 1971.
2. CVA. Add MSS 54, 508-D-1, File 5.
3. Ibid.
4. Ibid.
5. Ibid.
6. Ibid, File 8. Major Arthur Lloyd to James Skitt Matthews, July 1907.
7. Ibid, File 5.

Chapter 2

1. CVA. Add MSS 54, 508D-1, File 5.
2. Ibid.
3. CVA. Add MSS 54, 718-D-4, File 9, JSM to principal of Paraparaumu School, Jan. 2, 1960.
4. Add MSS 54, 508-D-1, File 5.
5. The area is still being farmed today. The original 1886 station is gone, but the second station remains and is now a bed and breakfast guest house. Information from the owners, John and Helen Wi Neera.
6. Add MSS 54, 508-D-1, File 5.
7. Ibid.

8. Ibid.
9. Add MSS 54, 508-D-1, File 2.
10. Ibid. A statement made by Maud's aunt and uncle, Gertrude and Douglas Hamilton.
11. Ibid.
12. Ibid.
13. Ibid.
14. Add MSS 54, 718-F-4, Files 6 and 7. Also, Add MSS 54, 508-D-1, File 2.
15. Add MSS 54, 718-D-3, File 8.

Chapter 3

1. *Province* and *Vancouver Daily World*, Nov. 4, 1898. Also CVA. Add MSS 54, 508-D-1, File 5.
2. *Province*, Nov. 5, 1898.
3. CVA. Archives Department, Chronological Files, Series 437, 37-A-1, File 1, JSM to the Hon. Royal L. Maitland, Aug. 9, 1931.
4. CVA. Add MSS 54, 508-D-1, File 5.
5. Add MSS 54, 718-F-4, File 7.
6. Series 437, #3073, JSM to General Victor Odlum, May 8, 1954.
7. Speech by JSM in 1955, cited by Chuck Davis.
8. Ibid.
9. Add MSS 54, 508-D-1, File 5.
10. *Penticton Herald*, May 9, 1967, p. 3.
11. Add MSS 54, 508-D-1, File 5.
12. Ibid. JSM's own list of publications, but newspaper and date not identified.
13. This column ran from at least Oct. 1904 to May 1909.
14. CVA. Add MSS 54, 508-D-1, File 5.
15. Cited by Eric Nicol in *Vancouver*, p. 124.

Chapter 4

1. Matthews, J.S., *Early Vancouver*, Vol. 1, 1931, p. 24.
2. Ibid, p.22.
3. CVA. Matthews collection, Genealogical Files, Add MSS 54, 508-D-1, File 5. Also Private Papers, Add MSS 54, 718-G-2, File 4.
4. Gould, Sgt. Leonard. *From B.C. to Basieux; Being the Narrative History of the 102nd Canadian Infantry Battalion,* ch. 1. 1919.
5. Ackery, Ivan. *Fifty Years on Theatre Row*, c. 1980, pp. 22, 23.
6. This story is told by both JSM and L. Gould, ch. 1.
7. Add MSS 54, 508-D-1, File 5.
8. Ibid.
9. Ibid.
10. Gould, ch. 3.
11. JSM, "My First Communion," *Church Family Newspaper*, July 13, 1917.
12. JSM, "Anniversary Regina Trench, Where 102nd Won Undying Glory," *Province*, Oct. 21, 1918.
13. Gould, chapter 4.
14. JSM, "Anniversary Regina Trench." (JSM quotes higher figures than Gould.)
15. Ibid.
16. Add MSS 54, 013.03141, "An Officer's Tribute to his Batman."
17. *Province*, June 1, 1918.
18. Add MSS 54, 508-D-1, File 5.

Chapter 5

1. CVA. Add MSS 54, 508-D-1, File 5.
2. *Evening Observer*, La Grande, Oregon, April 11, 1918.
3. Add MSS 54, 508-D-1, File 5.
4. Ibid.
5. NAC. CEF regimental documents.
6. Add MSS 54, 506-D-1, File 4, #187, John Worden to JSM, Nov. 16, 1930.
7. Add MSS 54, 506-D-1, File 5.
8. Matthews, *Early Vancouver*, Vol. 1, p. 94.
9. Ibid, p. 95.
10. Add MSS 54, 718-D-3, File 8. JSM was in sympathetic correspondence with Barry's daughter, Rita Vaughan, from at least 1963 to 1967.
11. *Province*, March 18, 1948, p. 6.
12. MSS 54, 508-D-1, File 5.
13. Add MSS 54, 718-G-4, File 8.
14. JSM always described Emily's 1914–1915 Medal as the Mons Star, but he may have been mistaken in this, for the Mons Star appears to refer only to service in 1914, and she did not enlist until 1915.
15. Add MSS 54, 508-D-1, File 5.

Chapter 6

1. CVA. Add MSS 54, 508-D-1, File 5. Also *Province*, Nov. 25, 1922, p. 1; Nov. 28, 1922, p. 17 (verdict of coroner's jury).
2. Add MSS 54, 508-D-1, File 5.
3. *Province*, Nov. 27, 1922, p. 7; Nov. 30, 1922, p. 17.
4. CVA. Add MSS 54, 718-E-6, File 1. Also 508-D-1, File 5.
5. Ibid.
6. Add MSS 54, 508-D-1, File 5.
7. CVA. Add MSS 54, 718-E-6, File 1. Also 508-D-1, File 5. After his father's death Martin cabled his mother's lawyers to discuss her position. Martin had been in real estate from 1918 to 1921, but had then retired except for some small-scale tobacco growing.
8. Ibid.

Chapter 7

1. An article in an unidentified newspaper, May 1925, describes the work of this company.
2. CVA. Add MSS 54, 508-D-1.
3. CVA. Series 347, 37-A-1, File 4, JSM to Provincial Archivist John Hosie, March 17, 1934.
4. CVA. Add MSS 54, Fiche 013.03141, #1, unsigned letter to Ministry of Marine and Fisheries, Nov. 21, 1929.
5. Add MSS 54, 506-D-1, File 4, #188, John Worden to JSM, Nov. 16, 1930.
6. CVA, Add MSS 54, 508-D-1, File 7.
7. Series 347, 37-A-5, File 1, #3904, JSM to Marion Woodward, June 11, 1960.
8. Ibid, 37-A-1, T.P.O Menzies (Curator of the Vancouver City Museum) to JSM, Aug. 24, 1929.
9. CVA. Archives Department, Chronological Files, Series 437, 37-A-1, File 3, John Hosie to JSM, Sept. 27, and JSM to Hosie, Sept. 28, 1933.
10. Ibid, #11, Hosie to JSM, March 9, 1931.
11. Ibid, #14, Hosie to JSM, March 13, 1931.
12. BCA. GR 1738, Box 174, File 1, Correspondence 1909–1979, JSM to Hosie, April 13, 1931.
13. William Henry Lembke (1870–1958) had been reeve of Point Grey, but was now an alderman on Vancouver City Council. He was listed in directories as dealing in real estate, loans and timber.
14. Series 437, 37-A-1, File 1, #15, JSM to W. Lembke, March 17, 1931.

Chapter 8

1. Matthews, J.S., *Early Vancouver*, Vol. 2, p. 315.
2. Ibid.
3. CVA. Archives Department, Chronological Files, Series 437, 37-A-1, File 1, #27, JSM to E.S. Robinson, June 15, 1931.
4. CVA. Library minutes, Series 482, #180.
5. Series 437, 37-A-1, File 1, #41, JSM to John Hosie, July 14, 1931.
6. Ibid.
7. Ibid, #38, JSM to Robinson, July 9, 1931.
8. Ibid, #29, Robinson to JSM, June 16, 1931.
9. Ibid, #59, JSM to Deputy Provincial Secretary, Aug. 5, 1931.
10. *Vancouver Star* and *Province,* Aug. 5, 1931.
11. *Province*, Aug. 11, 1931, p. 6.
12. Series 437, 37-A-1, File 1 and 2, Hosie to JSM, Oct. 14 and Dec. 30, 1931; Jan. 21, 1932.
13. Series 437, 37-A-1, File 2, JSM to J. Hosie, Aug. 4, 1932.
14. Series 437, 37-A-1, F1, E.S. Robinson to JSM, June 16, 1931.
15. Ibid, File 2, #147, Hosie to JSM, July 15, 1931.
16. Ibid, #146, Robinson to JSM, c. Aug. 29, 1932.
17. Matthews, *Early Vancouver*, Vol. 2, p. 315.
18. Series 437, 37-A-1, File 2, #308, Robinson to Hosie, Dec. 1932.
19. Ibid, #311, Hosie to JSM, Dec. 12, 1932.
20. Ibid, #291, Hosie to JSM, Nov. 21, 1932.
21. 1932. Library minutes, series 482, reel 1, May 12, 1933.

22. Series 437, 37-A-1, File 3, #347, Hosie to JSM, March 16, 1933.
23. Ibid, #360, Hosie to JSM, April 22, 1933.
24. William Harold Malkin (1868–1959), one of Vancouver's leading businessmen, was mayor from 1929 to 1930.
25. CVA. Vancouver City Council minutes, June 13, 1933. William James Twiss (1869–1953) was the district manager of Mutual Life Insurance Company of Canada, Vancouver branch, and had just retired from that position in 1932.

Chapter 9

1. Series 437, 37-A-1, F3, W. Malkin to JSM, July 5, 1933.
2. Ibid, File 4, Hosie to JSM, March 1, 1934.
3. Ibid, Hosie to JSM, April 18, 1934.
4. Marian Hosie to JSM, series 437, 37-A-1, File 4, Aug. 3, 1934.
5. Ibid, File 5, #906, Gladys Hutchinson to JSM, Dec. 17, 1935, annotation by JSM.
6. Ibid, another annotation by JSM.
7. Series 437, 37-A-1, File 3, #471, J. Hosie to JSM, Oct. 15, 1933.
8. Ibid, 37-A-3, #2433, JSM to Willard Ireland, March 7, 1942.
9. Ibid, 37-A-4, Ireland to JSM, Nov. 17, 1950, annotation by JSM.
10. Ibid, 37-A-5, #773, annotation by JSM.
11. CVA. Add MSS 54, 505-D-1, File 10.
12. Williams, David R. *Mayor Gerry*, 1986.
13. *Province*, Dec. 17, 1936, p. 5.
14. Series 437, 37-A-1, File 4, Hosie to JSM, Jan. 10, 1934.
15. Series 437, 37-A-1, #2463, JSM to D. McTaggart, May 22, 1942.
16. Series 437, 37-A-3, #2464, McTaggart to JSM, May 23, 1942.
17. CVA. Correspondence between JSM, City Council, Captain Annandale and Maggs Brothers Ltd., London, England, Sept. 22 to Oct. 6, 1936.
18. CVA. Add MSS 334, 541-G-1, File 13.
19. *Province*, May 8, 1956.
20. Series 437, 37-A-1, #1329a, JSM to City Clerk, June 29, 1937.
21. Series 437, 37-A-2, #1332, JSM and Emily Matthews to City Clerk, June 30, 1937.
22. Series 437, 37-A-2, F4, #1646, memorandum of agreement, clause 6, Dec. 30, 1938.
23. Series 437, 37-A-2, #1538, JSM to City Council, June 30, 1938, #1538, memo on his letter.
24. Series 437, 37-A-3, F6, #2870, JSM to Archives trustees, March 20, 1948.
25. Ibid, 37-A-5, File 3, #4204, JSM to Ruth Woodward, March 19, 1967.
26. Series 437, 37-A-3, #2445, JSM to Willard Ireland, April 13, 1942.

Chapter 10

1. CVA. Archives Department, Chronological Files, Series 437, 37-A-1, #1378, JSM to W. Kaye Lamb, Oct. 18, 1937.
2. Ibid, City Comptroller to Board of Industrial Relations, April 30, 1938.
3. CVA. Add MSS 54, 013.03141. Department of National Defence to JSM, June 14, 1954.
4. Series 437, 37-A-3, File 1, #2088, JSM to W.A. McAdam, agent general, London, Aug. 28, 1940.
5. Ibid, #2447, City Clerk to JSM, April 14, 1942; #2453, Royal Trust Co. to JSM, May 6, 1942.
6. CVA. Series 437, 37-A-3, File 6, Roy A. Hunter to the governors and trustees of the City Archives, Feb. 10, 1948.
7. Series 437, 37-A-3, #2865, JSM to R. Tupper, March 12, 1948.
8. Ibid, File 6, #2867, Tupper to JSM, March 15, 1948.
9. Ibid, #2879, Justice W.B. Farris in Supreme Court, May 18, 1948.
10. Series 437, 37-A-4, File 1, JSM to R. Rowe Holland, Oct. 21, 1952. Also #3002, JSM to Denis Love, Feb. 18, 1952.
11. Add MSS 54, 518-D-5, File 6. This note of Emily's did not constitute an official will, but when JSM presented it to the bank manager, he replied at once: "This is good enough for me."

12. Series 437, 37-A-4, File 2, #3221, JSM to Ruth Woodward, Dec. 22, 1957.
13. Add MSS 54, 013.05027, notes by JSM and quotation from undated letter by Ruth Woodward.
14. Series 437, 37-A-4, JSM to R. Rowe Holland, Oct. 21, 1952.
15. CVA. Add MSS 54, 718-G-2, File 4.
16. *Province*, Oct. 19, 1957, article by Wilton Hyde.
17. Series 437, 37-A-4, File 1, #2958, Holland to JSM, Jan. 16, 1951.
18. Series 437, 37-A-4, File 1, #2982, JSM to Robert Maitland, Oct. 10, 1951, quoting Robert's father, Royal Maitland.
19. Ibid, 37-A-3, File 6, #2877, JSM to W.J. Barrett-Lennard, May 3, 1948.
20. Series 437, 37-A-4, JSM to Victor Odlum, July 16, 1956.
21. Ibid, 37-A-4, #2465, JSM memo, May 24, 1942.
22. Series 437, 37-A-4, File 1, JSM to R.A. Harrison, March 8, 1952.
23. *Province*, Oct. 19, 1957, article by Wilton Hyde. Series 437, 37-A-4, #3827, JSM's sworn declaration, July 15, 1959.
24. Ibid, #3827, JSM's sworn declaration.
25. Series 437, #2998.
26. CVA. Native Sons of BC, Post No. 2, Add MSS 334, File 6, K.A. Waites to Chief Factor, Sept. 21, 1949.
27. *Province*, July 11, 1959, p. 1A.

Chapter 11

1. CVA. Archives Department, Chronological Files, Series 437, 37-A-4, JSM to Howard Green, Oct. 29, 1956.
2. Ibid, 37-A-4, JSM to R.B. Worley, executive assistant to the premier, Nov. 13, 1956.
3. Series 437, 37-A-4, File 1, JSM to Robert R. Maitland, Aug. 20, 1951.
4. Series 437, 37-A-4, #3090, JSM to Society of Archivists, Reading, England, April 29, 1955.
5. Ibid, 37-A-4, W.T. Ward to JSM, Sept. 20, 1955.
6. Ibid, 37-A-4, #3108, JSM to Victor Odlum, April 9, 1956.
7. Ibid, 37-A-4, JSM to Society of Archivists, Reading, England, Oct. 15, 1956.
8. Ibid, 37-A-4, JSM to Worley, Nov. 13, 1956.
9. Ibid, 37-A-4, JSM to Bruce Ramsey, Feb. 18, 1957, and Ramsey to JSM, March 30, 1957.
10. CVA. Add MSS 54, Private Papers, 718-E-4, Box 10, File 4. Applications for an archival assistant.
11. Series 437, 37-A-4, File 1, #3163, Mayor Hume to City Council, April 12, 1957.
12. Series 437, 37-A-4, File 2, JSM to City Council, Aug. 1, 1957.
13. Ibid, JSM to W. McAdam, Sept. 18, 1957.
14. *Sun*, Sept. 9, 1959, p. 27.
15. Series 437, 37-A-4, #3871, JSM to J.L. Monk, assistant personnel director, Nov. 4, 1959, annotation on copy of the letter.
16. Ibid, 37-A-4, File 1, #2974, JSM to Robert R. Maitland, Aug. 20, 1951. Robert Reid Maitland (1917–1976) was the son of Royal Lethington Maitland (1889–1946).
17. Ibid, 37-A-4, #3141, JSM to City Comptroller, Nov./Dec., 1956.
18. Unidentified newspaper clipping, Nov. 23, 1956.
19. *Province*, Feb. 11, 1959.
20. Matthews, *Early Vancouver*, Vol. 1, p. 166.
21. Series 437, 37-A-4, Victor Odlum to JSM, March 13 and April 9, 1959.
22. Ibid, 37-A-4, JSM to James E. Eckman, Aug. 12, 1959.
23. Ibid, 37-A-4, JSM to James E. Eckman, Nov. 14, 1959.
24. Ibid, 37-A-4, #3000, JSM to Harold Merilees, BCER, Jan. 20, 1952.
25. Series 437, 37-A-4, F2, #3108, JSM to Victor Odlum, April 9, 1956.
26. Series 437, 37-A-5, File 1, #3978, JSM to Howard Green, Dec. 16, 1960.
27. Ibid, 37-A-5, #4064, W.G. Leithead's report, March 20, 1961.
28. Ibid, 37-A-5, #4052, JSM to Leithead, March 12, 1961.
29. Series 437, 37-A-5, File 2, #4111,

JSM to Deputy Agent General G.S. Gibson, Sept. 29, 1961.
30. Ibid. 37-A-5, #4091, JSM to George Buscombe, June 15, 1961.
31. CVA. Add MSS 478, 565-A-4, File 6, Leithead to Joseph C. Lawrence, President of the Vancouver Historical Society, Dec. 2, 1969.
32. Series 437, 37-A-5, File 3, #4190, JSM to City Clerk, July 13, 1964.
33. Series 437, 37-A-4, #3088, JSM to Society of Archivists, UK, March 8, 1955.
34. Stated by JSM to Jack Birt, public relations officer for Imperial Oil. Quoted by Birt in the *Sun*, Dec. 30, 1970, after JSM's death.
35. Ibid, 37-A-4, JSM to Odlum, Sept. 25, 1955.

Chapter 12

1. CVA. Archives Department, Chronological Files, Series 437, 37-A-4, File 2, #3201-3202, petition to Supreme Court, Sept. 17, 1957.
2. Series 437, 37-A-4, JSM to Col. and Mrs. W.C. Woodward, Dec. 27, 1956.
3. CVA. Add MSS 54, 507-C-2, File 8, #603, Rosalynde and Charles Latimer to JSM, c.1965–1969.
4. CVA. Add MSS 54, 508-D-1, File 15, R. Latimer to M.I. Beveridge, Jan. 12, 1971.
5. Add MSS 54, 507-C-3, File 10, inscription in one of many undated valentine cards from Edith Murray to JSM.
6. *Province*, Oct. 24, 1961, p. 21. Himie Koshevoy article, "The Major Fights for History."
7. Series 437, 37-A-5, File 2, #3985-9, Victor Odlum to JSM.
8. *Province*, Sept. 2, 1952, "Old document found."
9. Unidentified press clipping, June 13, 1952.
10. Ibid, Oct. 14, 1954, p. 5.
11. CVA. Add MSS 590, 599-D-4, File 1, JSM to R. Latimer, Jan. 29, 1966.
12. Ibid, Feb. 12, 1966.
13. *Province*, Dec. 3, 1964, p. 27.
14. Add MSS 590, 599-D-4.
15. BCA. Sound recording SD 0244: 0001-0002, Parts 1–4, presentation of Boyd paintings to Richmond municipality, June 11, 1947.
16. *Province*, Oct. 18, 1961.
17. CVA. Series 503, 22-G-6, File 5, memo by M.I. Beveridge, May 11, 1971. CVA. Council minutes, Dec. 1, 1970, motion by Alderman Halford Wilson.
18. Series 437, 37-A-4, #3197, notes by JSM, Aug. 27, 1957.
19. *Province*, March 1, 1961.
20. City Council meeting, Dec. 28, 1961, a motion by aldermen Rathie and Fredrickson (discussed, but not put).
21. Council in-camera meeting, May 31, 1966.
22. *Province*, Sept. 6, 1968, p. 5.

Chapter 13

1. *Vancouver Sun*, May 22, 1921, p. 40.
2. CVA. Archives Department, Chronological Files, Series 437, 37-A-5, #4034, JSM to Victor Odlum, Feb. 16, 1961.
3. Series 437, 37-A-4, JSM to Society of Archivists, Sept. 10, 1956.
4. CVA. Add MSS 54, 718-E-6, File 2, JSM to R. Tupper, May 14, 1950.
5. Author interview with Evelyn Walser.
6. Add MSS 54, 718-D-3, File 2, JSM to Sydney March, Dec. 11, 1961.
7. Interview with Leonard McCann, 2005.
8. Interview with Mildred Nelles, née King, 2003.
9. Mildred Nelles family archives. Correspondence with JSM, Aug. 16–Dec. 20, 1965.
10. Series 437, 37-A-5, File 3, #4188, City Clerk to JSM, July 10, 1964.
11. *Province*, Oct. 28, 1968, p. C1.
12. Series 437, #4211, JSM to City Clerk, Oct. 12, 1967. JSM maintained that "New Brighton" was a name that never existed. It was merely a jocular colloquial reference, one of several other names for the Hastings townsite.

13. *Sun*, April 27, 1968.
14. *Sun*, Aug. 5, 1968, p. 11, quoting Alderman Marianne Linnell.
15. Council meeting, Aug. 13, 1968, motion by aldermen Linnell and Alsbury (carried).
16. Ibid, 37-A-5, File 3, #4227-8, JSM to City Clerk of West Vancouver, May 13, 1969.
17. *Province*, Sept. 5, 1969, p. 5. Also *Sun*, Sept. 5, 1969, p. 10.
18. *Province*, Oct. 1, 1969.
19. CVA. Add MSS 54, 508-D-1, File 15, Hazel L. Bartlett to M.I. Beveridge, Oct. 12, 1970.
20. CVA. Mayor's Office, Series 483, File 3, Hazel V. Abbott to Mayor, Sept. 15, 1970.

Chapter 14

1. BCA. GR-0285, Box 7, File 8.
2. Keirstead, Robin G., "J.S. Matthews and an Archives for Vancouver, 1951–1972," in *Archivaria*, Winter 1986–87, p. 101.
3. CVA. Series 503, 22-G-6, File 6, Willard Ireland to R.H. Tupper, Oct. 14, 1971.
4. M.I. Beveridge's inventory, July 7–8, 1970.
5. CVA. Archives Department, General Correspondence, Series 58, 80-F-2, File 2, Robert D. Watts to various correspondents, Oct. to Dec. 1971.
6. Ibid, File 1, R. Lynn Ogden to records department, Philadelphia, Oct. 30, 1973.
7. Series 503, 22-G-6, File 6, memo from Ogden to Doug Little regarding JSM's trust funds.
8. Series 58, 80-F-2, F1, R.L. Ogden to Al Vitols, Dec. 11, 1973, quoting an unnamed person.
9. Plaque outside the Vancouver City Archives building.
10. CVA. Imredy fonds, Series 1371, 620-C-3.

Epilogue

1. JSM, "Anniversary of Regina Trench," *Province*, Oct. 21, 1918. Also: JSM, *Early Vancouver*, Vol. 1, p. 116; Series 437, 37-A-1, File 1, JSM to Royal Maitland, Aug. 9, 1931; JSM to Kitsilano Ratepayers Association, March 2, 1960.

SELECTED BIBLIOGRAPHY

Primary Sources

BC ARCHIVES

BC Vital Statistics
  Births, marriages and deaths.
Divorce records.
GR-0285, Box 7, File 8.
  J.S. Matthews and W.A.C. Bennett, Apr. 26, 1968, agreement.
MS-1115, Box 2, File 14
  Correspondence, Bruce McKelvie (1924–1960). Letters from J.S. Matthews
MS-0781, Box 2, File 58.
  J.S. Matthews to Hon. R.L. Maitland (1889–1946), Attorney General of BC. Correspondence, 1940s.
MS-0001, Box 26, File 5
  Correspondence, Bruce McKelvie (1889–1960). Letters from J.S. Matthews, 1940s and 1950s.
Probated wills.
Sound recording SD 0244: 0001-0002.
  J.S. Matthews' speech, presenting pictures to the City of Richmond.

CITY OF VANCOUVER ARCHIVES

Archives Department:
  Chronological Files, Housekeeping Subject Files.
Elek Imredy fonds.
Heinrich report.
J.S. Matthews Collection: Topical Files, Genealogical Files, Incoming and Outgoing Correspondence, Private Papers.
Leithead report.
Major Matthews' albums of clippings.
Mayor's Office, Correspondence.
Native Sons of BC, Post 2, fonds.
Vancouver City Council Minutes.

National Archives of Canada
CEF regimental documents

Matthews Family Archives
Correspondence
Matthews family Bible entries

Published Sources

Books

Ackery, Ivan. *Fifty Years on Theatre Row.* North Vancouver, BC: Hancock House Publishers Ltd. 1980.
Armitage, Doreen. *Burrard Inlet, a History.* Madeira Park, BC: Harbour Publishing, 2001.
Burke's Peerage and Baronetage, 105th edition. London, England: Burke's Peerage Ltd. 1970.
Davies, David and Lorne Nicklason. *The CPR's English Bay Branch.* Vancouver, BC: Canadian Railroad Historical Association, Pacific Coast Division Inc., 1975 and 1993.
Davis, Chuck. *The Vancouver Book.* North Vancouver, BC: J.J. Douglas Ltd., 1976.
Ewart, Henry. *The Story of the BC Electric Railway Company.* North Vancouver, BC: Whitecap Books, 1986.
Francis, Daniel. *L.D.: Mayor Louis Taylor and the Rise of Vancouver.* Vancouver, BC: Arsenal Pulp Press, 2004.
Gould, Leonard McLeod. *From B.C. to Basieux: Being the Narrative History of the 102nd Canadian Infantry Battalion.* Victoria, BC: Thos. R. Crusack Presses, 1919.
Harker, Douglas E. *The Woodwards.* Vancouver/Toronto/Chicago: Mitchell Press, 1976.
Hayes, Derek. *Historical Atlas of Vancouver and the Lower Fraser Valley.* Vancouver/Toronto/Berkeley: Douglas & McIntyre, 2005.
Henderson. *BC Directories.*
Hull, Raymond, Gordon Soules and Christine Soules. *Vancouver's Past.* Vancouver, BC: Gordon Soules Economic and Marketing Research, 1974.
Jenkins, J. Geraint. *The Welsh Woollen Industry.* Cardiff, Wales: National Museum of Wales; Welsh Folk Museum, 1969.
Keirstead, Robin G. "James Skitt Matthews and an Archives for Vancouver, 1951–1972." From *Archivaria,* Vol. 23, Winter 1986–87.
Kluckner, Michael. *Vancouver, the Way it Was.* Vancouver, BC: Whitecap Books Ltd., 1984.
Kluckner, Michael and John Atkin. *Heritage Walks around Vancouver,* Vancouver/Toronto: Whitecap Books, 1992.
Luxton, Donald. *Building the West.* Vancouver, BC: Talon Books, 2003.
Matthews, J.S. *Early Vancouver,* Vols. 1 and 2. Vancouver, BC. Self-published, 1932.
Morgan, Roland. *Vancouver Then and Now.* Vancouver, BC: Bodima Publications, 1977.
Morley, Alan. *Vancouver, from Milltown to Metropolis.* Vancouver, BC: Mitchell Press, 1961.
Nicol, Eric. *Vancouver.* Toronto, ON: Doubleday Canada Ltd., 1970.
Odlum, Roger. *Victor Odlum, a Memoir.* Vancouver, BC: Roger Odlum, 1995.
Reeve, Phyllis. *Every Good Gift, a History of S. James' Vancouver, 1881–1981.* Vancouver, BC: St. James' Church, 1981.
Richards, Maurice. *An Outline of the Newtown Woollen Industry.* Newtown, Wales: M. Richards, 1971.
Roy, Patricia E. *Vancouver, an Illustrated History.* Toronto, ON: James Lorimer & Co. et al, 1980.
Williams, David Ricardo. *Mayor Gerry, the Remarkable Gerald Grattan McGeer.* Vancouver/Toronto: Douglas & McIntyre, 1986.
Wrigley. *BC Directories.*
Vancouver Historical Journals. Vancouver, BC: Compiled by Major J.S. Matthews.

Newspapers

British Columbian
Vancouver Daily Province
Vancouver Daily World
Vancouver Sun

Unpublished Sources

Read, Stanley. *The History of the Vancouver Public Library.* Typescript. c. 1975.

Index

The Author

Daphne Sleigh was born in Ewell, Surrey, England. She received her master's degree from Somerville College, Oxford, and was a librarian at the Royal Institute of British Architects. She moved to Vancouver in 1957 and became interested in BC history during the province's 1971 centennial, for which she co-wrote a history of Maple Ridge. She was the first curator of the Maple Ridge Museum, from 1975 to 1981, and she won the Lieutenant-Governor's Medal from the BC Historical Federation in 1984 for her book *Discovering Deroche.* She has written six other books, including a biography of the explorer Walter Moberly. Sleigh lives in Deroche, BC, with her husband, Francis.